DATE DUE

FEB 0 3 1998			
SEP 06 06			
FEB 0 6 07			

DEMCO 38-297

SEX WITHOUT LOVE
a philosophical exploration

SEX WITHOUT LOVE
a philosophical exploration

Russell Vannoy

Prometheus Books

Buffalo, New York

Published by Prometheus Books

Library of Congress Catalog Card Number 79-57534
ISBN 0-87975-128-2 (cloth)
ISBN 0-87975-129-0 (paper)

Printed in the United States of America on acid-free paper.

Acknowledgments

I am deeply grateful to my colleagues in the Philosophy Department of the State University of New York (College at Buffalo) for allowing me to establish a decade ago what was then a daring experiment in the philosophical world: to teach a course called "Philosophy of Love and Sex." That course and the thousands of students who subsequently enrolled in it were the inspiration for writing this book.

I have been fortunate to have had several gifted and inspiring teachers, including Professors Henry David Aiken, my mentor at Harvard, and Richard Taylor of the University of Rochester. I am also indebted to Dr. Seymour Weissman, a deeply learned psychiatrist, who generously shared with me his insights into human sexuality. I must also mention the many creative philosophers who have done so much to make love and sex valid subjects for philosophical study. These include Thomas Nagel (Princeton), Irving Singer (M.I.T.), Janice Moulton (Duke), Robert Solomon (Texas), Alan Soble (Southern Methodist), and many others.

I am also deeply indebted to Dr. Paul Kurtz and Cynthia Dwyer of Prometheus Books for their generous and expert editorial assistance. Finally, I should like to thank my typist, Mrs. Marilyn Coyne, for her devoted efforts.

Russell Vannoy

For Eric Lindstrom

Contents

Foreword: Some Preliminary Reflections on Sex and Love   1

Part One
The Philosophy of Sex

Chapter One.   SEX WITH LOVE VS. SEX WITHOUT LOVE
      1. The Difficulty of Combining Sex with Love   7
      2. Some Arguments for Sex with Love   12
      3. Some Arguments for Sex Without Love   23
      4. Summary and Conclusions   28
Chapter Two.   SEXUAL PERVERSION: IS THERE SUCH A THING?
      1. Introductory Considerations   30
      2. The "Harmony of Opposites" Principle   33
      3. Is Perversion "Unnatural"?   34
      4. Perversion: Linguistic, Moral,
        and Psychological Considerations   39
      5. De Sade and Sartre on Sex and Sadism   43
      6. Some Arguments Against Rape   52
      7. Thomas Nagel's Theory of Perversion   60
      8. Robert Solomon's Theory of Perversion   69
Chapter Three. WHAT IS "GOOD SEX"?
      1. Some Difficulties with "Transcendent" Orgasms:
        Reichian and Tantric Sex Compared   79

	2. Moulton's Feminist Critique	
	of Conventional Sexual Intercourse	93
	3. On "Sex for Sex's Sake"	97
	4. A New Theory of Sexual Immorality	101
	5. Sex and Privacy	107
	6. Can Masturbation Be "Good Sex"?	111
Chapter Four.	TYPES OF SEXUAL PHILOSOPHY: A SUMMARY	
	1. The Conservative Point of View	118
	2. The Liberal Point of View	120
	3. The Radical Point of View	125

Part Two
The Philosophy of Love

Chapter One.	EROTIC LOVE: IS IT A VIABLE CONCEPT?	
	1. Some Preliminary Difficulties	129
	2. Is Erotic Love a Contradictory Ideal?	131
	A. Ecstasy vs. Endurance	132
	B. Altruism vs. Self-Interest	132
	C. Choice vs. Emotion	138
	D. Security vs. Insecurity	140
	E. Oneness vs. Twoness	142
	F. Opposites Attract vs. Like Attracts Like	145
Chapter Two.	CAN ONE DEFINE "LOVE"?	
	1. Some Preliminary Difficulties	148
	2. Love as an Emotion	153
	3. Love as Knowledge of the Beloved	156
	4. Is Love Benevolent? Fromm, Plato, Aristotle	159
	5. Can We Distinguish Love from	
	Infatuation and Friendship?	181
	6. On Defining "True Love":	
	Some Concluding Reflections	189
Chapter Three.	FOUR PHILOSOPHERS OF LOVE: SINGER,	
	SCHOPENHAUER, FREUD, AND SARTRE	
	1. Irving Singer: Love as Bestowal of Value	192
	2. Schopenhauer and Freud: Love as Derived from Sex	197
	3. Jean Paul Sartre: Love as a Contradictory Ideal	203
Chapter Four.	EROTIC LOVE: A FINAL APPRAISAL	212

| Suggestions for Further Reading | 220 |

| Index | 224 |

Foreword

SOME PRELIMINARY REFLECTIONS ON SEX AND LOVE

It may reasonably be asked just what a philosopher, supposedly committed to rationality in all things, could have to say about something seemingly so non-rational as sex or love. How could one, for example, be expected to construct a philosophical system around something so elementary as an "itch in the groin," as sexual desire has so often been described? How can one hope to find the philosophical essence of love, when everyone knows that love comes in so many varieties, ranging from the passionate to the merely affectionate? How can one hope to define the ideal sex act, when it can be argued reasonably that no one sex act is ideal for everybody?

Yet anyone with any acquaintance at all with twentieth-century philosophy knows that it is no longer concerned primarily with reducing all things to a coherent, rational philosophical system, that it is not necessarily committed to searching for the one true ideal of anything, be it the good life, love, sex, or whatever. And it is certainly not clear why something that is seemingly as non-rational as love or sex cannot be discussed in a rational way. Sociologists and psychiatrists certainly feel that they have something rational to say about such subjects. Why should not philosophers have the same opportunity to focus their own distinctive rational approach on love and sex?

It has never ceased to amaze this writer how people who are so demanding of precision, conceptual clarity, and rational arguments in their professional lives are nevertheless so often shallow and uncritical in their private lives. They commonly assume that what is good sex for them is good sex for everybody; or they say "do your own thing" to rationalize their own tastes, while labeling as "perverts" those whose "thing" is different from theirs. It is common among even my philosophy students to write a paper condemning rape as an objective evil, while concluding the same paper with the contradictory claim that morality is just a matter of taste. The young desperately want to be open-minded and yet vigorously condemn the insincerity, role-playing, and sexism that infects so much sexual intercourse.

Perhaps a few examples will illustrate how deeply our confusions go in such matters. Many would say that one cannot give a conceptual analysis of love, that it's just an emotion and that when it comes you'll know that it's love; yet they also say that infatuation is not love, despite the fact that, as emotions, they may both feel the same. Some say that one "falls" in love—much as one would fall in a ditch—and yet they also say that they *choose* their love. The most common claim of all is that "sex with love" is best, despite the fact that millions of husbands who love their wives nevertheless engage in a rapid, simple type of sex act that leaves their wives orgasmically unfulfilled.

Some people say that rape is evil because it harms a helpless, innocent person, while maintaining that the decision to request or perform an abortion should be left to individual conscience. The pro-choice proponent may have a valid case, but to be consistent with what one thinks about rape, one would first have to prove that a fetus is not also a helpless, innocent person. Do pro-choice people have a clearly developed rationale for distinguishing a person from a non-person? Indeed, the entire abortion controversy is itself riddled with philosophical questions that a philosopher of sex might want to explore. It is not clear, for example, that either those who are for or against abortion have a philosophically sound definition of what it is to be a human being, such that one could then decide whether or not a fetus has any rights. And even if one could prove the fetus is a human being, what philosophical basis is there for deciding whether or not fetal rights should take precedence over the rights of the mother? Furthermore, if one should hold that there are in many cases good reasons for having an abortion, what criterion would one use to determine when a reason is a good reason? These questions are fundamentally philosophical in nature, and surely are not the exclusive province of religion, biology, or the law.

Finally, one finds that authors of books on psychology, religion, women's liberation, and the law glibly toss around vague, value-laden terms (mature, adult, decent, wholesome, sane, normal, natural, a threat to family life: the cornerstone of society, insecure, dehumanizing, sexist, liberated, perverted, sick, deviant, human integrity, *truly* fulfilling, a richer and more meaningful experience, the "true" purpose of sex, true love) without giving any clear criteria for the use of such terms or without any awareness of the particular life-style they are presupposing as the best, to the exclusion of all others.

A case in point is the politics of sexual liberation. It is sometimes argued that vaginal orgasms (those taking place deep in the interior of the vagina as a result of the thrusting penis) are somehow unreal, and that the only "true" orgasms are clitoral. This claim is made despite the fact that many females report a distinctive difference in the feel of the two orgasms, and some go further in saying that vaginal orgasm is the more deeply satisfying. But since one of the goals of some sexual liberationists is to make women less dependent on so-called male oppressors, the clitoral orgasm—which can be produced by masturbation—would permit this. Is the claim that vaginal orgasms are "unreal" more of a political than a physiological claim, having to do with a recommendation for a change in women's life-styles?

There are, to be sure, claims from certain physiologists that the inner vagina is incapable of sensations and that all orgasms originate in the clitoris. Thus, the vaginal orgasm is claimed to be something purely psychological, based perhaps on the female's joy in pleasing the male. But there is more to reality than the purely physiological; if the sensation is there, it is there, even if it is only psychological in origin. For the essence of orgasm rests on its being a certain kind of experience, regardless of its causes. Once again it seems that there is a confusion between what seems politically or morally desirable in liberating females, and what is the status of the reality of something that is thought to impede liberation. It might, however, be argued that when we probe the causes of the vaginal orgasm, we will find that it is a masochistic thrill, the product of a self-hate that is in turn the product of women's oppression. It might then seem that the exquisite sensation of a vaginal orgasm is simply too high a price to pay for the continued sexism that feeds it; when we eliminate sexism, the vaginal orgasm (that is, the thrill of pleasing the male master) will simply disappear—and good riddance. However, even if this highly speculative analysis of the vaginal orgasm were correct, it would not follow that a liberated woman must content herself solely with clitoral manipulation. For a woman who is truly liberated in a sexual way can play whatever role she chooses in the bedroom, including a passive role, without its following that she must also be reduced to being a masochist in her public life.

It should be evident by now that the philosopher is deeply concerned with analyzing the underlying presuppositions, assumptions, and biases that most persons are hardly aware of making and which the moralist or psychologist rarely explores in depth. It is of little use for the psychologist to investigate what causes love unless he or she has some clear idea of precisely what love is—if indeed there is any common essence of love in virtue of which all instances of love are so labeled. People often assume that "true love" is forever, that it is unselfish, that it can't be found in a mature form between a teenager and an older person or between persons of the same sex, that its noblest expression is in marriage, and so forth. If love is discovered to have some fault, such as the desire to possess the beloved, then the defender of love would simply say it is not "true" love or that it is merely infatuation. We simply define out of existence any exceptions to this claim that love is a perfectly beautiful thing; the claim thus becomes true but only by definition.[1]

Furthermore, the philosopher would ask: What does it mean to say that X is "in love with" Y? Is sex with love really better than sex without love? Indeed, could there be a winner should one engage in a debate on such a question, or is one side of such an argument as valid as the other?

The philosopher would also ask whether or not there are any necessary conditions for saying that a sex act was a "good" one. Simlarly, are there any conditions, such as sex, emotion, self-sacrifice, selectivity, fidelity that are necessary conditions for saying that one is "in love"? Can love be distinguished from friendship and infatuation? For if love can be defined, it should be possible to distinguish these three states. Do any of these conditions for love conflict with each other, for example, unselfishness, on the one hand, and such things as the desire to be loved and selectivity, on the other? If so, would this mean that the concept of love is incoherent? Do any of these conditions for love conflict with other needs we have: fidelity and self-sacrifice versus our duties to ourselves as free, independent beings? If so, love is a potential source of conflict and is not an absolute good.

Finally, let me give one more illustration by returning to the politics of sexual liberation. The philosopher would be particularly concerned with what is implied by the term *liberation* when it occurs in a sexual context. One knows what it means for the United States to liberate itself from British oppression; the colonies declared their independence and split from Britain. But for a woman to become liberated sexually need not mean that she divorce herself from all amorous contacts with men. What then must she do to be liberated?

Actually, all that she need do is make an "authentic decision" what she is going to do sexually,[2] to be utterly open to the sort of sexual fulfillment that

---

1. Another related argument that one commonly finds in discussions of love and sex are what may be called double-standard arguments. If the life of a single person has certain difficulties, it will be argued that this is proof that the life of the single person is inferior to married bliss. But if a married life involves certain difficulties, it will be argued that this proves nothing against married life as such; rather, the parties involved are merely too immature for marriage or that such problems will be conquered if only they seek proper counsel. Those who defend married life as the best life will thus define away crucial difficulties it might face as an institution but will claim that any difficulties with single life prove its invalidity as a life-style.

2. According to Peter Koestenbaum, there are four criteria for an authentic decision: (1) that it is a decision made by the individual himself, with a minimum of external influences; (2) that it is a decision made deliberately and not unconsciously, a decision one clearly knows he has made and for which he is willing to assume full responsibility; (3) that it is made with a maximum of understanding of the sort of person one is and of the nature of man; and (4) that it is a decision that "feels" right, that brings a sense of relief and joy and freedom. See Koestenbaum, *Existential Sexuality* (Englewood Cliffs, N.J.: Prentice-Hall, 1974), pp. 13–14.

In utilizing Koestenbaum's criteria one must be very careful not to load the term *authentic* with a specific sexual program that would be claimed to be the only one that a woman could accept if she were truly liberated and fully understood her unique nature. It might be argued that some women who feel a sense of "relief and joy and freedom" when they decide to prefer a passive sexual role cannot have made an authentic decision; they merely think they are free when they are only responding to the way they have been conditioned by a sexist society. But this need not be true at all; to choose a passive role in the sexual sense of the term does not mean that one has failed to make an authentic decision. If one has chosen to be unequal, one might suspect brainwashing. But a passive sexual role does not necessarily mean one is unequal; both passive and active roles can have equal dignity and provide equal sexual satisfaction. Of course, if a woman has no other choice than the passive role, then she can rightly accuse her mate of being sexist.

is best for her, and to make sure that her partner respects her wishes or is at least willing to make a decent compromise so that both will be fulfilled. It does not follow that in order for a woman to be truly liberated she must scorn vaginal orgasms because they somehow suggest feminine passivity and servitude; or that she must become sexually aggressive, unless she enjoys doing so; or that she must have an orgasm whether she wants it or not; or that she must become obsessed with whether she is being viewed as a sex object in the bedroom. (Many things that sound utterly awful from a moralist's point of view can be quite thrilling in the bedroom.) We should, therefore, study very carefully those who insist that their sexual outlook is the only one that is "liberated" from "hangups"; they may be a new breed of absolutists claiming that what they have found fulfilling is the only way for everyone.

At this point it might seem as if philosophers are merely concerned with defining terms or pointing out fallacies in the arguments of others; but this is not the case at all. Philosophers also create new theories of their own or recommend new ways of looking at familiar concepts. Such contemporary philosophers as Jean-Paul Sartre, Thomas Nagel, Michael Kosok, Janice Moulton, and Robert Solomon give us quite different ways of looking at traditional theories of sex and sexual perversion. Plato, Aristotle, Freud, Stendhal, Irving Singer, Sartre, Schopenhauer, and Erich Fromm also provide us with new ways of looking at love. These and other theorists and writers will be examined in the pages that follow.

Finally, brief mention must be made of the choice of words I sometimes make. In a work such as this, which deals largely with relations between the sexes, the words *he, she, his,* and *her* will inevitably have to be used frequently. This can give rise to misunderstandings; if, for example, I say "He kissed her," the reader might think that I am reflecting the sexist assumption that males always take the active role in sexual or love relationships. I intend no such thing; words like *he* and *she* are ordinarily to be read interchangeably. When specific reference is made to gender roles the words *male* and *female* are used instead.

The term *lover* also causes some difficulties, since in some circles it has come to be a euphemism for two persons who are having a purely sexual relationship. In this book, however, I use the word *lover* in its strict sense, to refer to the person one is *in* love with. And, with the exception of those sections that deal specifically with friendship, the love that I discuss here is erotic love, rather than love of God, parents, country, ideals, and so forth.

One

Sex with Love vs.
Sex without Love

1
The Difficulty of Combining Sex with Love

If anyone defends, say, a humanist philosophy of sexuality that upholds the dignity of the human person, must he draw the traditional distinction between "sheer lust," on the one hand, and the supposedly richer and more fulfilling experience of having sex with someone who is loved? *Love* is, to be sure, often a mere code word for marriage in some circles, but this surely need not be true for all sexual philosophies. Yet it might very well seem that respect for the human person would demand that a humanist roundly condemn sex without love. For is this not the sort of sex in which two partners have traditionally been said to be merely manipulating each other in order to satisfy their own selfish lusts and then quickly saying farewell? Instead of a deep form of communication between two human beings, in which each one is touched to the depths of his emotional core, there is, it is often claimed, a mere "contact between two epidermises," or a quick ejaculation where gratification is temporary at best.

The traditional claim that females feel themselves degraded by loveless sex is certainly confirmed by surveys in my own undergraduate class, "Philosophies of Love and Sex," taught to more than two thousand students over the past ten years. Nearly 80 percent of the young women in my surveys clearly preferred sex with someone who loved them. The young men, on the other hand, registered quite the opposite view; slightly less than 20 percent found deep emotional involvement to be of any significant importance.[1]

Would this prove that women are the true humanists in the world of sex, and that males cannot be relied upon to practice any such view?

Certainly distinguished male theorists of sexuality have widely argued that sex without love is vastly inferior to sex with a lover. It is well known that Freud, who regarded sex as essentially a mere release of sexual tension, nevertheless regarded the combination of tenderness and sensuality (which for him was rarely achieved) as the ultimate form of sexual fulfillment. C. H. and Winifred Whiteley make it perfectly clear that they feel sex with love is superior when they write: "Sex has beyond all the human experiences the power to exalt, to produce ecstasy, to give people the sense of being carried beyond themselves to a higher level of feeling—not, of course, when it is a mere physical tumescence, but when it is associated with love and delight in another person."[2]

Peter Koestenbaum, in *Existential Sexuality,* goes to great lengths to claim that sex without love fully qualifies as an "authentic choice," despite the fact that he refers to sex as a mere itch in the groin that yields momentary pleasure and nothing else. He does not seem to be able to bring himself to say that sex without love is fully meaningful, and one wonders if he really does think that sex without love is as authentic a choice as sex with love:

> The problem of Rhoda and Ruth is the fragmentation of sex. Both expect sex to have *meaning* (other than pleasure) by itself. In fact sex has meaning only in connection with love. Meaning stands for integration: meaning refers to a total life and to the fulfillment of its potential. Both Rhoda and Ruth want ideal sex but search for it as if it were an isolated physical rather than a total being-experience. . . . Existential sex is a total, integral experience, one which is built on a foundation of existential *love.*[3]

If, however, one probes a bit more deeply into the precise nature of love and sex, the easy reconciliation between the two made by many writers encounters some glaring difficulties. One clue is given by Oswald Schwarz: *"Although totally different in nature,* sexual impulse and love are dependent on and complementary to, each other. In a perfect, fully mature human being only this inseparable fusion of sexual impulse and love exists." (Italics mine.)[4]

1. This, of course, raises grave implications for the viability of heterosexual love if the two sexes really do have such divergent views on sex. Perhaps one or the other of the sexes is suppressing his or her own views to please the other in order to have sex or love at all. And in a sexist society, there is little doubt which sex is suppressing its views. The interviews also confirmed the point that males tend to prefer quick, sensual, hard, direct sex whose primary goal is ejaculation; the females tend to prefer the more lengthy and tender and sophisticated approach that might be described as sensuous eroticism. One female noted, interestingly enough, that if you have a 160-pound male on top of you, you'd certainly want to be sure he'd respect you as a lover would!

2. C. H. and Winifred Whiteley, *Sex and Morals* (New York: Basic Books, 1967), p. 48.

3. Koestenbaum, *Existential Sexuality* (Englewood Cliffs, N.J.: Prentice-Hall, 1974), p. 4.

4. Schwarz, *The Psychology of Sex* (Baltimore: Penguin Books, 1949), p. 21.

The problem raised by Schwarz's admission that love and sex are "totally different in nature" is, if valid, not easily resolved by merely saying they are "dependent on and complementary to each other." There is no a priori reason to think that things said to be totally different in nature are somehow going to complement each other—however much the differences may have been papered over by centuries of habit, conditioning, blindness to the more subtle differences between sex and love, the necessity of procreation, the maintenance of religious and social conventions, and so forth.

One example of a difficulty that confronts combining love and sex is that the attitudes we take toward a person when we wish to show our love may differ significantly from our mode of viewing a person sexually. James Barrel, for example, contrasts two different modes of viewing another person:

> The sexual excitement we feel is related to the way we look at the other person. To clarify the notion of the objectness viewing position, we shall contrast it with another position referred to as tenderness. When we feel tenderness we look at the other's body as a whole. Our gaze spends most of its time in the head area and *within* the body boundaries. However, this position involves penetration of the other beyond the object characteristics. The body is experienced as a whole rather than as separate parts. It is perceived as embedded in its natural environment. For example, the reflection of sunlight off the hair, the grass one is sitting on, or the creek that one is near, all facilitate the tenderness orientation. There is a desire to place one's arms around and embrace rather than to use one's arms as instruments to manipulate the other.[5]

By contrast with the tender or loving attitude, Barrel defines the "objectifying attitude" of sexual arousal in the following way:

> By contrast, in the objectness position we view the other as an object separate from and not embedded in the world. We see the body as consisting of parts; we see legs or bust rather than the total person. For the most part this objectifying gaze gives attention to the erogenous zones and body boundaries, avoiding the head and face (p. 99).

It is not clear from Barrel's paper whether he considers the tenderness and the objectifying orientation as merely alternative modes of sexual arousal, or whether he thinks they are incompatible with each other. There is, of course, the possibility that one might begin the act by first viewing the person as a whole and then moving gradually into the objectifying attitude. But it is clearly true that for many persons the "love attitude" and the sexual "objectifying attitude" could conflict because of the fundamentally different ways one views

---

5. Barrel, "Sexual Arousal in the Objectifying Attitude," *Review of Existential Psychology and Psychiatry* 13, no. 1 (1974): 98–99.

one's lover in the two modes. Switching from one attitude to the other could be very difficult, particularly if the lovers find it degrading to view each other as sex objects.[6]

But if they do come to see each other as sex objects, and if this is a necessary condition for sexual arousal, then the two lovers who have objectified each other would not vary one bit from two non-lovers who similarly view each other in this way. The only difference would be that in the former case a loving attitude may have preceded the sex act, while in the latter case there may be no such antecedent attitude. But once the lovers have switched from the loving to the objectifying attitude, love then has nothing to do with the act and they are sexually on a par with the non-lovers and can claim no superiority for their sex act because they also happen to love each other. For who thinks of love when one surrenders himself fully to lust and willingly becomes a sex object for another?

Perhaps the classic statement of the difference between love and sex is found in the writings of Theodore Reik, in which he tries to refute Freud's view that love is merely sublimated or "aim-inhibited" sex.

Between love and sex are differences of such a decisive nature that it is very unlikely they could be, as psychoanalysis asserts, of the same origin and character. These differences are best realized when both phenomena are contrasted in their purest form; here are a few examples: sex is a biological urge, a product of chemistry within the organism; love is an emotional craving, a creation of individual imagination. In sex there is a drive to get rid of organic tension; in love there is a need to escape from the feeling of one's own inadequacy. In the first there is a quest for physical satisfaction; in the second there is a pursuit of happiness. One concerns the choice of a body. Sex has a general meaning; love a personal one. The first is a call from nature; the second from culture. Sex is common to men and beasts; love or romance is unknown to millions of people even now. Sex is indiscriminate; love is directed to a certain person. The one relaxes the muscles; the other opens the floodgates of personality. Also the sexually satisfied individual can feel love-starved. The sex drive is extinguished; there is a tension, a spasm, a release. The ultimate act of pleasure cannot later be recalled, just as the taste of a food cannot be vividly recalled. No such ultimate indifference to the object is to be

---

6. Freud argued that one has difficulty in having sex with a loved one because one was severely scolded in childhood for having incestuous wishes for the mother. This causes a man to feel guilt in the presence of women when he grows up, and he is compelled to degrade them in his mind so they will not remind him of his beloved mother and thus arouse the subconscious feelings of guilt at violating the incest taboo. But perhaps the explanation for having difficulty with sexual intercourse with a loved one is much simpler. It is that when one objectifies the female (often a necessary condition for male arousal), one feels the same sort of horror when he finds a beloved object, such as a car, dismantled into its component parts. There is the further possibility that, when one reduces a female into her component sexual parts of breasts, vagina, rump, thighs, and so forth, such objectification of the female is somehow linked to *conquest* of her; and this could cause guilt feelings in a particularly sensitive male. (For does not one break up an object and destroy its wholeness in order to better conquer it, he might ask.) Freud's theory is expounded in greater detail in "The Most Prevalent Form of Degradation in Erotic Life," *Sexuality and the Psychology of Love* (New York: Collier Books, 1972), pp. 58-70.

observed in the phenomenon of love. Every word and every gesture of your sweetheart is deliciously remembered. Sex is dramatic; love is lyric. The object of sex is desired only during the short time of excitement and appears undesirable otherwise; the beloved person is the object of continued tenderness.[7]

One who defends sex with love might argue that the crude form of sex Reik discusses is precisely what results when love is divorced from sex. Yet, if the differences between sex and love are as drastic as Reik suggests, one wonders how one could possibly be an expression of the other. If one thinks that sex without love is "animalistic," then how does it suddenly become a satisfactory vehicle for expressing the tenderer emotions of love?

To be sure, sex that expresses love may become more tender and sensuous. But what then becomes of its cruder aspects, which so many participants desire? They regard anything else as insipid and excessively refined. Indeed, just how does a penis that is vigorously thrusting up and down in a vagina express anything at all, with the possible exception of dominance (which is hardly the same thing as love)? If one moves the penis slowly, is this an expression of love? The absurdity of this line of thinking is evident.

Can love and lust really be combined in a perfect harmony? Reik notes that when love and sex are united "it is sometimes difficult to know which of the needs has the lion's share, but they can usually clearly be separated in our perception."[8]

But if the two can be distinguished clearly, what then becomes of the perfect unity between the two, where they are said to form an indistinguishable unity that is richer than sex alone? Indeed, if one does surrender oneself to lust in the act, is there any awareness of some higher unity of love and lust? One's lust-clogged perceptions are hardly in a position to say that the purely lustful experience really was enriched by love; perhaps its ecstacy came from lust alone, and one only fancied that love made it better.

Furthermore, Reik himself suggests that there is no such thing as crude sex at all, that lust is a myth in human beings. "How is it possible to exclude the factor of emotion, to remove the influence of thoughts and fantasies connected with sex as we know it, to eliminate the effects of other drives? [Reik includes power and ego drives as part of human sexuality.] It seems that we can never reach the psychological expression in its crudest, most primitive form (p. 12)."

Although Reik speaks of the "factor of emotion," this certainly need not refer only to love; for there are many other emotions that can enrich sex other than just the emotion of love. Reik's admission, therefore, that there is really no such thing as sheer lust in human beings—what with all this psychological complexity, associations, and so forth—undercuts the familiar claim that the

---

7. Reik, *The Psychology of Sexual Relations* (New York: Grove Press, 1945), pp. 17–18. See also Reik, *A Psychologist Looks at Love* (New York: Lancer Books, 1944), pp. 31–36.

8. Reik, *Psychology of Sexual Relations,* p. 19.

only alternative to sex with love is "sheer lust." For if sheer lust in human beings is a myth, this opens the intriguing possibility that there are richer, more complex forms of human sexuality that need not involve being with one's beloved at all.

Before proceeding to a hypothetical debate between those who want sex with a lover and those who defend sex with a person one is not emotionally involved with, it is important to recall the point that love, as well as sex, comes in many forms. Alan Lee's work, *The Colors of Love* (Toronto: New Press, 1973) has, for example, made a strong case for a pluralistic analysis of love. Each of his love types has quite different notions of what "good sex" is. Although Lee was not specifically concerned with the problem we face here, a closer analysis of what he discovered from his sociological studies of what is considered good sex by differing kinds of lovers gives cold comfort to those who think that love and sex invariably have a humanistic connection.

Lee's "eros" type, for example, seeks beauty and immediate and prolonged sensuous and sensual rapport; yet, while the *experience* of sex with such a type may be beautiful indeed, the insistence on high standards of beauty and sexual sophistication could generate anxiety (even during the sex act) as to whether one will be able to maintain the high standards the eros-type demands. Lee's "ludus" type is the playboy who regards sex as a game of conquest and seduction; whether the sex act itself is of any real importance to him is dubious indeed, and fidelity is out of the question. (His "ludic-eros" type merely combines the disadvantages of the two types.)

Lee's "manic" lover is perhaps the worst of all; the manic is so obsessively attached to his beloved, so lacking in a sense of self-worth, that his sex acts are generally an utter failure. The "storge" or "family man" type of lover lacks the romantic ecstasy of eros and sees sex largely as a routine matter for a quick relief of tension or for producing a family. "Pragma" has an obsession with performing sex according to the mechanical procedures outlined in sex manuals. Only one type—"storgic-eros"—seems to fulfill the requirement of humanistic sex; he has idealism, personal warmth, tenderness, and a sense of self-sacrifice for the beloved's happiness. Yet Lee notes, without comment, that the storgic-eros type confines himself mostly to tender embraces, the gentler forms of affection that would hardly be satisfying to women who demand more intense forms of sensual gratification than he could provide.

2
Some Arguments for Sex with Love

Let us now imagine a hypothetical debate between a defender of sex with love and a defender of sex with a person one is not in love with. By *love* I shall mean the kind of affiliative love that suggests emotional ties deeper than just friendship, where there is usually fidelity of one partner to another. With such a love there is at least the theoretical possibility of marriage, although the partners may not be married or never will be married.

In order that the debate be fair and not plagued by narrow-minded arguments, both partners should be capable of an "authentic decision," as defined by Peter Koestenbaum in the Foreword; that is, it is a decision made with a minimum of external influences, a decision made deliberately and not unconsciously, a decision based on knowledge of the kind of person one uniquely is.

Further conditions for making a fair decision between sex with and without love would include:

• That one have an open mind and not see sex as so sinful that it can be redeemed only by love.

• That one should have no guilt or hangups about either love or sex. One should be open to the possibilities of both love and sensual pleasure.

• That one should have experienced both forms of sex—with and without love.

• That one should be a secure person, one who does not need to be "loved" in order to feel self-acceptance and self-respect. A man should also feel secure, in not needing to prove his virility with an endless string of sex acts with or without love. Furthermore, a woman who is secure will not be afraid to reveal herself to a non-lover.

• That one should have experienced stimulating, responsive, considerate partners in both love and non-love sexual relationships.

• That one have experienced both forms of sex in an equally favorable setting. It would hardly be fair to have one's ideas about sex with love shaped by love-making on a bearskin rug in a romantic, elegant setting, while one's experience of love without sex took place with a self-centered partner in the back seat of a car in some dingy section of town.

• That one have a clear awareness of just what it is one is enjoying in the act. Some partners don't really care for sex at all—it's just an excuse to enjoy the feeling of being loved and wanted. Such people are like those who pour spoons and spoons of cream and sugar in their coffee; they don't really enjoy coffee as coffee.

• That one be aware of the fact that sex can be a "loving act" even though one's partner may not be in love with you. Such an affair may last for one night or several months, but no permanence or fidelity is necessary. For example, such a partner, if he is a man, would show the woman courtesy and attention even though he might be a total stranger. Nor would he exploit the woman; he would give her as much or more than she gave him. This would indicate that a partner's having a good character is as decisive (and perhaps even more so) than his loving a woman.

Let us now consider some of the arguments in favor of sex with love.

• Perhaps the most common defense of sex with love is that it is deeply *personal.* One forms a unity not only with the body, but also with all the other aspects of what constitute a complete experience: the mental, emotional, and spiritual. One not only gives pleasure but receives pleasure in giving pleasure; one feels not only one's own pleasure but the pleasure of the beloved as well.

And the experience is enriched by memories of prior satisfactions and the anticipation that the joys will continue. There is, for the woman, the knowledge that one has been chosen above all the rest—not the feeling that one's lover wanted just any woman. Sex with love is thus claimed to be a rich complex of mental, emotional, and physical attributes that are lacking in sex without love. Another way of putting this is that sex *as* sex is pleasure only; only love (as Koestenbaum argues) has *meaning* and can make sex a meaningful and rich experience as well as a pleasurable one.

• It follows from this that sex with a beloved would be very important for those who must be quite certain they aren't being treated as an object. But is it not true, the defender of sex without love might argue, that when one is in the throes of lust one is often said to become completely "embodied," that is, one has submitted conscious control of one's acts to bodily desires? But then it would seem that even in love one reaches a state where one has become a certain kind of object, as it were, that takes pleasure in being manipulated and surrendering to the wishes of the partner. What, then, would be the difference between sex with a lover and a non-lover, once both reach this objectified state? For, as I noted earlier, who thinks of *love* when they are overwhelmed by *lust*?

Perhaps, the defender of sex with love would reply, when one is embodied one does not become so totally divorced from all consciousness that one does not remain unaware that this partner is one's lover. Furthermore, there are those moments of foreplay and afterplay that precede and follow embodiment—clasping palms, stroking hair, holding each other tight, kissing tenderly, and so forth; and it might be argued that non-lovers skip these preliminaries or else do them in a crude way to arouse themselves instead of their partner. Yet lovers often do skip these preliminaries. One need only think of the millions of weary husbands who seek sex with their wives as a form of quick relief from their tensions. And a non-lover might very well engage in such foreplay as a way of expressing appreciation for the partner's beauty or as a way of expressing gratitude for having been selected as a sexual partner.

• Good sex is often something one would like to continue, maybe permanently with someone. Sex with a lover is often claimed to be more likely to lead to future emotional security; men and women don't have to worry constantly about whether or not they will find a new "one-night" stand. (This would be important as they grow older and find themselves rejected by "swinging singles.") Perhaps because the lover accepts the partner more for what he or she is (or perhaps because love is blind), it is claimed that the lover will be aroused by the partner at any age. (Perhaps love is a kind of eternal aphrodisiac—or is it that one is really making love to a *memory* of what the older person once was and not to that person in the here and now?)

It should be noted, however, that the rejection of older single people by "swinging singles" is more a malady of our social mores than it is an inherent flaw in sex without love. Nor is it always true that sex with a non-lover is a mere one-night stand. Furthermore, the stability of sex *amongst* lovers depends on how they view each other; if they only love one another because of certain qualities that fade with age, then aging lovers are going to be rejected just as much as aging non-lovers. (One need only examine the divorce statistics to confirm this.)

• Even if one is not interested in emotional aspects and just wants good sex, it might be argued that a lover is still best at the purely physical level. Won't a lover put more of him or herself into the act and do his best to please the partner, knowing this is not just a one-night affair but involves someone whom he or she wants to please and to keep? He *selected* you, the argument goes, and selectivity implies *concern* for your happiness as well as his.

Furthermore, if you do happen to perform poorly one night, the lover won't dump you in the middle of the act. A lover is more forgiving of your failings, knowing from past experiences that this is just an off night for you.

However, given the statistics on the infrequency of orgasm among a large number of wives and the crudity of the sex practiced by the average "storge" lover, or man, as described earlier from Alan Lee's book, one wonders if the *average* lover is really as noble as the preceding description implies. Once again the key factors depend more on the partner's *sexual sophistication* and *innate generosity* than it does on whether that person happens to be one's beloved. Becoming a lover or a spouse does not—alas!—turn a man into a knight in shining armor or a woman into Queen Guinevere. *Indeed, it seems clear that one who is committed to humanistic principles as to the intrinsic worth of the individual person and who has some degree of ability to provide an exciting sexual experience will perform equally well and generously with a lover or non-lover.*

On the other hand, a selfish person who "falls in love" or who marries may (for a time) treat the beloved much more tenderly and generously than a mere sex object; but it is often a mark of selfish persons to treat their possessions with great care because they are proud to own them and because of the prospect of greater satisfaction received in return for such attention.

Indeed, if it is claimed that sex without love is selfish, how do we explain all those persons who engaged in sex *before* they fell in love? For if their sexual activity had been selfish, then it could never have contributed to their falling in love at all; for neither person would love someone whom they perceived as being primarily concerned with self-gratification of mere lust. Furthermore, even at the crudest physiological level, there is a kind of giving and receiving that need not be one-sided provided that the partners have mutually agreed to desire each other solely for simple sensual gratification. For to receive a man's penis, a female must "give" of her vagina, and vice versa. Thus, there is a kind of mutual give-and-take, even if only at the level of lust.

• It is sometimes argued that if all one wants is sex for sex's sake, and not as an expression of love, why not just masturbate? A clitoral orgasm, for example, is allegedly more intense than the vaginal orgasm produced by the thrusting of the male penis. Why do we seek out another person when we want the "best sex"? Isn't this because we want to unite with, relate to, communicate with another human being? If interpersonal communion is part of what is involved in the best sex, wouldn't the most profound and meaningful communication of this non-verbal, bodily type be with someone we love, someone who understands or who wants to understand us best, someone to whom we have something to say that mere words cannot convey? Sex would thus be a kind of body language, in which two lovers communicate emotions that lie beyond the powers of language to convey.[9]

When such communication is the central focus of the sex act, all the worries about premature ejaculation or simultaneous orgasm (or even whether one will have an orgasm) will disappear, whereas in sex without love performance and ejaculation are often said to be everything.

While this view has much to commend it, it is not clear why love needs to be the only beautiful thing that can be communicated by sex. For example, one can communicate gratification for having been selected to engage in such a beautiful experience, even though erotic love is absent. There is also the problem that emphasis on "communicating" emotion may direct attention from the sensual aspects of sex in which two persons surrender themselves to sexual feeling. The distraction is wondering if one is succeeding in communicating an emotion of some sort which the other may not even share or understand. Sex is complex enough without worrying about what or whether one's bodily language is actually communicating. Indeed, a penis thrusting up and down in a vagina may actually "communicate" dominance and aggression more than it does love, and this could disturb a sensitive person who is trying to communicate love, at least if he is doing it in a very self-conscious sort of way to show his intentions. Finally, there is the possibility that sex used primarily as a tool for communicating emotion would come to devalue the purely sensual aspects of sex.

• One student of mine argued in a paper that sex with love was clearly best for him since, for him, love is the "ultimate aphrodisiac" and that he is not aroused by someone he cannot love. But one wonders what "love" means in this context. Love is ordinarily defined as a love of the total person for his or her own sake alone. But when one speaks of love as an "aphrodisiac," can one really be sure that one is not merely responding in a lustful way to a complex of particular qualities the "loved" one is fortunate enough to possess (physical beauty, evidence of being sexually responsive and adept, and so forth)? Can he really be sure that he is loving his partner in some total sense that includes non-erotic as well as sexually stimulating qualities? If he claims that he loves all her other qualities as well, how does he know that this is not merely because he associates these qualities with the erotic ones which are really of primary significance to him? These questions arise because when love is described in aphrodisiacal terms, one wonders if it is not really being confused with lust—an all-too-common phenomenon.

9. See Robert Solomon, "Sex and Perversion," *Philosophy and Sex,* ed. Robert Baker and Frederick Elliston (Buffalo, N.Y.: Prometheus Books, 1976), pp. 279-282.

• A further argument for sex with a lover that constantly recurs is the claim that a non-lover is too "insecure" to give himself in total fidelity to a loved one. But this sort of psychologizing can cut both ways, for it could equally well be argued that the one who insists on love is too insecure to give oneself to the adventure of having sex with a stranger. Actually, security has no necessary connection with someone who prefers one form of sex or the other.

In a recent paper, Michael Kosok presents a highly intricate argument advocating a return to a kind of love relationship that will rescue sex from a variety of evils he thinks has befallen it.[10] He first imagines a kind of primordial paradise in which male and female mate with a simple animal awareness involving a natural harmony of opposites without any consciousness of tension or conflict with each other. However, with the progressive development of civilization, simple animal consciousness develops into ever more abstract forms of knowledge in which the thinker becomes an independent, self-conscious subject and others become objects or mental images or abstractions. This is a product of the human being's attempt to master nature rather than be united with it in a harmonious way.

An additional aspect of this process is the divorce of feeling from thought. Feeling, the feminine principle, is now condemned as animalistic and irrational, and thought, the controlling principle, is identified with the male. Thus male and female are alienated from each other, and the oppression of the female begins; male and female now become self and other, and their primordial unity of mating is destroyed.

In this situation, what becomes of sexual relations? Kosok distinguishes four types of failure that arise from our alienation from each other in civilized society. Just how do these isolated ego centers try to bring off a satisfying sexual act and perhaps even overcome this isolation?

The first attempt is to mimic the original natural act of mating by a simple animalistic act that Kosok labels "fucking." Here one attempts to break down isolation and to overcome the oppression of the male by the female by simply trying mutually to possess each other as if each were an object. Treating each other as objects is an attempt to mimic the primitivism of the original male-female harmonious unity, where neither was an object at all. Trying to possess each other represents the female's attempt to assert her dominance and thus rescue herself from dominance by the male and the male's attempt to try to maintain his dominance by assimilating the female. Kosok writes:

Fucking is a sexual act in which each attempts to *devour* the other in an impossible attempt to *be* the other, without either giving himself or herself to the other. Blind passion is mistaken for genuine intimacy. . . . Indeed, fucking *reinforces* civilized (alienated) behaviour in that it serves as a sedative and temporary relief *from* the antagonisms of civilization and

10. Kosok, "The Phenomenology of Fucking," *Telos*, no. 8 (1971): 64–76.

makes one all the more ready to continue the rat race of public existence. . . . The failure of fucking to re-establish genuine natural unity increases the self-conscious distinction already present; and in order to bear the pain of separation, the separation itself tends to become normalized into a socially approved form of mutual *alienation* (pp. 66–67).

The second form of sexual act arises directly out of this "socially approved mutual alienation." In such a society people forget their aloneness by becoming images of each other. Each one sees himself only in terms of how others see him. The sexual act becomes a kind of dignified role-playing, whose socially validated form is marriage. Kosok scornfully refers to this as mere "intercourse" instead of fucking. Here each one is highly self-conscious as to whether he is playing his proper social role—even in bed—and there is no genuine unity or oneness between the two. As Kosok says:

Whereas fucking is a blind unity of two objects *mutually possessed* and void of genuine consciousness, intercourse is the reverse side of this double immediacy, an empty unity of two projected images *mutually dispossessed,* a state of *mere* consciousness . . . whereas fucking attempts to merge two into one, intercourse is a game in which there is only the distance of recognition but nothing is recognized! . . . Fucking is a combination of two attempting to become one (which is complete but inconsistent), whereas intercourse is a combination of two seen only as *two* (which is consistent but incomplete) (p. 67).

As for masturbation and rape, Kosok sees them merely as logical extensions of the alienation between persons we have already noted. The masturbator sees him or herself as the only real self, while the other is a mere fantasy. Furthermore, the image of the other appears objectively invisible and subjectively unreachable. In rape, on the other hand, "the idea is to conquer the other in order to find the objective identity you have denied yourself to be"; the rapist "denies his own reality and immediacy and functions as an image within the reality of the other" (p. 71). Thus in both rape and masturbation, the relation is with "half-persons": the masturbator's partner is a fantasy with whom he cannot truly communicate, and the rapist is a fantasy-like half-person who tries to find his own reality by robbing that of the other. If either person is content with what he is doing, the alienated state of each is only further reinforced.

What is Kosok's solution to these forms of intercourse which seem inadequate to him? He denies wanting to return to some primordial state of unity between male and female; the problem is to resolve the dilemma within the terms of civilized society, but a society that is radically different from the one that breeds or is bred by alienation and mutual exploitation. A loving sexual act, for Kosok, would be one in which self and other would achieve a "true unity," in which they are somehow "both one and yet two, that is, a state in which each comes to know himself in a mutual relation through the other in real intimacy" (p. 67). Thus the oneness sought through "fucking" would be preserved but in a loving rather than a mutually enslaving act; and they would also be two, but not as in the impersonal "intercourse" mentioned earlier. The oneness Kosok seeks is not, therefore, an attempt to make each one the same as the other; the female does not have to become a kind of male in order to avoid exploitation, for example. Kosok argues that a genuine unity is "precisely that which makes passion, individuality, differences, and uniqueness grow . . ." (p. 69). He adds:

> A true unity is achieved only when *each* member gives birth to and brings into view its contrasting companion or opposite and hence gives rise to a higher type of interaction. Through genuine love and unity, the inter-acting polarity of life will *increase* as each *generates* the other in itself and does not only *confront* it externally as "the enemy." Conversely, only through this unity can each dynamic element express *itself* and its "will" most fully by giving birth to itself *through* the other (p. 69).

As an example, Kosok suggests that such "unity of sexuality might bring into existence *physical* sexes much more complex than our simple two-valued variety: male-females and female-males and other subtle combinations can produce an infinite variety of sexuality, making the standard distinctions into heterosexuality, homosexuality, bisexuality . . . a poor image of what a *truly* erotic universe would be like" (pp. 69–70).

Has Kosok proved that sex with love is superior to sex without love? The difficulty in answering this question lies in whether or not he has given a sufficiently clear definition of love to distinguish it from other close forms of human interaction that need not involve the erotic love we have been discussing in this section. His conception of love is sufficiently broad, for example, to include friendship or a "loving society," in which there is respect for individual differences along with a sense of communal interaction. But this is entirely compatible with sex being a "loving act" without the two partners being emotionally involved with each other. Indeed, such partners often avoid a closer sort of intimacy because they feel that it leads to emotional entanglements that involve mutual possessiveness, something that is as mutually devouring as the "fucking" Kosok condemns. When Kosok speaks of intimacy, can his ideal couple avoid this possessiveness that deeper emotional involvements seem to lead to?

Of course, Kosok would insist that in his liberated, communal society there would be no need to possess, that love would be a state of oneness in which each partner's individuality would be enhanced by interacting with the other. Desirable as this may be, it still does not follow that two sexual partners need be in love with each other in order for them to enjoy a temporary intimate liaison that does not possess the mutual exploitation, alienation, and so forth that Kosok condemns. It does not follow that, if two strangers enjoy the exquisite sensation of lustful oneness with each other, they are somehow trying to possess or devour each other. (Unity exists at levels other than that of just love.) Indeed, those who willingly allow themselves to become sex objects or the instruments of each other's satisfaction may appear to a moralist like Kosok to be doing something that is crassly dehumanizing. But surely those who willingly do these things feel that they are achieving a certain kind of sexual pleasure that bypasses rather than violates the ideals Kosok defends, that is, a non-alienated unity of persons in true communion.

Kosok might still argue that a purely lustful oneness is a mere escape or sedative that makes us all the more ready to continue the "rat-race of our existence." But whether sex serves or undermines society is not relevant to a criticism of it *as sex*. Indeed, even in an ideal community of non-alienated persons one might still want relief from time to time from the community by engaging in, say, masturbation or by seeking a mutually absorbing lustful state with another person.

One of the most vigorous defenses of sex with love is found in Rollo May's *Love and Will* (New York: Dell Publishing Co., 1969). May's argument is the familiar claim that sex with love is "profoundly personal" while sex without love is impersonal and obsessed with techniques at the expense of spontaneity and emotional surrender. His development of this theme does, however, raise some important philosophical difficulties. "We have," he says, "to block something off, exact some effort to make it [sex] *not* personal" (p. 312). This suggests that sex will not be fully spontaneous, that one will always hold back some important element of oneself unless the act is *personal,* a term that May uses interchangeably with *love.* But with this rather broad use of the word *love,* sex could be a loving act and thus be profoundly personal, even though the partners were not "lovers," in the narrower sense of the word.

Furthermore, it is not clear that "blocking something off" or withholding some aspect of one's self (by which May means the absence of love) means that one will not totally surrender to those aspects of one's being that are relevant to sex *as sex*; that is, the total surrender to lustful feelings. Certainly love is not the only aphrodisiac, nor even necessarily the most powerful aphrodisiac for all persons; otherwise there would be no sex between non-lovers at all. Thus, one may be totally involved with another person in ways that are relevant to a mutually agreed upon sex act; the emotion of love may be absent, but it does not follow that the partners need treat each other in a cold, withdrawn manner that is merely an excuse to display sexual techniques.

May further argues that "for human beings the more powerful need is not for sex per se but for relationship, intimacy, acceptance, and affirmation" (p. 311). This, however, suggests that sex is being used to gratify those needs that are so often missing in an impersonal society, and one wonders if the relative brevity of the sex act can carry its share of the burden that is placed on it to fulfill these needs. If one adopts the view that sex is primarily a mutually pleasurable experience, it is not clear that one who also expects sex to fulfill his needs for "relationship, intimacy, acceptance, and affirmation" is going to emerge with a very lasting feeling that these needs have been fulfilled. If one is repeatedly disappointed with sex for this reason, this would be a possible basis for a return to the old antisex attitudes the modern world thought it had overcome.

Another benefit that May claims for sex with love is that it fulfills our need to become totally absorbed with another person, to overcome our separateness and isolation. "The paradox of love is that it is the highest degree of awareness of the self as a person and the highest degree of absorption in another" (p. 311). The difficulty with this paradox is that it is not at all clear just how I become most aware of myself as a person while also seeking to lose myself in another. May seems to mean that my giving of myself totally and simultaneously receiving gratification of my deepest needs makes me more of a person, even though I am absorbed in another. He speaks of a resulting increased sense of self-awareness: "We normally emerge from the act of lovemaking with renewed vigor, a vitality that comes not from triumph or proof of one's strength but from the expansion of awareness" (p. 314). Yet, curiously enough, May sees this increased sense of self-awareness as contributing an element of sadness to the sex act.

> This sadness comes from the reminder that we have not succeeded absolutely in losing our separateness; and the infantile hope that we can recover the womb never becomes a reality. Even our increased self-awareness can also be a poignant reminder that none of us ever overcomes his loneliness completely. But by the replenished sense of our own personal significance in the love act itself, we can accept these limitations laid upon us by our human finiteness (p. 314).

It is, however, odd that someone who praises so highly our increased sense of self-awareness should add that this contributes sadness to the act. Despite the fact that he calls this need for total absorption infantile, it seems that what May thinks is most valuable is a total loss of self. He gives his highest praise, for example, to the moment of climax, where all sense of separateness between lover and beloved is lost (p. 316). May thus seems confused as to what value he wants to place on total absorption versus an increased sense of self-awareness. It is certainly not clear that everyone wants to totally lose himself in absorption with another in the sex act; for some, retaining conscious control over the sex act and directing or manipulating one's partner's feelings and actions can be as sexually exciting as a loss of identity and self-control. On the other hand, if the emphasis in sex is on total surrender to lustful feelings, to a sense of being identified with one's own on each other's bodies, it would seem this would provide the sense of total loss of self-consciousness he seems to be seeking. These latter things do not, of course, require love; indeed, one's concern for making sex also provide "relationship, intimacy, acceptance, and affirmation" by means of love may actually interfere with a total surrender of self to lustful feelings. For the more demands one makes of the sex act, the more self-conscious one may become about whether all these needs are being met.

Rollo May's most vigorous attack on what he takes to be current sexual trends occurs, however, in the chapter "Paradoxes of Sex and Love." He lists three paradoxes that he feels will eventually lead to society's turning against sex, a phenomenon that he calls the advent of a new form of Puritanism. The first paradox, he claims, is that emancipated sexual partners report that they are having more sex but somehow are enjoying it less. He thinks that there is a lack of feeling and passion, even though Victorian repression is gone. Indeed, he says that people feel guilty if they don't have enormous quantities of sex, and the female is made to feel guilty if she performs poorly and does not have a powerful orgasm that will impress her mate with her tremendous sexual potency.

The second paradox, according to May, is that there has been an over-emphasis on sexual technique at the expense of spontaneity and passion. There develops a "mechanistic attitude towards love-making that goes along with alienation, feelings of loneliness, and depersonalization" (p. 43). There is, for example, the desperate attempt to so structure the sex act that the couple will achieve simultaneous orgasm. "I confess," May writes, "that when people talk about the 'apocalyptic (simultaneous) orgasm,' I find myself wondering, why do they have to try so hard? What abyss of self-doubt, what inner void of loneliness, are they trying to cover up by this great concern for grandiose effects" (p. 44). What is missing in an act based on technique is "the sheer fact of intimacy . . . the meeting, the growing closeness with the excitement of not knowing where it will lead, the assertion of the self and the giving of the self" (p. 45). He notes that the "technical preoccupation robs the woman of what she wants most of all, physically and emotionally, namely the man's spontaneous abandon at the moment of climax" (p. 44).

The third paradox May labels the "new Puritanism." Whereas the traditional Puritanism sought to have love without falling into sex, the new form of Puritanism seeks to have sex without falling into love. The coldness that one associated with traditional Puritanism is now defined in terms of a withdrawal of feeling and passion, a new kind of duty to have sex whether one wants it or not, and the use of the body as a kind of sex machine that one carefully manipulates without daring to let oneself go in any kind of passionate commitment. May concludes by arguing that the sex machine who views himself as someone to be "turned on, adjusted, and steered" eventually loses the feeling he has either for himself or his partner. The loss of feeeling, May argues, also eventually causes a loss of sexual appetite and ability. "The upshot of this self-defeating pattern is that in the long run *the lover who is most efficient will also be the one who is most impotent*" (p. 55).

What is the reason for the shift from love to technique that May deplores? Is the only alternative to sex with love that of becoming a heartless sex machine? Perhaps the answer to the first question is that we are or have been going through a transitional period, in which modern man felt obligated to be liberated, yet was still saddled with a subconscious distaste for sex inherited from his Victorian past. Thus, out of fear of a total surrender to lust, he withdraws into the use of technique, which permits him to go through the obligatory motions of being sexually active but without the attendant guilt of a full surrender to lust. (May himself suggests a similar sort of explanation, p. 52.)

May further suggests there may eventually be a withdrawal from an obsession with technique and a combination of lust with a meaningful love relationship. But his insistence on a commitment to love one's sex partner is probably an inheritance from our Puritan past that is still lurking in May's attitude. His constant theme that two persons who simply surrender themselves to each other's bodies are devoid of "intimacy" and "mutual give and take" is itself the old Puritanism described in a new language—no longer that of "sinful lust."

Can it not also be true that two people who are not in love can be totally absorbed in a union of lust and mutually gratify each other's needs, not just for momentary sexual release but for mutual acceptance of each other's worth as well? Those who are interested in sex for sex's sake often look for many things in a partner other than just the presence of sexual organs. Lust can be aroused by many features of a human being, including personality, intelligence, and physical attractiveness. Lust thus has its own kind of selectivity (except, of course, for the desperate), and it is not just love that confirms my worth to myself. Indeed, if I am secure in my own sense of self-worth, my need for the acceptance and intimacy that May insists sex must provide should not matter at all. Merely to be chosen as a desirable sexual partner should be enough.

Finally, May's insistence on the split between "surrender to each other" and "technique" is a false dualism that constantly recurs in books advocating sex with love. Technique need not be the cold, self-centered phenomenon it is often described as being. The skilled exercise of technique, provided it does not become an end in itself, can be an all-absorbing phenomenon that is very lustfully arousing. One need not become a cold, withdrawn sex machine, as May suggests happens when one places great emphasis on technique. Its exercise can be so spontaneously performed and so integrated into the sex act that technique itself becomes a kind of lustful—or even loving—phenomenon.

May's book, therefore, exhibits a total lack of understanding of the infinite possibilities for gratification that sex without love can offer. Furthermore, it is far from clear that everyone's deepest needs are those that May suggests or that sex with love can gratify the needs May lists. Finally, he seems unaware that sex can be a "loving act" without the two partners being bound to each other in some profound, enduring emotional commitment, which he suggests should lead to procreation. This seems a giveaway to May's underlying desire to return to a more traditional form of love-making.

3
Some Arguments for Sex Without Love

I shall now present some arguments to show that sex without love may be, in certain circumstances, superior to sex with a lover. Some quotations from my students' papers illustrate this view:

• "I get so hung up on giving pleasure—or trying to—to my beloved that I don't think of my own pleasure. And I wonder if my lover is asking himself, 'Is she really enjoying it or is just she trying to please me?' "

• "I prefer sex with just friends. There are no worries about possessiveness or jealousy. The lover wants him to be a part of you and for you to be a part of him—permanently, and with all others excluded. The deeper the relation went and the deeper the emotion became, the more I ceased to be a separate person."

• "My lover gets 'cocksure' and makes demands, and apparently says to himself, 'She'll understand. She's my lover, after all.' Sometimes I have to do it even when I'm not horny: am I being selfish and inconsiderate if I refuse or is he being selfish for asking me when he knows I don't want to? I haven't figured that one out yet. But things like that don't bug me when I'm having sex for a good time with a stranger."

• "In reality those who demand sex with love should say, 'I'm copping out. I don't really like sex at all . . . but, if I must have it I'll set limitations and only have sex with someone I love.' They don't really believe sex with love is better than loveless sex—they are only choosing the lesser of two evils."

• "Once you've shown a lover all you know about sex you will have to repeat. With a non-lover there is a new demonstration of yourself each time and a new experience of each other's approach each time."

• "When I have sex accompanied by love my conscience directs me to self-sacrifice. When I perform sex without love there is a kind of intoxicated splendor with life and the feeling of well-being which spontaneously arises in me; and it becomes easier to be gratified and to gratify the partner."

• "When two people just start dating they are more concerned with each other's feelings. There is the novelty of a new romance. But as the romance progresses each person seems to become less of an individual. They think of the other as being almost physically attached to them. They are one, and each has no individuality. One may begin to think the other has the same desires and needs in love-making, but they really don't. [This apparently refers to differences between male and female conceptions mentioned earlier.] The mate falls into the category of 'the person I married' or 'my girlfriend.' These people gradually appear as numbers or faceless entities to each other."

• "You choose a lover according to how you wish to be loved, and you choose a sex partner according to how you wish to be laid. There is no guarantee whatever that the person you love and the person whom you find most sexually desirable are one and the same. There are just certain things a lover may not be able to give you, and it may be good sex."

It is tempting to give a "Dear Abby" reply to these student comments and to say that they are immature persons who do not know what "true love" is (as if anyone really knows!). But while such objections may be valid in some cases, such replies usually sidestep any objections to sex with love by simply defining away any objections to love by saying that such difficulties do not really hold for true or mature love. Thus the perfection of sex with love is upheld by simply being made true by definition.

In a recent paper Lawrence Casler has argued that the *need* for love is based on personal insecurity, a need for sexual gratification, and a need to conform to societal norms dictating that those who are not loved are among the damned.[11] Casler does not seem to disapprove of love as such; a secure person possessed of self-respect would feel no need for it, even though he might very properly choose to love. But Casler's thesis, if correct, certainly shakes many forms of love at their foundations; indeed, it suggests that the fundamental requirement is a solid sense of self-worth. Perhaps this is what is needed to make sex a valid, fulfilling experience rather than "being in love."

Furthermore, it is clear that if someone is loved for the reasons Casler suggests, that person would simply be one who is *used* to overcome the lover's lack of self-worth; and such a person would be making overt or subconscious demands that could make the sex act most unfulfilling. Or if one did wish to continue such a relationship, one would have to keep the person weak or dependent in order for her or him to continue to have the *need* to be in love.

The most devastating attacks on love, however, have come from certain recent feminist writers, who argue that love is merely a kind of masochistic worship of a woman's oppressor, the male.[12] They certainly have a point. If women have been relegated to an inferior position down through the ages, what can one say of the genuineness of a love where one partner keeps the other "in her place," even though he has showered her with passionate love letters or exotic balcony or bedroom scenes? One can, after all, shower affection on puppies, but this is hardly a mature love between equals. That there is a kind of love possible for those one treats as inferiors shows that a mature love between equals is perhaps more a function of the character of the lovers than it is of emotional involvement. But then a non-lover who is also a person of character may show a woman much greater consideration than would her sexist husband.

If these charges against certain forms of love are valid, then one could hardly claim that such love somehow ennobles sex. Certainly such charges require a reply from the countless male writers who extol the beauty of love combined with sex.

Those who defend sex with a lover say that love expresses deep emotions for another person, whereas sex with a non-lover is superficial and crude. We have already seen that many husbands who in some sense love their wives are equally superficial and crude in the bedroom. That is, there is an important difference

11. Casler, "Toward a Re-Evaluation of Love," *Symposium on Love,* ed. Mary Ellen Curtin (New York: Behavioural Publications, 1973), pp. 1–36.

12. "The most common escape (from their imprisonment in the female role and the denial of their humanity) is the psychopathological condition of love. It is a euphoric state of fantasy in which the victim transforms her oppressor into her redeemer: she turns her natural hostility against herself—her consciousness—and sees her counterpart in contrast to herself as all powerful (as he is by now at her expense). The combination of his power, her self-hatred and the hope for a life that is self-justifying—the goal of all living creatures—results in a yearning for her stolen life—her self—that is the delusion and poignancy of love. 'Love' is the natural response of the victim to the rapist." Ti-Grace Atkinson, "Radical Feminism," *Notes from the Second Year: Women's Liberation* (Boston, 1969), pp. 36–37.

between (1) whether two people love each other; and (2) whether two people are capable of sexually satisfying each other, especially when the rose-colored glasses of the honeymoon are removed by time.

Certainly not all husbands (especially of Alan Lee's storge type) see sex or could even enjoy sex as an expression of anything. Using vigorous penile-vaginal intercourse to express the tenderer emotions of love would be for many people two different realms that are as difficult to relate as it would be difficult for a dancing fat lady to "express" grace.

Furthermore, for many persons, just bringing off the sex act on the physiological level is enough of a challenge, much less simultaneously worrying about whether one is also succeeding in expressing any emotions and thus possibly offending one's lover if one fails to express what was intended. And at the moment of orgasm one is so lost in the ecstasy of the moment—the familiar sense of momentarily being outside space and time—that it is not clear that one is in any mental condition to be aware of anything other than one's own ecstasy. (I am not thinking of the relatively infrequent phenomenon of simultaneous orgasm; here there could perhaps be a shared sense of joy, but this could hold for lovers and non-lovers alike.)

Is sex without love superficial, as compared with the unity of heart, mind, and body that is claimed to exist between sex and love? Suppose that at a San Francisco night club I find myself overwhelmed by an attraction for someone in both a sensual and sensuous sense. Such a person's beauty need not, of course, be physical. There are many things about this person which may stir my emotions, even though I may have no desire to become emotionally involved with her in the sense usually meant by erotic love. The experience is enriched by the beautiful setting, by the hopes of sharing an evening with her, by memories of previous encounters with such charming individuals, by the prospects of meeting her or someone like her again, by the thought of having sex with an utter stranger with whom I may have a unique and fresh experience of her and my sexual abilities, by the fact that she has been sensually aroused and has responded to my stare, and so forth. Is this merely a description of a ludic playboy on the prowl for a sex object? It could be, but it need not be. For people who are concerned with persons as persons can experience such rich complexity of thought, emotion, and sensuality as much as anyone else; and so long as the object of one's affections shares one's views, an evening may be spent together that can be totally free of mutual exploitation.

It can be an evening of sensuous eroticism that may continue for hours and include all the foreplay, afterplay, kisses, and caresses that actual lovers enjoy, perhaps done simply out of deep mutual admiration for each other's sensuous qualities and out of gratitude for having been chosen by the other for such an evening. Yet the pair may go their separate ways in the morning and never see each other again, perhaps because they prefer their own independence and singlehood to permanent emotional involvement and marriage. The claim, then, that sex with love is a rich, complex phenomenon and sex without involvement is a mere sensation in the groin is a fallacious dualism.

Indeed, if there were only a lustful attachment between two strangers who are not wholly sure of each other's motives, the evening might still be an exciting and rewarding one. Robert Solomon writes:

> The fact that excitement is essential to sexuality explains how it is that many people find danger highly sexual . . . (short of terror, which understandably kills sexual enthusiasm) . . . It allows us to understand one of the most apparent anomalies of our sexual behaviour, the fact that our most satisfying sexual encounters are often with strangers, where there are strong elements of tension—fear, insecurity, guilt, and anticipation. Conversely, sex may be least satisfying with those whom we love and know well and whose habits and reactions are extremely well known to us.[13]

Moralists have traditionally drawn a sharp either-or distinction between sex with a lover (hoping thereby to preserve the institution of marriage) and sex with a non-lover, which they picture as something crude, selfish, animalistic. The idea that sex can be a loving act and that even loveless sex can be fun under certain conditions, they never admit. They falsely think that the only loving, unselfish act can be between two people who are in love, married, or going to be married.

Perhaps the young female has been so conditioned by the value system which maintains that either one is in love or else it's going to be vicious and dirty, that she truly believes an encounter has been vicious and dirty when it may not have been so in reality. And perhaps the male has been conditioned in the same way. He says: "I don't love her, so this means I'm going to exploit her; for this is what society expects me to do with someone I don't love." But if he had not been conditioned to view sex without love as selfish and animalistic in the first place, perhaps his unselfish side could assert itself naturally and he could provide the woman with a loving act even though he wasn't romantically involved with her at all.

As I noted in an earlier section, one can hardly say that sex with love is always superior, since millions of husbands practice only a crude form of the sex act that leaves their wives unfulfilled. The reply might be that such husbands do not really love their wives. But perhaps the husband simply does not (and, indeed, could not) care for the kind of sex his wife does—perhaps females in general prefer sensuous eroticism and males in general prefer the lustier, more "manly" type of sex. The husband might defend his love for his wife by saying that lovers need not share mutual interests in all areas, that love is a give-and-take proposition, and that he shows his love for her in other ways to make up for his wife's lack of fulfillment in the bedroom. But if he can thus prove that he does love his wife, then sex with love is not going to be the best for females who are married to this type of man.

13. Solomon, "Sex and Perversion," p. 278.

Is the person who feels that the only good sex is with a lover someone who feels that basically sex is dirty and can only be indulged in if it is done in a socially approved way (that is, it is only "nice" if it is bathed in the holy water of "love")? But, if deep down they think that sex without love is ugly or dirty or animalistic, then won't this perhaps unconscious attitude carry over even with a lover, and won't it be sensed? Will sex in such circumstances ever be open and spontaneous and guilt-free? If this is true, then only someone who can first enjoy sex for its own sake can really provide his beloved with a joyous experience.

There are, furthermore, certain things available to a non-lover that are often not available to a lover:

• There is the fun of seducing someone. One does not seduce a lover.

• One need not feel obligated to perform sexually except when one feels like it. But lovers often feel that they *owe* their beloveds the satisfaction of each other's needs even when they are not in the mood for sex.

• One can experiment with new partners or with new sex techniques without feeling guilt or fear of offending one's beloved. Furthermore, if sex is an appetite, as many claim, it seems odd to think that one could go through life satisfying an appetite in only one way. One's appetite for food cannot be permanently satisfied by hamburger, no matter how many different ways one tries to prepare it. Could not the same thing also be true of the sexual appetite? Isn't there a need for a variety of partners, and isn't our claim that we can be satisfied with one person forever a product of social conditioning used to preserve and protect the institution of marriage?

• One need not fear performing inadequately, ejaculating prematurely or not having an orgasm with a stranger whom you'll never see again. But if these things happen too often with a lover, one will feel that one has failed the loved one. This can be quite disheartening even if the lover is forgiving of one's faults.

• Perhaps the most basic difficulty of using sex to express love is that one is often merely using sex as a means to an end: expressing love, rather than enjoying sex for sex's sake. The focus tends to be on the emotions of love rather than lust itself. The sensual aspects of sex thus tend in many such cases to be sacrificed to tenderness, something which has its own worth and beauty, to be sure, but which may not be the central focus many sexual partners would prefer.

4
Summary and Conclusions

In this chapter I have tried to show that the old distinction between sex with a lover and crude, manipulative, exploitative sex (which I shall dub "loveless sex") is a false dualism, and further, that another type of sex is a loving act of mutual gratification and consideration without emotional commitment. In addition, I have tried to show that old distinctions between "noble and unselfish love" and "crude, selfish, simple lust," and between "warm and tender love" and "cold and mechanical" technique are vastly overdrawn in the traditional literature.

Who would win the argument between sex with love and sex without love? It is often argued that there is no winner in philosophical debates, and it may very well be true of this little debate also. Could it be that the preference for sex with love over sex without love is merely one of taste—tenderness versus raunchiness, predictability and security versus adventure and novelty, attachment versus independence? I am reminded of those who prefer their coffee straight and those who must have it mixed with cream and sugar. In each case something is gained and something is lost. The one who likes it only with cream and sugar will never savor coffee with its full "kick," and the one who likes it straight will never know how rich and sweet it tastes with cream and sugar.

Yet this conclusion is not really satisfactory either, for I have tried to show that there are forms of sex without love that are as rich in their own way as sex with love. (And I have also tried to show that many of those who prefer sex with love are really only interested in the "cream"—the feeling of being loved—and do not care for the coffee at all.)

Even if one is not able to decide the winner of such a debate, this chapter reveals that terms like *more meaningful, mature, wholesome,* and *richer* are not the exclusive domain of sex with love, if indeed they really do describe many such experiences at all to the exclusion of other forms of sexuality.

Two

Sexual Perversion: Is There Such a Thing?

1
Introductory Considerations

One of my students once insisted that he could conclusively prove that homosexuality was immoral. "What," he asked, "if everyone were a homosexual? The human race would perish." My own response was to ask, "Since you are a deeply religious person, what if everyone became a priest? The human race would also perish." It seems that the very sort of argument that proves that homosexuals are immoral also proves that priests are immoral as well—an odd conclusion indeed. (Of course, not everyone is going to become a priest, but not everyone is going to become a homosexual, either.) Arguments of the purely hypothetical "what if everybody did it" sort are very common in accusations against sexual deviancy, yet in this instance it goes nowhere. Just how does one prove that perversions are immoral or "sick." Can one even prove that there *are* such things as perversions—some of society's and some psychiatrists' convictions notwithstanding?

Another example of perversion given by a student was that of necrophilia or sex with a dead body, an example that immediately sent a shock wave of disgust through the lecture room. But if one uses the criterion that an act is immoral if it causes pain to the victim, such a criterion would hardly be applicable to a corpse! Of course such sex suffers from a distinct lack of responsiveness from the object of one's affections, but this is hardly a *moral* objection to such sex. One seems to be left only with one's shock, horror, and disgust with such a phenomenon, but this is hardly a criterion either; for conservative people are shocked by the sight of innocent lovemaking in a public park. Disgust seems to reveal more about the nature and conditioning of the one who is disgusted than it does about the object of one's disgust.

Even certain enlightened writers about sexual morality who avoid superficial moral arguments nevertheless insist on finding strained arguments to attack homosexuality. The Whiteleys, for example, do a brilliant job of exposing the manifold fallacies in condemnation of homosexuality as "unnatural," yet they persist in labeling such sex "unfruitful":

> In family life, two parents are biologically necessary to produce children, and it would seem, psychologically desirable to bring them up. The homosexual is usually a person who opts out of family life and parenthood, provides no children, and deprives whoever might have been his wife (or her husband) of the opportunity for family life. *A community of such people stands apart from and at odds with the rest of society. A selfish, pleasure-seeking pattern of living is common among them, not because they are constitutionally like this, but because their manner of life leaves them less incentive for the taking of responsibility.* They rarely achieve the full personal relationship between partners marriage makes possible. Love affairs are common amongst them, but they are usually short-lived; they lack the support of law and custom. . . . They can hardly avoid some degree of estrangement from their normal associates. . . .[1] (Italics mine.)

But the Whiteleys never stop to think where the real blame for the estrangement of homosexuals lies. For is it not the heterosexual majority who formulate the laws and customs that force homosexuals into a group alienated from the rest of society? Does this rejection not breed the self-hate that prevents long-lasting love attachments between homosexuals? (One must love oneself before one can love another.) And if the homosexual feels his creative accomplishments will be rejected by society because he is homosexual, will he not be driven to "selfish pleasure-seeking" as a form of compensation and to find some degree of happiness?

If homosexuals can be accused of being perverts because they are isolated from the rest of society, we can imagine an even more extreme case of lonely sex. Joe, for example, is a loner, who finds that reality is no match for the beautiful fantasies and orgasms he can have while his Accu-Jac machine masturbates him. What could be more in tune with this world of labor-saving devices, he asks, than to sit back and to avoid the hassle and expense of putting up with the demands and unpredictable whims of other people? Can we say that Joe is a pervert if he prefers this form of sex to the exclusion of penile-vaginal intercourse? Or must we say that if Joe is satisfied with his Accu-Jac,

1. C. H. and Winifred Whiteley, *Sex and Morals,* (New York: Basic Books, 1967), p. 91.

then that, for him, is the best sex? Nor should we call it perverted or even "bad sex" if it harms no one and brings him the gratification he seeks.

It might, however, be argued that even if we do not wish to label Joe a pervert, his is nevertheless "bad sex"; for bringing relief from sexual tension is surely not the same as full sexual gratification. We can imagine someone who likes steak more than anything else but then discovers that he can eat a certain kind of pill that gives him identical nourishment and a sense of a full stomach. But although his hunger has been relieved, he has not been truly satisfied in the way he would have been had he eaten steak. Is his case like Joe's?

But this reply would not hold for someone who prefers sex of a very simple sort to one who wants a "full course" treatment. In aesthetics we sometimes contrast a "thin" sense of aesthetic perception with a "thick" sense of perception; the former perceiver prefers to focus on the pure form of the work of art itself, while the latter prefers to enrich his perception by bringing to it all the associations the work calls to his mind, such as memories of his childhood, the tragedy of the human condition, and so forth. Yet each experience can be as intense and rich in its own way as the other. The advocates of "thin" aesthetic experiences feel that the intensity of such experiences is diluted by having one's total absorption in the work for its own sake distracted by irrelevant associations. Someone who prefers masturbation to other forms of sex could then be said to prefer a "thin" sexual experience for reasons similar to those who prefer thin aesthetic experiences of works of art.[2] Nor need masturbation always be viewed as a "thin" form of sex concerned solely with an orgasmic release of sexual tension. For when it is accompanied by fantasies or by one's sensuous caresses of one's own body or by the enjoyment of sexual arousal for its own sake, it may be as rich or "thick" an experience as any other form of sex.

One's response to Joe's preference for masturbation does, I think, tend to reveal more about the life-style and value system of Joe's critic than it does about Joe himself. Can Joe be refuted in any objective way by saying that his sex life is lonely, non-productive, impersonal, self-centered, or mechanistic if Joe himself has tried both types of sex and has decided on the type he thinks is best for him? Does this sort of example reveal that the concept of a non-perverted act has built into it a concept of what "good" sex is, what the good life is, what is presumably necessary to hold society together into a community

---

2. This "thin" versus "thick" example of sexual experience is also aptly illustrated by the dark-room orgy example that we might use to prove that "an orgasm is an orgasm," that is, that one orgasm is as good as another no matter how obtained and that there is thus no such thing as a perversion or bad sex. Suppose, for example, that a heterosexual male were placed in a dark room which, without his knowing it, contained a man, a woman, and perhaps even a sheep. Suppose further that he had sexual intercourse with each person or animal and that he could not tell which was which. Wouldn't he be equally satisfied with each? Of course, for those who want just an orgasm, the example is perfectly apt; but for those who want to know precisely whom they are having intercourse with, with all the psychological associations that entails, the example would not work. Whether they *should* be concerned about whom they have sex with, and whether they should not rather learn that any object is a potential object of sexual enjoyment if one only tries to learn to enjoy it is another question. De Sade, as we shall see in a later section, would regard our selectivity as merely the product of our own socially conditioned hangups.

of procreative, interacting individuals? If so, it is far from the clinically objective term it is often presented as being, and it is riddled with value systems that are subject to dissent and disagreement without one's necessarily being sick or perverted if he does dissent from what society considers to be healthy or normal sex.

Let us now look at some of the things that have been called sexual perversions, a phrase that has been used to cover such diverse phenomena as sadism and masochism, sex with corpses, homosexuality, voyeurism, exhibitionism, erotic attachments to certain types of clothing, or any sex that departs from the usual penile-vaginal sort, such as oral or anal sex. From time to time we receive mysterious pronouncements from psychiatrists that certain of these acts have been "declassified" as sicknesses; for example, psychiatrists (by a majority vote!) no longer classify homosexuals as sick, provided they have successfully adapted to and accepted their condition; oral and anal sex between heterosexuals has similarly been declassified, on grounds that they are commonly practiced by humans and animals. But many psychiatrists will still condemn such practices if they are allowed to take predominance over "normal" penile-vaginal intercourse, rather than being occasional supplements to the "normal" routine.

A philosopher who is looking for some clear principle to distinguish the perverted from the normal will obviously find this to be a chaotic situation, indeed. He may well wonder how many more such acts will be similarly freed from the stigma of being labeled as perverted. Is the concept of perversion, after all, perhaps an all-too-human interpretation or value judgment placed on certain sexual phenomena rather than an objective or descriptive term? Can we, for example, see the perverted quality of a sex act in the way that there can be a consensus in seeing the awkward quality of an inept dancer? Can we see the disorder in perverted sex in the same way we can see the disorder of someone undergoing an epileptic seizure? Surely there is no consensus that this could be the case, except among those who have already been conditioned to believe there must be something disordered in perverted sex.

2
The "Harmony of Opposites" Principle

One of the most commonly offered criteria for perversion is that it is somehow a violation of the natural order of things. It has been argued, for example, that nature is governed by a "harmony of opposites" between the male and female principles. The male is active, the female passive; the active male penis is a shaft, which by nature "fits" its opposite, the passive vaginal emptiness. The male is the aggressive provider who goes forth into the world to provide for the family; the female's role is stay home, raise the children, and with her feminine tenderness help her husband relax after a long day. Each gives what the other presumably lacks, and this is supposed to be a beautiful phenomenon indeed.

It is clear, however, that the entire principle as traditionally expressed rests on sexist stereotypes of "active" males and "passive" females that have been vigorously challenged for several years now. Furthermore, the defenders of the principle overlook the obvious fact that there can be a harmony of opposites that need not involve differences of gender at all. Opposites can take many forms; between a passive and an active male, for example, an opposite exists on the psychological as well as on the physiological level. The possibility of sodomy between two males, with one male preferring the active or masculine role of penetrating the anus and the other preferring the passive feminine role of being penetrated, is but one illustration of how there could also be a harmony of opposites between homosexuals. The fact that traditional defenders of the principle speak of "male and female genders" rather than "masculine and feminine temperaments," two sets of concepts that need have no connection, shows clearly that the defenders of the principle have interpreted it to rationalize their heterosexual preferences that antedated the formulation of the principle itself. Indeed, if defenders of such a principle could be brought to see the validity of forms of sex other than the traditional penile-vaginal sort, they would discover many sexual practices that do not require the two partners to take "harmoniously opposite" active-passive roles at all. For example, certain forms of mutual oral stimulation of the sexual organs can be performed in the lateral position by partners of the same or opposite sex. Both are active; neither dominate the other.

Indeed, as I have noted before, my own research from student term papers reveals a decided difference in sexual philosophy between males and females, with the former preferring the more aggressive, quick sexual act and the latter preferring the more prolonged, relaxed "loving" sensuous eroticism. If there is any "harmony" here, it is apparent that one of the two sexes is subordinating its wishes to the other, and in a sexist society it is no mystery which gender is doing the surrendering.

Furthermore, there is the curious phenomenon of males wooing females in the most devoted fashion, yet also condoning or fostering a sexist society where women are not treated as equals. It is as if men down through history said, "I love you, but stay in the kitchen where you belong and take care of the children." If true love is love between equals, each complementing the other in a harmonious attitude of mutual respect for each other's dignity, then one wonders how much true heterosexual love has existed in history.

3
Is Perversion "Unnatural"?

Perhaps the most familiar use of the term *natural* in a sexual context is the claim that the sexual organs have a certain natural purpose: that nature or God intended them for procreation. It is, however, apparent that nature also gives sexual desires and sexual pleasures to those who cannot procreate, either temporarily or permanently, such as those who are too young or too old, or those who are sterile or who are in a temporarily non-reproductive cycle.

The reply might be that non-reproductive intercourse could still be "natural," provided it is the sort of intercourse that could lead to procreation *were conditions normal.* But this reply would mean that a female who is in a temporarily non-reproductive cycle is somehow abnormal. Yet the period of the month when she is fertile and the years of her life when she can bear children are quite brief compared to the times she cannot reproduce. Her fertile period could then just as easily be characterized as an abnormal phenomenon. Furthermore, the number of times people have sex for pleasure so vastly outnumbers the times when sex is meant for procreation that one could argue that sex for procreation is kind of statistical abnormality. And if our sexual desires come from nature, the abnormality is not merely statistical.

Indeed, the ability to have sexual pleasure rather than the ability to or the desire to reproduce would seem to be what defines us as sexual beings. For if we could only reproduce but not have sexual feelings, we would not speak of sexual acts or sexual organs at all; rather we would speak only of reproductive acts or reproductive organs.

But the main difficulty is that there seems to be a contradiction in nature, in giving us desires for non-procreative sex when procreation is said to be its *sole* sexual purpose. What then becomes of the claim that an act that violates nature is a sexual disorder if nature is confused about its purposes? And what becomes of the theory that nature is created by a deity or presided over by a biology that arranges all things in an orderly means-end relationship directed toward procreation if nature is contradicting herself in also allowing—indeed making us desire—non-procreative sex?

The deeper question, however, is whether and how anything unnatural can happen in the world of nature at all. Is there some point in the universe where nature ceases and the unnatural begins? We might, for example, compare the universe to a solid bowl of pure Jello; wherever we bite into the gelatin, we will find that its creator has included in it nothing other than Jello. There would thus be no basis for saying that one should eat only the Jello and avoid anything that deviates from what its creator intended the bowl to contain. Thus, just as one would be puzzled as to how anything that is Jello could be non-gelatinous, one might equally well wonder how anything in the world of nature could be unnatural. For if something were unnatural it couldn't be part of our universe at all; the universe *is* nature, and thus everything in it is natural.

If, then, one feels an urge to commit sodomy, has one discovered some mysterious gap in the world of nature where nature does not exist? Or cannot one say that the prompting is as much a part of nature as any other? Such an urge may be unusual and widely deplored, but so is a hurricane, which is a perfectly natural phenomenon. Perhaps what we should say is that the only thing that is sexually unnatural is whatever nature does not allow us to do. A man might, for example, have the desire to ejaculate by penetrating someone's ear canal and engage in thrusting motions of the penis much as he would in a vagina. But nature clearly makes this mode of ejaculation out of the question; thus it would be unnatural. One could, of course, masturbate and shoot his semen into someone's ear (or onto any part of someone's body, for that matter). Such an act would be natural, since nature does not forbid it by making it impossible to do so.

It might, however, be argued that such an argument about the naturalness of all things that are possible destroys a perfectly familiar distinction: that between the natural and the antinatural (or artificial or synthetic). Self-preservation is a natural phenomenon, yet why is it that so many people kill themselves? Isn't suicide "unnatural"? Germs are a part of nature, yet we develop manmade (that is, unnatural) drugs to destroy germs.

Indeed, if all these things were natural, wouldn't nature be contradicting herself if both disease and the drugs to conquer disease were natural, or if nature gave both the desire for self-preservation and, to some, a desire for self-destruction?

None of these considerations, however, necessarily disprove the principle that whatever exists and whatever we desire and can do is natural. Nietzsche, for example, argued that nature is a battleground of conflicting wills to power, with each one trying to expand its influence and strength and destroying whatever stands in its way. A virus or cancer, for example, is a phenomenon of nature that tries to conquer the body, and we try to conquer the virus and cancer in turn because of another phenomenon of nature—our instinct for self-preservation. The materials we use to conquer disease may be man-made, but their ingredients can be traced back to nature, as well as the natural ingenuity we use to create these materials. Furthermore, there may not be only an instinct for self-preservation; as Freud once noted, there may also exist a natural death wish, of which suicide would be the most extreme example.

It is clear, therefore, that the term *natural* can be defined to refer to many things, even if one still wanted to insist that some things are unnatural. Those who claim that only one kind of sex, procreative sex, is natural are simply selecting one aspect of our sexual nature to suit their own moral presuppositions about what the purpose of sex ought to be. Furthermore, those who attempt to give a religious or moralistic backing to such sexual doctrines make the following questionable assumptions.

• They assume that they know exactly what God's will is in sexual matters, that He intended sex only for the purpose of procreation, despite the fact that the deity has clearly created us with many other sexual needs and desires.

• They assume that whatever is natural is good, despite the fact that nature daily, through no fault of man's, inflicts on us catastrophes of all sorts. Furthermore, many would hold that aggression is a perfectly natural instinct: witness infants' screams and kicking of feet and pounding of fists when they are frustrated. Babies didn't learn to be aggressive; and if one holds that one learns aggression from society, how did society come to be aggressive in the first place and require endless laws to keep the social order? But if aggression is natural and if whatever is natural is held to be good, then under the "obey nature" philosophy, one would be driven to the highly unwelcome conclusion that rape is natural and therefore good.

• Defenders of the philosophy that nature intends sex only for procreation assume that all men have the same basic nature, even though some men (they say) willfully violate nature. This overlooks the fact that nature has clearly made us all different in some respects; could it not therefore be true that nature has created some persons with a unique sexual nature of their own that has nothing to do with procreation? But if this is true, then under the "obey nature" philosophy one should allow such persons to fulfill their own individual natures (so long as they do not harm others) rather than accuse them of having committed so-called crimes against nature.

One can therefore say that if someone who differs from what is usually considered natural and who commits acts most persons would find perverted, then the fact that such a person was endowed by nature with (1) the imagination to conceive the act, (2) the desire to perform the act, (3) the ability to carry it out, and (4) the ability to enjoy it, makes that act perfectly natural for him or her. If nature had not intended a person to perform such acts, it would have been impossible to acquire these four abilities. (If some persons claim they do not desire or cannot enjoy something that deviates from the norm, this may only mean that their unique nature has been buried under layers of repressive social conditioning.)

• It should be noted further that to reduce human sex to procreation is, in effect, to reduce sex to the purely animal level where sex is performed in only one way for one purpose—the reproduction of the species. But men and women are also beings with free will and powers of reason and imagination, and these are completely overlooked when one reduces sex to a purely animalistic function. If nature gives man freedom and imagination, doesn't nature want him to use these talents to conceive of and freely choose forms of sex other than the purely animal one? Some defenders of procreation try to meet this charge that they are reducing sex to an animal level by allowing sex to have a secondary function: sex as an expression of love. Then they condemn sex with a non-lover that is for pleasure alone, even though nature clearly gives pleasure to non-lovers, as well. Nor can one call sex for sex's sake animalistic, for it seems to be uniquely human. This is particularly true if such sex is performed with imagination, thereby utilizing a distinctively human ability.

• If sex for procreation were a law of nature implanted in all living creatures by, say, an all-powerful God, it is difficult to see why defenders of procreation have to write elaborate treatises and deliver endless sermons telling us we ought to obey the dictates of nature. For if there is a natural law regarding procreation, it would seem plausible to assume that we would all have to obey it automatically as a matter of course, just as we must all obey the natural dictates to breathe, defecate, and eventually die. But the fact that defenders of nature have to struggle to convince us to procreate (or else face eternal damnation), and the fact that so many heterosexuals do not procreate (nor do any homosexuals) indicate that there are no natural laws compelling us to procreate or even to be heterosexual.

• Defenders of procreation make the mistaken assumption that if X results from Y, X was the purpose of Y. Babies, of course, do result from sex quite frequently (although not, oddly enough, during a female's infertile period, despite the fact that nature gave her sexual desires during this period, a fact the procreation theorist cannot explain). But, once again, because X results from Y, it does not follow that X was the exclusive or main goal or purpose of Y. All sorts of things result from sex, everything from ecstatic pleasure to venereal disease. (Certainly one would not say that gonorrhea is a purpose of sex, even though it is an all too common result of sex.)

Turning from this brief critique of traditional moral and religious views on the one true purpose of sex, we also find that there are those who have questioned the idea that sex is a natural instinct of all—whatever its purpose. Ti-Grace Atkinson, for example, argues that the desire for sex is really a function of the male's desire to dominate the female in the bedroom. When this need to dominate—and the correlative culturally conditioned desire in the female to surrender—is obliterated in some future era when the sexes are equal and feel no need for the dominance-submission syndrome, sexual desire will reveal itself for the culturally conditioned phenomenon it is and, according to Ms. Atkinson, will simply disappear.[3] The difficulty with Ms. Atkinson's theory is that she, like the conservative defenders of the natural-instinct philosophy, has assumed there is only one motive for sex: the culturally conditioned desire for dominance and submission. The fact that sex can have many purposes escapes both Ms. Atkinson and the defender of a natural instinct for procreation alone. In response to Ms. Atkinson's argument that sex will disappear when the dominance-submission syndrome is ended by overcoming sexist social conditioning, one could hold that since there are many other purposes sex might have (be they natural or socially conditioned), desires for sex will continue even after sexism is eliminated.

Finally, it might be noted that those who give up any attempt to define perversion as something that violates nature often turn to another criterion: A pervert is someone who disobeys social norms. But adultery violates a social norm, and it is not considered a perversion. Furthermore, such things as kissing in public and oral sex once violated social norms, though they are now widespread social phenomena that only a few conservatives would condemn. Basing a concept of perversion on disobedience to what is often a narrow-minded society, therefore, commits a person to basing his philosophy on the shifting sands of obedience to current fashions in sex. Anyone who prides himself on thinking for himself and on being able to transcend social conditioning would be revolted (and justifiably so) by such a socially defined concept of perversion.

---

3. Ms. Atkinson's views are summarized in Elizabeth Rapaport, "On the Future of Love: Rousseau and the Radical Feminists," *The Philosophical Forum* 5, nos. 1–2 (Fall-Winter, 1973-74): 188.

4
Perversion: Linguistic, Moral, and Psychological Considerations

Not all forms, alas, of the so-called perversions are as innocent as some of the unusual forms of sexual conduct. There is, for example, the question of sadistic acts of rape. Does a case such as this prove that *perversion* is a term that really does describe an objective feature of the world—some quality of rottenness in the act that one can see, in the way one tastes the rottenness of an apple? Yet many philosophers down through the ages have claimed that moral judgments are merely reports on expressions of a certain individual's or society's feelings, and that such feelings reveal only certain facts about that person's particular psychological perspective in responding to the world about him rather than to supposed moral "facts" of goodness or evil in the world itself. *Perversion,* they might argue, is merely a term that reveals our horror and disgust over the performance of certain acts; and even here, society is not consistent since it labels homosexuality a perversion but does not so label adultery or a heterosexual couple fornicating in public view in a park, despite the fact that society also disapproves these acts.

Certainly an act such as rape or sadism does pose a serious challenge to a "do my own thing" morality. For what if "my thing" is rape? Defenders of such a view might qualify this by saying: "Do your own thing so long as it does not violate the rights of others." But with "do your own thing" morality, who is to decide what the rights of others are or when there are overriding considerations that require that others' rights be violated? It would seem to be up to the individual himself who wants to do his own thing. Or one might say, "Do your own thing, so long as it does not *needlessly* harm others." (The term *needlessly* is important since it is sometimes necessary to harm others, as in self-defense). But once again, who is to decide when harming the other person is needless or not; perhaps the rapist felt his needs overrode the female's need to be left alone. Thus, while "you do your thing and I'll do mine" sounds like a very liberal live-and-let-live philosophy, there are simply too many circumstances where "my thing" involves some conflict with another human being's "thing." Such a philosophy is bereft of any way of resolving the issue except to leave it up to the individual to decide for himself whether to honor his own rights or the rights of the other. The individual deciding on a course of action may be a peace-loving liberal who leaves others alone, or he may not be; yet each may be doing his own "thing."

Consider, for example, a rape that is absolutely clear in its horror—the rape of a helpless infant. If one dares to question the claim that there are any perversions at all, isn't a sadistic act of this sort clear evidence to the contrary?

The rape of an infant is, to be sure, a brutal act, but how shall we describe the person who did it? Once he would have been unanimously described as possessed by demons; now he might be described as mentally ill (in liberal circles) or as a "notorious sex pervert who must be held responsible for his acts" (in conservative circles).

One difficulty that immediately arises is how to compare the raper of infants with others who are also said to be "perverts," if perversion is said to have a common "essence" in virtue of which they all may be so labeled, and thus condemned. Homosexuals, for example, who do not assault others and who consort only with those in their own age group, are often described by society as being perverted and mentally ill as well. But there is surely a confusion here since it is not clear how Leonardo da Vinci or Andre Gide was mentally ill, unless we so dilute the phrase to cover any alternative life-style whatever. Would we still want to say that Leonardo was a pervert, even if we drop the charge that he was mentally ill? But one who held this view would be driven to say that there are degrees of perversion, that some perverts are not really quite as perverted as others, since some are violent while others conduct their lives in a socially useful and self-fulfilling, integrated way.

But while it makes perfectly good sense to say that one person is more mentally ill than another, or more immoral than another, there is a kind of linguistic oddity about saying that Smith is more of a pervert than Jones is—unless we simply mean that Smith is somewhat more flagrant or frequent in the performance of his perverted acts. Perhaps this linguistic oddity is simply due to the fact that down through the ages society has decreed that a pervert is a pervert and that's it, regardless of whether he is Socrates or the Marquis de Sade. But then it is blatantly inconsistent and unfair of society to put all perverts in the same group, while simultaneously being willing to speak of degrees of mental illness and immorality and treating the differences accordingly.

More enlightened persons might, however, grant that there are differences among perverts that allow of differences in the way we are to view them. We might say there are "sick" perverts, who harm others, but also non-violent perverts, who are creative and socially beneficial in many ways. But why speak of non-violent persons who are socially beneficial as perverts at all? The phrase "alternative life-style" that has become so common in liberal circles in recent years would seem to be far more apt.

That is to say, it would not be fruitful to make perversion a generic concept in which perverted acts are subdivided into harmless and harmful or sick ones. For as long as mental illness or immorality is associated with perversion in any way whatever, the harmless perverted acts between mutually consenting adults will continue to be stigmatized by association with the so-called sick ones, however sharply we may try to draw the line between the two. Thus the only solution would be to declassify homosexuality, not only as an illness but as a perversion as well.

At this point, let us consider an article on sexual perversion in the *Encyclopedia of Sexual Behaviour*. Note the value-laden terms *right* and *wrong*, which the author uses: "It is mainly in the mode of expression and the nature of the sexual object that something goes wrong in the sexual pervert; either he behaves *wrongly* to the *right* object or he chooses the *wrong* object.[4] (Italics mine.)

4. Clifford Allen, "Sexual Perversions," *The Encyclopedia of Sexual Behaviour,* ed. Albert Ellis and Albert Abravanel (New York: Hawthorne Books, 1967), p. 803.

Behaving wrongly to the right object would include relations between a man and a woman. In such cases Allen lists the fetishistic injuring of another person (sadism), being injured (masochism), or oral-genital or anal-genital relations as an exclusive substitute for penile-vaginal coitus. Choosing the wrong object would include such things as homosexuality, pedophilia, coprophilia. If we accept Allen, it is clear that *perversion* is not the descriptive, scientific term it is purported to be, but is laden with value judgments that would be quite controversial among critics of the concept of perversion. Allen continues: "From a biological standpoint, the primary aim of sex is pleasure and reproduction, and includes at some stage, coitus between a man and a woman. When these aims are entirely sidetracked and, out of fear or fixation, the usual modes of heterosexual intercourse are entirely omitted, then the individual's behaviour is deviant."[5]

However, to base perversion on violations of biology is dubious. With the arrival of test-tube babies and ever more sophisticated forms of extrauterine fertilization and incubation, the use of intercourse for reproduction could theoretically become obsolete. With penile-vaginal intercourse dethroned from its key position of being the only way to reproduce, its only remaining role would be for pleasure, which Allen says is also a natural or biological aim. But since there are many ways of achieving sexual pleasure other than by penile-vaginal intercourse and since Allen has granted that sexual pleasure is natural, these other forms of sex, be they heterosexual or homosexual or whatever, should then be given equal status with penile-vaginal intercourse and not be condemned as perverted or unnatural.

Allen, however, goes on to modify his position in some important ways:

> It must be emphasized that sexual oralism, analism, and other extra-vaginal forms of sex are by no means perverted or neurotic under all or even most circumstances. Virtually all normal human beings have perfectly normal tendencies to engage in these kinds of sex acts (as well as mildly masochistic or sadistic activities). As Kinsey pointed out, manifestations of oralism, analism, and extravaginalism are part of our mammalian heritage, and it would be rare, and in some sense an emotionally disturbed or perverted, individual who had *no* such tendencies.
>
> Perversion occurs when the individual under no circumstances other than engaging in oral-genital or anal-genital relations can come to orgasm; or who participates in these acts because he is irrationally afraid of penile-vaginal copulation; or who compulsively drives himself to these activities in a self-destructive manner—this individual is truly perverted. But his brother or sister who thoroughly enjoys extravaginal engagements, but enjoys them as a significant part *but not the whole* of his or her sexual activity, this individual may not be in the least abnormal or

---

5. Ibid., p. 802. However, if one were to insist (as many psychologists do) that man is by nature bisexual, then would not Allen have to add that "if out of fear or fixation, the homosexual side is entirely omitted, then the individual's behaviour is deviant"?

perverted and may actually be more "normal" than a person who can, under all circumstances, enjoy only penile-vaginal intercourse (p. 80).

It is now clear, however, that once Allen has admitted that fellatio and sodomy and mild degrees of sadomasochism are all right under certain circumstances—for example, as supplements to penile-vaginal intercourse—there seems no reason for labeling as perverts those who engage exclusively in these activities, except for a question-begging preference for penile-vaginal intercourse. The most that one should say is that such persons are quite limited in the ways they can find sexual satisfaction. Indeed, many heterosexuals can, under no circumstances, have an orgasm except by engaging in penile-vaginal intercourse, yet Allen stops short of labeling them perverts; he says only that they may simply be somewhat less "normal" than those that can engage in a variety of alternate activities. Furthermore, someone who only engages in homosexual acts need not be "irrationally afraid" of penile-vaginal inter-course; he or she simply finds no enjoyment in it, anymore than some people have no taste for ants. (Significantly, Allen does not label as perverted those who are irrationally afraid of homosexual acts.)

Much more challenging is his claim that those who compulsively drive themselves to these activities in a self-destructive manner are truly perverted. (By "these activities" he mentions only oral-genital or anal-genital relations.) Society, however, is curiously ambivalent about how it describes those who are self-destructively compulsive. An artist or inventor who compulsively drives himself to complete his work to the neglect of his mental or physical health is often praised as a heroic, dedicated person. And significantly missing from Allen's account is any reference to heterosexuals who compulsively engage in penile-vaginal intercourse.

What, for example, of those husbands who make excessive demands on their wives, causing them mental anguish, and themselves neglecting their other duties to thus engage in conduct harmful to themselves? Or what of the heterosexual playboy or nymphomaniac who compulsively engage in endless sexual activity, often to their own detriment? As long as their compulsive activities are heterosexual and do not involve rape, society tends to describe such persons in more benign terms; they are commonly said to be simply too demanding or promiscuous. (Or if such persons are labeled "perverts" it is usually merely because society resents the fact that they are obtaining so much sex.) It seems clear, therefore, that it is not compulsiveness that is the criterion for perversion, but rather acts that deviate from society's norms. And someone who compulsively engages in sexual activities of which society disapproves would consider it blatantly unfair for society to label him or her a pervert, while tending to excuse those who compulsively engage in conventional heterosexual acts.

Perhaps, however, there is a further description of compulsive sexual behavior that may offer a more persuasive criterion for perversion. What of the person who engages in non-violent sexual acts of which society disapproves, who desires to change but finds he cannot, who cannot handle his behavior, and cannot integrate it successfully into his life's activities? Shall we say that he is a full-fledged pervert or that he is simply maladjusted or unable to accept what he is? Many of those who are unhappy with what they are, are simply the victims of a society that conditions them to feel that what they are doing is evil; someone who accepts such a judgment may very well develop neurotic traits mentioned. (Compulsive sexual behavior, for example, is often an attempt to seek relief from the self-hate engendered by society's disapproval of one's tastes, just as alcoholics seek forgetfulness of their sorrows in drink.) But if so, then perhaps society itself is "perverted" for causing those who have unusual sexual preferences to develop such traits that follow from a lack of self-acceptance. There are still, however, acts that harm others against their will; these will be discussed in the following section.

5
De Sade and Sartre on Sex and Sadism

Thus far we have argued that such traditional criteria for perversion such as an act's being abnormal or unnatural will not work. For example, a teen-age boy who finds a woman over eighty years of age sexually attractive might be said by society to have abnormal or unnatural desires; yet he is surely not a pervert. Sexual attractiveness is in the eye of the beholder, and his tastes could only be labeled odd, but not perverted. Or in a small Southern town a white female who is only attracted to black males would be labeled as having abnormal, unnatural, and even "sick" sexual desires. Yet she is surely not a pervert. Examples such as these tend to show that terms like *unnatural, abnormal,* and *sick* are merely expressions of society's distaste for certain sexual preferences, and do not refer to anything objectively present in the desire itself.

The supreme test of this thesis, however, comes when we turn to sexual acts of violence. There are, to be sure, many types of sadists. There is the sadist who only tortures a consenting masochist; there is the rapist who forces his victim to have sexual intercourse; and there is the sadist who may or may not rape his victim, but who tortures and mutilates her body and may eventually murder her. It might be argued that such acts, while perverse, are not really perverted in a sexual sense, since they are motivated solely by the desire for conquest and degradation. However, as I shall argue later, conquest and degradation can be quite arousing sexually. Many would argue that a picture of a nude female with her legs spread apart is a degradation of the female; yet males who read magazines containing such pictures clearly do so with sexual motives. Many males and females who masturbate report that they are aroused by rape fantasies. Thus the fact that the sadist's motive may be for conquest does not rule out sexual motives as well. And even if his original motive was not for a sexual thrill, the fact that such acts commonly produce a sexual thrill still makes them sexual phenomena.

The philosophical problem posed by sadism is this: How can we reconcile a claim that perversion is a term based on a purely human perspective invented by normal or conventional people to express their disgust with unusual sexual acts, with the other claim that violent perverts are doing something that is objectively evil? One could, of course, still say that there are no "objective" values in the nature of things, and that "perversion" as a term applied to violent crimes is still a human invention that is a *protective* form of terminology we invent to justify our punishment and prevention of such crimes. (Indeed, it is clear that the term *perversion* as traditionally applied to nonviolent sexual acts refers to nothing objectively evil in the act or to anything that makes the act bad in a non-moral sense. It is itself only a kind of protective terminology designed to safeguard a simple, traditional mode of family life where sex is meant primarily for procreation. To do this, society thinks it must stigmatize any act as being perverted that it thinks, rightly or wrongly, threatens conventional family living.)

However, some would argue that sadism poses no moral or philosophical problem, but only a psychiatric one, since the violent form of pervert is mentally ill and not responsible for his behavior. This may, of course, be true of some forms of particularly brutal perverts who don't just rape but who also mutilate or murder their victims, perhaps because they are symbolically trying to take revenge against an overprotective mother whom they resented in childhood.

Yet it need not necessarily be true that all rapists engage in totally involuntary behavior and thus present no moral or philosophical problem. There is, for example, the amoral delinquent who rapes but does not mutilate his victims, and who feels he is beyond conventional good and evil. Rape is merely a case of his "doing his own thing." Or there is the "double-standard" rapist, who idolizes "nice" girls but who regards females from the lower classes as perfectly proper subjects for exploitation. One must be very cautious about claiming that all those who relish violence and brutality are somehow mentally ill. Those who are disgusted by violence, for example, might label those who enjoy watching or participating in boxing matches or bullfights as having sick desires; but it surely does not follow that such persons are all mentally ill. *Sick* is used here simply as a term of moral disapproval.

De Sade himself thought there were three classes of sexual partners.[6] There is the normal, conventional type of person, whom he scorned as unimaginative and inhibited by social conventions. Such persons limit themselves to one very simple type of sexual act needed for procreation or for the quick relief of sexual tensions or to express love. To them, sex in itself is disgusting, and they would probably not practice it at all were it not the only means to procreate or to prevent sexual frustration. Yet—applying Nietzsche's theory of

6. The major statement of the Marquis de Sade's philosophy, although scattered throughout his writings, is found in *Three Complete Novels: Justine, Philosophy in the Bedroom, Eugenie De Franval; Other Writings*, trans. Richard Seaver and Austryn Wainhouse (New York: Grove Press, 1965), pp. 318–329. See especially *Philosophy in the Bedroom.*

conventional morality to sex—it is the inhibited masses of people who develop our codes of sexual morality. In Nietzsche's view, the masses are frightened of anything new or imaginative or bold, though they are secretly jealous of those who are strong enough to commit bold deeds. But since the inhibited masses know that they can never be imaginative or commit acts of daring, they rationalize their weakness by proclaiming that their way of life is superior and that the bold ones must submit to their constricted morality. The masses then escape feelings of inferiority by making, as it were, a virtue of necessity, the necessity being that they are weak and cowardly and unimaginative. This would be Nietzsche's theory of how our constricting, guilt-producing concept of what is sexually moral arises, and de Sade would heartily approve of the general outlines of Nietzsche's theory.

The second type of sexual being, for de Sade, was what he called the "natural pervert." Such a person can only find sexual satisfaction in some one limited way that deviates from what is considered normal. De Sade, however, argued that such persons are born with such proclivities, cannot help what they do, and should therefore not be condemned.

The third class is the one de Sade idolized: the sexual libertines. For him, these persons constituted a group of free spirits who use their imagination and free will to engage in any sexual thrill possible. They were, in contemporary slang, "try-sexuals"—try anything for a thrill. Like the amoral delinquent mentioned earlier, they thought of themselves as being beyond conventional good and evil, and as constituting a sexual elite. Society might consider them animalistic, but they would reply that it is the conventional people who are animalistic since, unlike the libertines, they do not use their distinctively human free will and imagination to choose to commit bold, imaginative sexual acts.

Unlike Nietzsche, however, in de Sade's case it is not clear that he thought only a special group of persons were naturally strong, and that the masses could never be anything other than what they are. For his writings are addressed to the masses as well as to the libertines, and he constantly calls on those who are inhibited by social conventions to throw away their shackles and be fully natural. Thus, unlike Nietzsche, he did not think conventional persons were by nature inhibited, but rather that they were the victims of repressive social conditioning. Once they were liberated, they could with practice find any object or person or sexual practice fulfilling. And, in de Sade's theory, all such practices would be natural and hence not perverted. All desires, he claimed, come from nature and nothing that it is possible to do would offend her. Otherwise nature would have made it impossible to conceive of or desire or be able to perform the act and receive pleasure from it. Although de Sade himself often defended a kind of "might makes right" philosophy to try to justify rape, he nevertheless felt that all persons, male and female, had certain strengths that entitled everyone to full sexual gratification. (In mentioning Nietzsche in this context, I do not mean to suggest that he would consider de Sade's libertines as examples of free spirits. What Nietzsche would think of de Sade will be discussed later.)

Let us now construct a debate between a sadist who develops arguments derived from de Sade (or which would be heartily approved of by de Sade's type of philosophy) and a female liberationist, who is convinced that rape is objectively abominable. For de Sade acts of violence yield such exotic sexual thrills that the end justifies any means of attaining them, but for the female liberationist, rape is the ultimate degradation of the female's dignity. The basic question is, of course, whether or not rape or other sadistic acts are perverted. Since sadism is usually considered a perversion when it involves forcing one's will on another, the concept of perversion here seems to rest on a moral issue. Thus our debate will be essentially about the morality of sadism. Of course, not all acts that are immoral are considered perverted; adultery is an example. But the degree of viciousness of sadistic acts, as contrasted with adultery, has apparently been the reason rape has been considered a perversion rather than a mere violation of a social norm.

Could either side win such a debate in the presence of a panel of neutral judges on the matter? (I am not assuming that such judges or ideal observers could be found, which is an additional problem that defenders of objective morality must face.) But let us see how such a debate might go, and let the reader judge for himself who has the better argument. The defender of de Sade might present the following arguments.

First, an act may be judged in terms of what caused it, what it "feels" like as it is immediately experienced, and what its consequences are. The sadist will doubtlessly focus on the immediate phenomenological "feel" of the experience and report that if the setting is just right, if the victim has little chance of contacting help, and so forth, then his sexual thrill may be intense indeed. But, it will be argued, any intense thrill is *to that extent* a good—the consequences for the victim notwithstanding. If it is claimed that the victim's pain and suffering are more intense than the sadist's pleasure, the sadist will challenge his opponent to prove how one can draw qualitative differences in immediate experiences of pleasure versus pain. Can a panel of judges get into the mind of each person and make such a comparison?

Once again it must be noted that what is at issue is the immediacy of the experience as it takes place during the act, not the consequent anguish the victim may feel for years later or the consequent sense of victory the perpetrator may relish in memory for years later. (These consequences are, to be sure, also equally difficult to measure in a pleasure-pain balance.) Furthermore, the sadist would ask, even if the victim does suffer prolonged mental anguish how does one prove that the *quantity* of that anguish outweighs in evil the *quality* of his exquisite feelings that can be savored for years? (This sort of argument can, of course, cut both ways since the victim of rape can equally well challenge the rapist to prove that his pleasure outweighs her pain and suffering.)

The second argument is pure de Sade and rests on his concept of nature as a vicious, violent realm and on his claim that one nevertheless ought to obey its dictates. For de Sade, the world is populated by the strong and the weak, and, by giving some persons (males) greater physical strength, nature thereby showed its intention to endow them with the right to temporarily possess the weak (specifically, women) for their own sexual gratification. But if, as de Sade argued, one should obey nature's dictates (and even Aquinas accepted this general principle although certainly he would not have agreed with de Sade's conclusions), then it is positively unnatural for a woman to resist the demands of any man who wants her. All women belong to all men, he argued, and it is positively selfish of a woman to give herself exclusively to one man for life. Although he did not say so, he might have added that in nature any mature penis will fit any mature vagina, and it probably is not nature's idea that we should search until we find the one perfect "fit."

De Sade might be classified as a classic case of male chauvinism pushed to its logical extreme, yet he also argued that women had an equal right to sadistically gratify their desires on men; indeed, he felt that women were stronger than men in one important respect—that their sexual desires were insatiable.[7] To compensate for women's lesser physical strength, houses of sadistic pleasure would be established in his utopia where men would be legally compelled to submit to women. But if de Sade had any true respect for what he thinks is the lustier female sexuality, he should realize that rape often makes it impossible for women ever to enjoy sex again.

How seriously de Sade meant any of his so-called philosophical arguments is unclear; perhaps he was simply tweaking the noses of those who argued that nature or instinct intends sex exclusively for procreation between those who have consented to marry one another. To do this, perhaps he felt that one could just as well show that nature equally gives men desires to seek sex for pleasure, with any means whatever or with the nearest victim available. "No inclinations or taste can exist in us save the ones we have from Nature, that she is too wise and too consistent to have given us any which could ever offend her.[8] If de Sade is correct, the concepts of nature and instinct are Protean concepts indeed and can be used to prove almost anything one wishes in sexual arguments.

Of course, if de Sade were truly serious about his use of nature as a criterion to sanctify sadism on the grounds that nature itself is a vicious realm, then he is being as unfairly selective in his interpretation of nature as are the conservatives who insist that nature sanctified sex only for procreation. For nature is surely not the wholly vicious, sadistic realm de Sade pictured it as being, as witness the self-sacrifice of animals for their young. Indeed, his admission that nature is vicious and violent would force him to concede that sadism is also vicious if sadistic desires are, as he claims, derived from nature. But this is hardly consistent with his glorification of sadism as being the ultimate sexual thrill.

De Sade was, furthermore, unclear about how it is that women have desires *not* to be assaulted and to choose a sexual partner they love. Would these

7. Curiously enough, Mary Jane Scherfey, a defender of a woman's right to all the sexual gratification she wants, argues the same view in *The Nature and Evolution of Female Sexuality* (New York: Random House, 1972), that women are capable of a virtually unlimited number of (clitoral) orgasms. Were it not for cultural conditioning, females would, like primate females, reveal themselves to be sexually insatiable and would cease soliciting men for sex only when physical exhaustion intervened. (pp. 134–35).

8. De Sade, *Three Complete Novels,* p. 326.

desires not be natural, too, if, as he has already claimed, all our desires are derived from or at least sanctioned by nature? Of course, he would condemn the resistance of women to his views as merely the product of conditioning by a narrow-minded society. But if all our desires derive from nature, would not society itself be a reflection of and thus sanctified by the nature de Sade uses as his model?

For Jean-Paul Sartre, the philosopher of existentialist freedom, the ideal human relationship is between two free *subjects*; exploitation of one person by another or mutual exploitation would thus be furthest from his ideal. It is in human sexuality that Sartre claims to see one of the clearest violations of his ideal, a violation that he feels eventuates in sadism. Through caresses, Sartre claims that sexual partners surrender their independence, subjectivity, and freedom and turn each other into lust-controlled objects, each manipulating the other for lustful gratification. But, more ominously, lust is not the real motive for sex; to Sartre, the real motive is an attempt to possess the other's freedom by trapping or incarnating it in the flesh. Sartre feels that conventional sex, for the reasons outlined below, fails to achieve this goal, and one is driven to violence and sadism to achieve the possession of the other's freedom.[9]

Thus Sartre's analysis, though certainly not a defense of sadism, nevertheless presents an interpretation of sex that must eventuate in sadism. Sartre argues that sadism itself also fails to achieve the goal of capturing the victim's freedom, a conclusion the defender of sadism would reject. What the sadist would find especially welcome in Sartre's analysis is the possibility that even voluntary sex—where each partner willingly becomes an object or instrument of the other's gratification in order to be in a position to possess the other—itself has sadistic overtones. He would then argue that full-fledged sadism merely carries these tendencies that Sartre claims to find in voluntary sex to their ultimate resolution.

For Sartre, interaction between persons is one of perpetual conflict. He speaks of the "stare" of others, whereby one finds oneself being judged or categorized in ways that one can never grasp, because it is impossible to penetrate the private consciousness of the person doing the "looking." One's own sense of self-possession and self-identity is thus constantly being threatened by the assessments of others over whom one has no control. This impenetrable gaze (that is, judgment) of others reduces one to feeling that one is a mere object or thing whose freedom and subjectivity have been stolen by the stare. The solution would seem to be to turn the tables on one's judge and to "look" at him in return. In this way one would recapture the freedom and subjectivity that has been stolen by others. But in staring at one's judge one will thereby have reduced him to a mere object whose freedom has been captured by one's gaze. Sartre's world is thus one of a perpetual struggle between persons, in which we can maintain our own psychological sense of freedom only at the expense of capturing the freedom of others.

9. Jean-Paul Sartre, *Being and Nothingness,* trans. Hazel Barnes (New York: The Philosophical Library, 1956). Sartre's concept of the "stare" is discussed on pp. 252–302. His discussion of sexuality is found on pp. 379–412.

Sexuality, for Sartre, is not essentially a matter of either procreation or lust, nor does it have any particular center in the genitals. Those who are eunuchs—sterile, or too old or too young to procreate—nevertheless feel sexual desire. Sexuality for Sartre is rather a way of relating to others by means of the body; sex is an attempt to capture the other person's freedom, for, as we noted, he thinks we can preserve our own freedom only at the expense of the freedom of others. In love, one wants to capture a *person's* freedom; but in sex one wants to focus on a person's *body* and gain possession of it. In normal, non-sadistic sex one does not want to enslave the other person in a violent fashion and thus risk reducing her to a mere piece of flesh whose freedom has been destroyed; for then there would be no freedom to capture. (The same line of reasoning, Sartre feels, lies behind the normal person's lack of interest in seducing the dead or the unconscious.)

In ordinary sex, one wants, therefore, to reduce the other person to an object to be possessed, yet one also wants her to be a subject whose freedom has not been utterly destroyed. Yet, if one has also reduced her to an object, one has destroyed the freedom one tried to possess, and one is left with a mere body that can only serve as an instrument for gratifying lust. We are thus left, Sartre concludes, with the contradictory ideal of trying to make the partner both a subject and an object, both a freedom that can be possessed and an object that has been reduced to a passive body, a quasi-slave of lust.

Although we are bound to fail, how do we, in Sartrean terms, try to trap the freedom of our partner without simultaneously destroying it? The goal in normal sex is to get the other person to submit freely to becoming totally identified with his or her own body, and to let its desires take control. The other's freedom becomes, so to speak, "incarnated" in the flesh, and is now available for my possession since the other person's consciousness is overwhelmed by lust and is hardly in a position to resist. This incarnation or embodiment of the partner's freedom is achieved by means of the caress. Sartre notes how a lover focuses on those parts of the body that are the least free to resist and are the most like objects: the fleshy, immobile parts such as the breasts, rump, stomach, and thighs.

Yet one finds it difficult to possess the other person for long, for in order to make his victim sexually desire him he must offer himself to her as an object of her gratification in order to be in a position to possess her. But then he becomes overwhelmed by lustful desire as a result of her caresses, and his own freedom is now trapped or incarnated in his flesh as well. But then, overwhelmed by his own lustful desires, he is as helpless as the one he was originally trying to possess, and he is now hardly in a position to capture the freedom he has incarnated in the other. And, being aroused by sexual desire, he now views his partner solely as an object of lust rather than as a freedom to be captured.

Furthermore, as soon as lust and orgasm take over, one will ultimately cease to relate to the other as possessor to possessed, and one will be lost in the privacy of one's own lonely pleasurable sensations. One will have lost interest in the other's body and the incarnated freedom one sought to possess; sexual sensations thus are counterproductive to the goal of sex as far as Sartre is concerned. Even if none of these things had occurred, we would still be left with a partner who is a mere object controlled by lust and whose freedom has vanished. What we had sought has thus eluded our grasp: the freedom of the other.

Sartre then adds that one may, in desperation, turn to sadism, a phenomenon that is already implicit in the normal sexuality outlined here. One could illustrate Sartre's description of sadism's goal by noting a daydream that many men have when they see a beautiful, graceful woman strolling down Fifth Avenue in all her dignity. They may mentally undress her and imagine her in bed, flat on her back, with her legs spread apart, panting and writhing with lust. But, more ominously, a few may take this degrading fantasy a step further and imagine her bound with a rope and forced to assume various awkward, immobile positions. For Sartre, what the sadist does is to actually transform grace into an obscene sight of awkwardness and immobility while maintaining control over his victim by not allowing himself to become incarnated or overwhelmed by lust.

But sadism, an attempt to force the victim to imprison her freedom in the flesh and thus capture it as one would a wild (that is, free) animal is, for Sartre, doomed to failure also. For example, she may still at any moment turn and "look" at her oppressor, thus once again stealing back the very freedom the sadist had sought to gain for himself. For the "look" contains a judgment that cannot be possessed or possibly even known by the torturer. The sadist then realizes that he has only possessed her body, but not her inner freedom to judge him as she wishes. In desperation, he may then try to beat her into such a stupor that she is no longer able to respond with such a "look" at all. But then one is left with a mere piece of flesh whose freedom has been destroyed; thus the freedom that the sadist sought has eluded him just as it did in normal voluntary sex.

Sartre has surely made a valid argument about the futility of attempts to possess the freedom of another. For a freedom that is possessed is no longer free. To possess another's freedom is as futile as trying to possess the steam on a window by touching it; the very act of touching the window makes the steam disappear wherever one touches it.

How could the sadist respond to Sartre's arguments about the futility of sadism? Of course, if the sadist is primarily trying to overcome some sense of inferiority and insecurity by robbing another person of her freedom (in some total sense of the word) and thus prove that he can completely master another by beating her into submission, then he may very well be frustrated for the reasons Sartre suggests. But there are many different kinds of sadists with differing motives for what they do. If capturing another person's freedom were his only motive, why wouldn't he simply bind her and lock her in a room and leave it at that? But if he engages in a sexual act with her, then considerations of lust must clearly enter into the picture. And if a certain strange kind of lustful thrill is his motive, he would not be concerned with whether he had conquered her inwardly as well as outwardly, and her "stare" would be of no great concern to him. For all that he would want is to capture a body and perform certain acts on it that provide him with the lustful thrills he seeks.

Sartre thinks that the sadist does not allow himself to think of lust, for to be overwhelmed by lust would cause one to lose control of one's victim. But one can be aroused by lust without necessarily being overwhelmed by it. Nor would the sadist allow his victim to become a mere helpless piece of flesh by beating her into a stupor, for he undoubtedly wants her to be sufficiently free to make some kind of response (such as screams of agony or resistance) to give him the sense of conquest and the lustful thrill this provides. Finally, if capturing her freedom were his primary motive, one would think the sadist would want to possess his victim permanently. Yet the rapist ordinarily finishes the act as quickly as possible and lets his victim go free, once again suggesting that he was primarily seeking a momentary lustful thrill.

A further argument for sadism, which de Sade would heartily endorse, is that there is, in many persons at least, a link between sexual pleasure and pain. A pacifist from another planet would be shocked at the sight of a huge man making rapid thrusts into a tiny female's vagina—giving her vagina a "beating," to use Marie Bonaparte's phrase. But the female would tell such a man of peace to go away, for she's positively enjoying what he is doing. What appears to be agony to an outside observer is really ecstasy to her. For example, a series of rapid thrusts of the penis in the vagina can be a pleasurable phenomenon, even though each individual thrust is painful in itself. Is there, therefore, really a sharp distinction between pleasure and pain in the sex act, provided one doesn't decide in advance that there must be this distinction and thus read into the act horrors that are only in his mind?

Indeed, every sexual act is at least mildly aggressive for the one who takes the active role: the vigorous thrusting of the male penis by a sexually excited male, giving one's partner a love bite, and even having the partner bear the weight of one's body—all connote dominance and aggression. One's partner may well find such things sexually thrilling, and would quite likely reject the timid moralist who resists such acts because he thinks they violate treating one's partner like a person.

At this point the sadist would try to push these phenomena to their farthest conclusion: If a mild degree of aggression and dominance such as that found in the conventional sex act is exciting for both partners, then total violence must be the ultimate thrill. And if causing and receiving a little pain can be thrilling (as in love bites), then causing and receiving extreme pain must be even more thrilling. Analogously, if one finds jumping from a tree an exciting experience, then sky-diving would be the ultimate thrill. Most of us are, of course, frightened by such extremes, but the sadist would assure us that such fears are utterly irrational since experience so often conquers them and opens up new possibilities for pleasures we never thought possible.

It should be noted, however, that this argument about the link between sexual ecstasy and agony would not work for a rapist whose victims also agree that violence and pain are wonderful things. For if the rapist's victims do not resist or express some kind of horror at the act, it then merely becomes sadism with a consenting masochist, and the rapist is robbed of his joy of the actual conquest of his victim.

Most persons, furthermore, would find it difficult to believe that because a small amount of pain or dominance might enrich a sex act, it would necessarily follow that vastly increased amounts of such things would make the sex act even better. To sprinkle a small amount of salt on one's eggs might very well make them taste better, but it would be a rare individual who would find that pouring an entire cup of salt on them would make them taste more delicious.

Finally, a possible argument by the sadist could perhaps go far in explaining why rape is such a common phenomenon, and why its significance transcends its importance in a hypothetical debate such as this. It is not so much an argument for rape as it is a commentary on our hypocritical society. The sadist might argue that in a world where people hide their true feelings—if, indeed, they feel anything at all—causing pain to another person is the one sure way by which one knows he has had a definite impact on another, that he has gotten an honest response. In a world of phoniness and "put on" smiles of gratitude and happiness, in a world where people rarely communicate honestly anymore, communicating degradation and pain is better than nothing at all. At last, the sadist thinks, one has gotten through to somebody and elicited a genuine feeling. Pain comes from genuine inner hurting, whereas happiness may be only a mask to please and flatter others.

6
Some Arguments Against Rape

Let us now turn to some of the arguments that might be given against rape.

The first argument will open with the abstract of a paper read at the American Philosophical Association in Chicago in 1975 by Professor Marilyn Frye:

Rape and Respect for Persons: The respect one has for another is reflected in what one deems to be in their *domain*—the space in which they do what they please. A person little respected is one whose domain is particularly narrow and/or restricted in certain ways.

From here we can see that what makes rape so odious a crime. Physical penetration without consent is the perfect and complete arrogance of *domain*. You act as if all the space(s) which might have been presumed to be in their domain are in yours. You act as though they have no domain, and it is therefore an act which reveals a total absence of respect for persons.[10]

10. This quotation is from the program notes for the convention. Ms. Frye also links rape with a revelation to the woman of just where she stands in a sexist society where women are considered inferior. She says: "The act of heterosexual rape is often seen as a degrading of the woman, but it is not a 'de-grading.' It is merely the assertion of the 'grade' she already had—her status as being without respect. Her real status is often obscured by the condescending 'kindliness' which often mark male-female relations. So rape is an *exposure,* a *revelation* to her of her status; and the well-timed revelation of disrespect can be as violent as the disrespect is base."

Does not the strength of Frey's thesis also rest on the fact that the rapist himself does not desire to be raped, and insists on the very thing he denies others: the right to have some domain of his own where he is free to do what he pleases, obviously a prerequisite for one who wishes to be free to assault others?

Yet de Sade might still insist that he has some special right to do as he pleases, and that others do not have a similar right to treat him as he treats others. But can he prove that he has special qualities that give him a special right to invade the domain of others while denying others a similar privilege toward him?

Consider, for example, the following manner of establishing a principle of freedom that might be used against the sadist: (1) Each person must say "My freedom is valuable." (2) One ought to make judgments about relevantly similar cases. (3) Persons are relevantly similar. (4) Each person must therefore accept the judgment: "The freedom of others is equally valuable to mine."

But the tricky phrase in this analysis is *relevantly similar*. Has not de Sade argued that men have superior strength to women and thus have a right to force them to submit to their wills?

Furthermore, the sadist might argue that he is perfectly willing to submit to the same punishment he inflicts on others. For is not sadism also linked with masochistic desires, as psychoanalysts maintain? (The sadist vents his hostilities, the psychoanalyst would say, to avenge the brutal treatment he received in childhood; yet he still retains a need for punishment since he has been conditioned to feel that he is so worthless and naughty that he deserve it and, indeed, comes to enjoy and expect it to assuage the sense of guilt induced by his parents.) Thus the sadist would say he cannot lose: if he inflicts pain without being caught, he wins; and if he is caught and punished, he wins also since his masochistic desire for punishment is also gratified.

Second, there is the familiar argument that if sadism became a common practice, society would disintegrate and return to a state of the jungle where, as Hobbes put it, life is "nasty, brutish, mean, and short." But de Sade himself argued that everything is ultimately derived from nature, that nature is a ruthless dog-eat-dog realm, and thus that society itself is based on violence in many subtle forms: ruthless competition for women, jobs, money, and power. The rich "screw" the poor and the government "shafts" the young in sending them off to brutal, senseless wars to which they never consented. (The sexually sadistic overtones of such slang words as *screw* and *shaft* that exist in our language indicates that we are not wholly in disagreement with de Sade's cynicism.)

Furthermore, does the failure of citizens to help victims of rape reflect not only the insensitivity bred by the cruel society in which we live, but also the notion that, in some subconscious way, they are akin to the rapist himself? Would they feel they are somehow also "turning themselves in" if they reported the rapist? It is certainly not fear of the rapist, since in many such cases the citizen could easily call the police from the security of his apartment. (Furthermore, if society is itself implicitly involved in its own crimes, there would be the further difficulty of finding a neutral court of moral appeal to which one could test the claim of the sadist that he has special powers that make the principle of freedom mentioned in the first argument inapplicable to him.)

It is, however, perhaps not true that the rapist is justified because his accusers are not so innocent themselves. To do something because everyone else is in some sense guilty does not justify the act; it only adds to the misery we have enough of anyway. But the problem, we must recall, was the one of finding a way to refute arguments for rape in a philosophical fashion—to refute the claim that morality is a matter of opinion and that one is as much entitled to one's own opinion as anyone else. Indeed, society itself claims that it is proper to invade the private domain of others and punish or confine them, provided there is a good reason for doing so—for example, if they constitute a threat to the welfare and safety of others.

De Sade, however, might reply by claiming that he has *his* good reasons for justifying the confinement and punishment he perpetrates on others, that the concept of "good reasons" is a value judgment, and that value judgments are up to the individual to decide for himself.

At this point it might be argued that de Sade's picture of society is altogether too cynical, and that even if there is widespread viciousness on the part of so-called good people, there still must be some degree of law and order. Further, de Sade's ideas would destroy what mutual respect for individual rights we do have now.

But some of de Sade's other ideas complicate this sort of response about the collapse of society. For de Sade wanted to establish a curious "community of law," in which houses of sexual pleasure would be established that all citizens, male and female, would be legally obligated to attend. There they would be compelled to submit to whatever sexual acts—no matter how "perverted" or sadistic—that others wanted to practice on them.[11] And they in turn could do the same to those who had practiced such acts on them. This is based on his view that no one could selfishly claim that he had a legal right to withhold his mate's sexual delights from those in need of them, whoever they might be. For in a truly unselfish society, everyone should be sexually available to everyone else, so that no one—men or women—would be sexually unfulfilled.

In his sexual utopia de Sade presumably would also have banned love and marriage, things which he thought were utterly possessive and selfish. Love and marriage, he argued, were selfish in that one claimed one's sexual partner exclusively for oneself, thus removing him or her as a source of enjoyment for others. (He had the curious idea that it was moral to satisfy one's sexual desires by possessing a woman temporarily, as in rape, but that it was immoral

---

11. There is clearly something odd about trying to legalize rape or trying to persuade society that it is a perfectly good thing. If a woman discovered that rape were legal and was a law-abiding person, then she would submit willingly to being raped. But to submit willingly is not to be raped at all. Or if a woman were to read de Sade's works (and they are addressed to both men and women) and, if she were convinced by de Sade's arguments that men have a natural right to rape women, then if she believed in respecting the rights of others, she would submit willingly. But this is, again, hardly what it means to be raped, for to be raped is to be forced to do something against one's will. And how could de Sade then fulfill his claim: "One must do violence to the object of one's desire; for when it *surrenders,* our pleasure is all the greater"?

to possess her permanently, as in marriage.) In holding that everyone ought to be sexually available to everyone else, he would reject the idea of only certain persons having sexual appeal as being merely the product of our social conditioning. With practice and an open mind, he thought we could find anyone, no matter how ugly, to be sexually appealing. Thus everyone in his utopia would be sexually fulfilled.

Indeed, de Sade might argue that Ms. Frye's defense of a sexual private domain does not necessarily concern itself with respect for persons at all. For she may be, in effect, defending a feature of our competitive atomistic society in which only those who are sexually attractive are invited into one's private domain. On the other hand, those who are old or ugly or who are dissatisfied with conventional sexuality are often condemned to a different private domain that is lonely and unfulfilling.

Indeed, if one separates out of de Sade's communal utopia his obsession with forcing others to submit to undesired sexual acts, then one could imagine a society that would perhaps be far more fulfillling than the lonely, selfish one in which we live, in which sexual satisfaction is denied to so many who do not fulfill the demanding criteria of those who refuse to admit anyone to their private domain until just the right one comes along who can satisfy their egos as well as their genitals.

There is, however, a third argument that might hit the sadist where it hurts him the most, namely that sadistic sex is actually bad (that is, inferior) sex. For non-consensual sadistic sex is not sexual *intercourse,* where one feels the joy of one's partner as well as oneself. Rather, sadistic sex might be claimed to be the lonely act of masturbating in someone's vagina.

Furthermore, can someone who is struggling with an unwilling victim really concentrate on sex? Can a man who is filled with fear of detection and hatred for his victim be open to sensual desires and their gratification? In existentialist terms, can he "become his body" and utterly surrender himself to lust when he must use his wits constantly to control the situation, manipulate torture devices, and otherwise occupy his mind with non-sensuous thoughts?

Perhaps the most the sadist could say in reply is that it is not necessary to turn off the intellect and become a pure body to enjoy sex. For he may find that using his wits to ensnare his victim and employ instruments of torture is quite erotically arousing. And he might add that fear of detection and hatred of his victim add to, rather than detract from, the degree of his erotic arousal. If his claims were correct, he could then have just as rich a combination of mental, emotional, and sensual elements functioning as lovers claim they have during a sexual encounter.

Since the author of this book is not a sadist, he is in no position to verify the sadist's experience as described. What the sadist has not proved, however, is that his momentary satisfaction outweighs in value the permanent damage he may have done his victim. And it is highly doubtful that he could prove such a thing, except possibly in a tiny minority of cases.

Who has won this argument between the sadist and the majority of society? This I will leave to the reader to decide. But I should like to add one further note as to whether rape or sadism should be called a perversion. We have already noted that it is highly dubious that any of the consensual acts (or solitary acts performed with such unusual objects as excrement) deserve to be called perversions in any objective sense of the word. Non-consensual acts, therefore, remain as the most powerful argument for "real" sexual perversions. But perverse as sadism may be, is it really a sexual perversion?

It might rather be argued that sadism is an act of *symbolic murder,* in which the sadist stabs his victim, not with a knife but rather with his penis. It is an act of hate and violence and thus is perverse; but it need not be termed a *sexual* perversion, despite the fact that there is penile-vaginal penetration. The argument against this point of view is that sex can have many purposes, including aggression (which can be sexually arousing), without ceasing to be sexual. Indeed, for a rapist to be able to obtain and maintain an erection while dealing with a screaming, struggling victim certainly might indicate that there is some degree of sexual arousal present. And if one wished only to conquer and degrade a woman, one could surely use far simpler means of achieving this goal than engaging in the relatively complicated and risky act of disrobing oneself and one's victim and performing a sexual act.

One is not, therefore, forced to conclude that rape must be either an act of lust *or* an act of violence against and degradation of women, as if these were mutually exclusive alternatives. Susan Brownmiller in *Against Our Will: Men, Women, and Rape* (New York: Simon & Shuster, 1975) cites a case of the rape of a seventy-year-old woman as evidence that rape is motivated not by lust but rather by contempt for women. Yet the elderly woman may have reminded the rapist of his hated mother for whom he had repressed incestuous wishes; thus even here it is possible that contempt and lust can exist side by side.

One might still argue, however, that rape is not a sexual phenomenon, on the grounds that the rapist did not enter into the act for the purpose of having a sexual experience. He merely discovered that the act was sexually arousing, so that the sexual arousal was only a side effect of the rape experience. Or one might argue that even if a sexual experience was part of his motive for raping someone, it was, at best, only a secondary consideration.

Neither of these arguments, however, destroys the claim that rape is, at least in part, a sexual phenomenon. One may ride a horse, for example, without having any prior thought that it was going to provide a sexual experience. Yet the rubbing of the groin against the saddle may very well arouse sexual feelings. Thus riding a horse could be said to be a sexual experience, even if the fact that it does so is the result of a discovery. And the claim that the rapist's having a sexual experience is only a secondary consideration certainly does not destroy the claim that rape is, at least to some degree, a sexual phenomenon.

In summary, it seems clear that many of the traditional arguments against rape are not going to prove that rape is evil in all cases. Yet this goes against all our intuitions that rape is an absolute evil. One might argue that if everyone assaulted others at will the fabric of society would be destroyed. In such a world everyone would live behind locked doors and the rapist would find no available victims for assault; nor would the rapist himself be free from assault. But a "what if everybody did it" argument would still allow the possibility that if only a few people were rapists society would not be destroyed. Still, our intuitions tell us that any instance of rape is evil.

If, on the other hand, we use a hedonistic scale to claim that the victim's pain far outweighs the aggressor's pleasure, there is still the possibility that a particularly hardened or imperturbable victim might shrug off the incident as being of no particular significance, so that the rapist's pleasure would then have outweighed her pain. But would not such a rape still be an unjust act?

Finally, if one holds that the rapist is being inconsistent in violating the rights of others while demanding that he himself not be assaulted, then one is faced with the case of the rapist who is captured, who can no longer vent his aggressions outwardly, and who then turns his aggressions against himself and becomes a masochist who welcomes being assaulted. Yet such a rapist would still be held to be unjust, however, much as he may avoid any charge of inconsistency.

Another way to avoid the charge of inconsistency would be for the rapist to hold that the strong have certain rights over the weak, but that if the strong one is caught he has thereby been proved to be weak. He might then grant that the stronger forces of the law can do to him what he did to his victim. This argument, though not violating the principle of consistency, still seems to give the rapist a right to do as he wishes so long as his strength is not disproved by his being caught. Yet whether he is caught or not, whether he is strong or weak, does not seem to have any bearing on the injustice of what he did. (It is important to note that this latter "might make right" philosophy allows the rapist to accept freely that others punish him in the way he has tortured others without his punishment being tied to some compulsive masochistic desire that would make such desires involuntary or signs of mental illness and thus remove the debate from the moral realm.)

Is there a moral framework which could prove—and not merely assert—that all cases of rape are evil? One seems to be left only with the notion of a basic right to have one's privacy respected and the claim that this right takes precedence over the rapist's claim that he has a right to force others to have sex. But where do rights come from? If one's right to be left alone comes from God or nature, why is it that so many have perhaps been endowed by this very same God or nature with aggressive impulses that violate this right? Indeed, what with all the disasters that have been inflicted on innocent persons down through the ages (hurricanes, earthquakes, plagues, and so forth) that are not the fault of man himself, one wonders if God or nature has any real concern for human preservation or human dignity at all.

If, on the other hand, our rights come from society, why is that so many societies are based on the kind of competitive struggle that fosters the very aggressions they claim they want to suppress? One might hold that society must defend human rights on the grounds that society would otherwise collapse into a primitive state. But this is a dubious foundation on which to base a respect for the human rights of *all* persons; for most societies in the world daily violate in one form or another the rights of a minority or even a majority of their citizens, and most such societies manage to survive quite nicely.

Appeals to God, nature, or society as a foundation of one's rights to be left alone seem, therefore, to yield inconclusive results at best. If we go on to argue that the nature of man himself has a certain kind of dignity derived from his rationality, his creativity, his free will, and so forth, then the sadist would simply point out that no philosopher has shown how these traits entail a moral claim about respect for persons, such that aggression ought to be repressed or sublimated in their favor. The difficulty is that many philosophers hold that moral claims are matters of judgment that vary from person to person, and thus belong in a different logical category altogether from any facts about uniquely human traits. Such facts, it would be argued, could therefore not entail any moral claims or rights. And if one does hold that facts entail values and rights, then one is confronted by de Sade's claim that the superior strength of the male entails a right to rape women. We thus seem to be left with a conflicting claim about rights. How is the argument to be adjudicated in a philosophical way?

One might argue against de Sade that mere physical strength does not entail a human right but only an animal right, and that human rights clearly take precedence over animal rights. But someone might try to rescue de Sade by arguing that the more complex forms of sadism in which he was more interested do require superior human imaginative powers. Such a sadist must conceive of ways to trap his victim without being caught, and he must use his imagination to conceive of ever new forms of torture. He would then claim that a person with such supposedly superior talents has a right to do as he pleases with those who lack such powers, be they male or female. He would argue that, ethical dogmas to the contrary, nature has not created all humankind equal and that the doctrine of equal rights is a myth.

It is instructive, however, to see how a philosopher like Nietzsche would respond to such an argument. Nietzsche himself sometimes argued that nature created two classes of beings: the strong and the weak and that the former have rights over the latter by virtue of their superior talents. But Nietzsche's minority of the strong were usually pictured as philosophers, poets, and artists, who sought the ultimate challenge to their powers in creating great works that would ennoble civilization. Even in his darker moments, when he claimed that conquerors such as Caesar and Napoleon could trample on the rights of the masses in their march to glory, such men could still be said to have had a kind of strength in facing the challenge of conquering entire nations. But how, Nietzsche would ask, could a mere sadist claim to be a man of strength when he chooses only helpless and weak victims? If de Sade has any claim to superior powers at all, Nietzsche would hold that it was proved by his having written literary works describing bizarre sexual fantasies. The sadist, Nietzsche would argue, is not a strong man at all; other critics would hold that the sadists' sexual philosophy is only an exotic version of that vulgar hedonism which is the opiate of the masses who are incapable of the self-discipline that the truly strong must undergo to achieve their destiny.

If the sadist cannot claim to have any superior human rights, then his philosophy can be refuted simply by noting that his pleasures must be foregone because the vast human misery his philosophy promotes far outweighs the pleasures of a few sadists. One might reasonably compel a certain number of people to suffer in order to defend their country's freedom and ensure the happiness of the majority of its citizens, but one cannot compel the sadist's victims to suffer in the name of one person's selfish desires. Finally, it should be noted that as long as women are regarded as suitable objects of exploitation and as long as male sexuality is defined in terms of dominance, there will always be those few who carry sexism and dominance to their ultimate resolution in rape. Were women treated with as much respect as men, and were male dominance redefined into some other form of strength (such as the ability to give a woman a good orgasm—no mean feat if the statistics are right), then perhaps rape would disappear.

Perhaps, however, the mere disappearance of sexism would not solve the problem. A critic might argue that if sexual violence is to be overcome, there must be a complete overhaul of the nature of society itself. If aggression is a natural trait, then society must be transformed so that every person can channel his aggressions in some constructive way. Or if society itself breeds aggression, then society must make certain that its members have at least a minimal degree of self-respect so that they will not be driven to project their own self-hate onto others in brutal ways. (It is a commonplace in psychology to hold that we treat others in ways that reflect our view of ourselves.)

Furthermore, I would like to propose that the use of sex as an expression of hatred and violence is perhaps due to the philosophy propounded by the sexual conservative, who would be the most horrified by de Sade's philosophy. The conservative's insistence that sex can only be redeemed by being used as a vehicle for reproduction or for communicating love reveals an underlying contempt for sex in and of itself. And if sex is viewed with scorn, then one can only expect that certain persons will use sex as an expression of hatred and violence. In my view, those who have a sense of self-respect and who can respect and enjoy sex for its own sake will never use it to brutalize another human being.

In summary, I should like to point out quite strongly that I have not presented both sides of the rape issue in order to condone in any way such a vicious crime. In the courtroom of philosophy, as in the courtroom of law, both sides must be allowed to state their case, however odious the criminal's views may be. I have presented the rape issue in this format to challenge the reader to think more deeply about the philosophical foundations of human rights and human dignity as they relate to sexual questions. There are, indeed, many difficulties with whatever philosophical theory we invoke to defend universal human rights. My argument that the sadist's philosophy results in a far greater balance of pain over pleasure would not, for example, work in all possible worlds. For one might imagine a society that was so legally structured that the vast majority of citizens, while they would not be permitted to assault each other, could force a small minority to submit to their sadistic whims. In such a society the sadistic pleasures of the majority would perhaps outweigh the pain and suffering of the minority, and would thus be justified in terms of the pleasure-pain argument. Yet we would still condemn such a society for its gross violation of human rights.

But where do human rights come from? We have already noted that an appeal to God, nature, or society is a dubious foundation from which to derive a concept of universal respect for human rights. So far as the natural desire to be free is concerned, this seems to be contradicted daily by the millions of persons who find making their own decisions too great a burden to bear and who gladly surrender their freedom to social conformity, religious cults, or even to a Hitler. And in hundreds of societies, being free to choose one's lover and sexual partner is unheard of and would be considered utterly unnatural. One's mate is chosen by one's parents or by the tribe, often even before one is born. (See Robert Brain's *Friends and Lovers,* New York, Simon & Shuster, 1977.)

But if God, nature, and society constitute a dubious foundation for human rights, one seems to be left only with the claim that human rights are based on some kind of inherent human dignity. But how do we prove that all persons have human dignity? To say that we have human dignity merely because we are human seems vacuous and circular. If man himself pronounces that he has human dignity, this would be, given man's love for himself, hardly a neutral evaluation. (A super-human race of beings from another planet might view us in the way we view cattle.) And to define human dignity in terms of uniquely human traits such as rationality, creativity, free will, and so forth would leave infants, the subnormal, the psychotic, and the senile without any dignity at all.

In the final analysis, perhaps we should say that human dignity is not a theoretical concept for which one can offer a philosophical proof. It is, rather, a practical concept in which we must all believe not only for our own self-preservation but also for our sense of self-worth as free beings. Indeed, even the sadist believes he has some kind of human dignity and the rights to protection derived therefrom; otherwise he would be unable to survive and engage in his criminal deeds.

7
Thomas Nagel's Theory of Perversion

In this section we shall return to our original question once again: Is there really such a thing as sexual perversion? It seems clear that any object can be the object of sexual interest to someone, but (with the possible exception of non-voluntary acts) it is still not clear how one can distinguish perverted acts from non-perverted acts.

Thomas Nagel, in a classic paper titled "Sexual Perversion,' argues that naturalness and some deviation from it must be the criterion for perversion if there is to be such a thing as perversion at all.[12] Yet the standard for naturalness is not to be found in some specific physical act, such as procreation. Those who are sterile do not procreate, yet they are not perverted. Nor can the criterion be taken from some deviation from a social norm. Adultery, he notes, violates sexual mores; yet it is not considered a perversion either.

For Nagel, it seems that the naturalness he speaks of is essentially tied to the *psychological* ways in which two partners relate to each other, along with the resultant bodily state this produces. Natural sex, he claims, essentially involves the way in which two partners relate to each other's desire to be desired sexually in turn and the extent to which each thereby reduces the other to a state of self-surrender to sexual desire that takes over the entire body.

What is the nature of this mutual feedback that, according to Nagel, leads to ever deeper levels of arousal? Feedback occurs when one person is aroused by another person, who is perhaps unaware of that person's arousal; but when the other person senses he is being stared at and is aroused also, one senses this other person's arousal and is further aroused. He is also aware that this further arousal is a response to him. As each partner continues to steal glances at the other, each one's sensuality and arousal is further increased in response to the increased arousal seen in the other. But there is also clearly a strong degree of ego-involvement, for each one is obviously flattered to know that he or she has made an impression on the other and is responsible for the increasing degrees of arousal in the other.

As an example of such feedback, Nagel considers the hypothetical case of Romeo and Juliet sitting at a cocktail bar:

Suppose a man and a woman, whom we may call Romeo and Juliet, are at opposite ends of a cocktail lounge with many mirrors on its walls, permitting unobserved observation and even mutual unobserved observation. Each of them is sipping a martini and studying other people in the mirrors. At some point Romeo notices Juliet. He is moved, somehow, by the softness of her hair and the diffidence with which she sips her martini, and this arouses him sexually. Let us say that X *senses* Y whenever X regards Y with sexual desire. (Y need not be a person and X's apprehension of Y can be visual, tactile, olfactory, and so on, or purely imaginary. In the present example we shall concentrate on vision.) So Romeo senses Juliet, rather than merely noticing her. At this stage he is aroused by an unaroused object; so he is more in the sexual grip of his body than she of hers.

Let us suppose, however, that Juliet now senses Romeo in another mirror on the opposite wall, though neither of them yet knows he is seen by the other (the mirror angles provide three quarter views). Romeo then

12. In *Philosophy and Sex,* ed. Robert Baker and Frederick Elliston (Buffalo, N.Y.: Prometheus Books, 1975), pp. 247–60.

begins to notice in Juliet the subtle signs of sexual arousal: heavy lidded
stare, dilated pupils, a faint flush. This of course renders her much more
bodily, and he not only notices but senses this as well. His arousal is
nevertheless still solitary. But now, cleverly calculating the line of her
stare without actually looking in her eyes, he realizes it is directed at him
through the mirror on the opposite wall. This is definitely a new development, for it gives him a sense of embodiment [that is, feeling like a lust-
filled body], not only through his own reactions, but also through the eyes
and reactions of another. Moreover, it is separable from the initial sensing
of Juliet, for sexual arousal might begin with a person sensing that he is
sensed and being assailed by the perception of the other person's desire
rather than merely by the perception of the person.

But there is a further step. Let us suppose that Juliet, who is a little
slower than Romeo, now senses that he senses her. This puts Romeo in a
position to notice, and be aroused by, her arousal at being sensed by him.
He senses that she senses that he senses her. This is still another level of
arousal, for he becomes conscious of his sexuality through his awareness
of its effect on her and of her awareness that this effect is due to him.
Once she takes the same step and senses that he senses her sensing him, it
becomes difficult to state, let alone imagine, further iterations, though
they may be logically distinct. Physical contact and intercourse are
perfectly natural extensions of this complicated visual exchange, and
mutual touch can involve all the complexities of awareness present in the
visual case, but with a far greater range of subtlety and awareness
(pp. 253–54).

To put Nagel's example into simpler language: I see you and I am aroused;
you see me and you are aroused; I then see that you are aroused by me and this
arouses me even further; you see that I am aroused by your arousal, and you
are aroused even further; this further arousal of yours then arouses me even
further, and so on.

Such a complex set of responses would, however, seem to be an exception to
the relatively simple and quick way most people signal their desire for another.
Nagel's couple seems positively to enjoy sitting and eyeing each other with desire
in a complex seductive ritual, while most couples would simply signal their intentions, chat for awhile, and then go to bed. Indeed, we can wonder if Nagel's
couple is aroused by sexual considerations at all; maybe it is their egos that are
being progressively aroused by noticing the impact each is having on the other.

Nagel, however, goes on to argue that, if the feedback loop illustrated by the
Romeo and Juliet example is successful, each person will become progressively
"embodied," a state in which consciousness becomes, as it were, incarnated in
the body and submits to the body's control. One is virtually taken over by lust,
and conscious self-control is supposedly limited to the bare minimum
necessary to give some direction to the sexual act. Nagel writes that "ideally
deliberate control is needed only to guide the expression of those impulses,"

but it would seem that if one's whole body is literally "saturated with lust," as Nagel claims, one's actions would become utterly involuntary. But would one then have any control over or awareness of what one is doing, or any awareness of or ability to respond to one's partner's needs.

Indeed, he writes: "What is perceived is one's own or another's subjection to or immersion in his body. . . . In sexual desire the involuntary responses are combined with submission to spontaneous impulses; not only one's pulse and secretions but one's actions are taken over by the body; ideally deliberate control is needed only to guide the expression of those impulses" (p. 255). But if there is to be the kind of deliberate control obviously needed to prevent one from becoming so enveloped in one's own sensations that he cannot relate to or sense his partner's needs, then one is not going to be able to fully submit to one's body's direction. And for those who insist on completely surrendering to lust, it is going to be terribly frustrating to have to control one's increasingly aroused lustful state. Thus Nagel's intense concern with interpersonal communication of sexual feelings, as illustrated in the Romeo and Juliet seduction scene, would seem to run the serious risk of being violated once Romeo and Juliet reach the bedroom.

What, then, does Nagel consider a perversion? A perverted act would occur when there is some violation of what he calls "complete" sex. Complete sex involves (1) the embodiment of both partners, where each surrenders fully to being directed by sexual desire, and (2) the creation of this state of embodiment by multiple levels of interperceptual awareness of each other's desire and increasing arousal. This can take place either on the visual level, as in the Romeo and Juliet example, or on the tactile level, as in foreplay.

Using the second criterion, there can be no feedback of the kind Nagel wants in masturbation, voyeurism, exhibitionism, or sex with animals, shoes, infants, or with those who are dead, unconscious, or asleep. However, it is not clear why someone who does not care to be desired by a sexual partner need thereby be considered perverted. Such persons may be shy or simply unwilling to endure the difficulties of trying to please someone else. But do they thereby deserve to be labeled perverts? Indeed, even ordinary heterosexuals are sometimes most stimulated, either in the cocktail bar or in the bedroom, by those who are aloof and do not respond with a desiring stare. Surely they are not perverted.

Furthermore, Nagel's second requirement would mean that those partners who are already highly aroused before they engage in a sex act would be perverted; for such persons do not need to stare at each with desire in order to become aroused. They are already, to use Nagel's terminology, fully embodied and do not need to be seduced. To demand, as Nagel does, that one become embodied only by being stared at with desire or by some other form of seduction is simply egoistic.

But if it is ridiculous to claim that partners who do not need to be aroused by Nagel's feedback loop are perverted, then Nagel's second criterion collapses as a basis on which to prove that those who violate it are perverted. Therefore, those who are voyeurs or who have sex with animals or inanimate objects cannot be called perverts either, even though they violate the second criterion. Nor can their acts be perverted under the first criterion, for there is no reason to think that such persons do not become as fully embodied as Romeo and Juliet were in the cocktail bar.

Indeed, the voyeur becomes highly aroused precisely because he knows he is not being stared at in turn; the fact that he is secretly violating someone's privacy is, for him, the ultimate sexual thrill. And those who have sex with a sheep or a shoe or a corpse or an infant can become just as fully embodied as Romeo and Juliet. Their embodiment derives not from being stared at with desire or sensing increasing levels of arousal in their partner, but from the thrill aroused either by the unusual or exotic nature of the object of desire or for some other reason known only to a psychologist. And the one who has sex with a sheep or a shoe might claim that he can become even more fully embodied than Romeo and Juliet, for he does not have to control his lustful arousal in order to be able to respond to his partner's sexual needs.

There is, of course, no embodiment of both partners in the sorts of acts just described. But a sheep or a shoe or a corpse is hardly worried about whether it is embodied as well. And a housewife who is too tired to be fully embodied in Nagel's sense may have sex with her embodied husband because she wants to please him, yet their act surely is not perverted.

Let us now examine more closely the first criterion for perversion, that is, embodiment. Perversion under this criterion would occur when there is excessive concern for controlling or manipulating the other person; when there is pretense; or when there is obsession with technique, as well as trying to fantasize while having sex or being concerned with some ulterior goal the sex act is supposed to produce, rather than surrendering to lust. All of these fall short of embodiment since they all keep the intellect in control and prevent one from surrendering to sheer sexual desire. Utilizing this criterion, Nagel would then claim that sadism is a perversion, because the sadist must be so concerned with using his intellect in controlling and manipulating his victim and devising various methods of torture that he cannot become embodied.

This criterion, however, yields rather curious results, since it seems to put someone who enjoys fantasizing into the same category as a sadist. The fact that someone fantasizes while enjoying sex surely does not make him a pervert; indeed, the mind can enrich one's lustful arousal if mind and body are properly integrated. The sadist himself could argue that the best sex involves the full use of one's mind in developing fantasies that he then perpetrates on his victim. Unlike the one who is embodied in Nagel's sense, he can stand back and be fully aware of all the ways in which his conquered victim is responding, something which he finds very arousing. Indeed, an aroused mind may be even more erotic than the groin. If one still insists that the sadist is going to have to frustrate his bodily lust somewhat so as to have enough presence of mind to manipulate his victim, the sadist would reply that his aroused mind more than compensates for his having to control his bodily lust.

But what of the sadist's victim? If the victim is not embodied, then the criterion of mutual embodiment is violated. However, in the case of an act between a sadist and a consenting masochist, it is surely true that the masochist becomes embodied as well. So long as the pain is not too severe, pain is sexually arousing for the masochist and can lead to just as deep a state of embodiment as any other sexual act. Furthermore, the sadist and consenting masochist can fulfill the second criterion of arousing each other by the awareness of each other's desire. The sadist will be aroused by the masochist's submissive stare, and the masochist will be aroused by the sadist's domineering stare. And in bed each succeeding blow and scream will progressively arouse the two partners as well.

In the case of rape, however, it would seem clear that both of Nagel's criteria have been violated. For the rapist's victim does not become embodied, and the victim obviously does not stare in desire in the way Nagel's Romeo and Juliet do. Yet these things can also hold true for a consenting heterosexual couple, as well. Housewives often fail to be stimulated or embodied by their husbands, but will continue with the act because they want to please their mate. In such a case there is no mutual responsiveness, but this does not mean the act is perverted. And, as I noted earlier, two persons who are already highly aroused do not have to engage in the progressively arousing exchange of stares described in the Romeo and Juliet example. (Indeed, the rapist becomes aroused not by a desiring stare, but by conquering a victim who resists.) But if Nagel's two criteria can be violated in these ways without an act's being perverted, then they cannot be used to prove that rape is perverted either.

To return briefly to Nagel's two concepts of (1) being mutually aroused by awareness of each other's desire for one another and (2) embodiment—it seems that there are certain difficulties in moving from (1) to (2), as Nagel wants. In Nagel's system one must become embodied by having a favorable response from someone one finds attractive. Yet it would seem that the demand that one's desires make a favorable impact on another contains a very strong degree of ego-involvement. (At one point in his paper he claims that such mutual recognition "involves a desire that one's partner be aroused by the recognition of one's desire that he or she be aroused (p. 255)," which is certainly a very egoistic demand.) Would not many persons find such ego-satisfaction an end in itself? This aroused ego-state could then militate against a surrender of the ego to a state of unselfconscious embodiment, the very opposite of what Nagel's theory requires.

A further criticism of Nagel that is related to the preceding point involves another possible conflict between embodiment as he describes it and the complex series of mutual perceptions that precede and accompany such a bodily state. The term *embodiment*—where consciousness becomes virtually shut off except possibly to give some kind of direction to one's impulses, where one becomes nearly overwhelmed by sheer desire and lust—suggests a state that is the very opposite of that rich combination of thought, emotion, lust, fantasy, and mutual arousal via sex techniques that can so enrich a sexual experience.

On the other hand, the complex series of mutual feedbacks between the two partners, where each progressively arouses the other through the awareness of the other's desire (along with the ego involvement of feedback, where one's desires are confirmed as being worthy of response) would seem to produce just such a rich inner complex as described above.

Furthermore, in this complex interperceptual exchange of stares there is the knowledge that one's desires are having an effect on another person, and this ego-fulfillment fills one with emotion and lustful desire. And there are fantasies of the delights that await one once one has made contact with the one who has been responsive to one's desires. This inner complex of thought, emotion, lust, and fantasy is miles removed from some kind of neo-primitivistic state of merely "becoming one's body" or being in a state of sheer lust. Once again, therefore, Nagel's two concepts of mutual perceptual feedback and sheer embodiment seem to work against each other, and it is not clear how the former state is going to produce the latter.

At this point one must now ask the question as to whether such concepts as embodiment and a mutual desire for sex constitute a suitable basis for reintroducing the concept of perversion, that is, that perverted acts are those that violate these criteria. One might agree that Nagel has defined his criteria for what "good" sex is (criteria to which a shoe fetishist would vigorously object). But does it follow that what constitutes perverted sex in Nagel's terms is also "bad" sex, in that it is less pleasurable sex? At the end of his paper (p. 259) Nagel somewhat reluctantly admits that his criteria have no necessary connection with increased pleasure and that there may be cases in which perverted sex is more pleasurable for some persons than non-perverted sex. (A fantasy-filled masturbator and shoe-fetishist could be examples; each surrenders some features that can make an act good in exchange for other features that make it especially good for him or her.)

But once these admissions are made, what becomes of the concept of perversion? Many would hold that some cases such as voyeurism or rape could still be called perverted, even if Nagel's criteria fail. Such phenomena could be called perverted simply because they violate the other person's right to privacy or because they violate human dignity.

One might, however, argue that Nagel's criterion for responding to another's desires and the implied endorsement of another's desires as being worthy of a response, really does entail a mutual respect for persons. Certainly Nagel's criteria will mean that both the male and female will be sexually aroused before intercourse takes place, thus eliminating the lack of respect that males so often show in not sufficiently stimulating the female. Thus the voyeur, for example, could perhaps be judged as perverted in moral terms in Nagel's system, as well, even though Nagel did not intend his concept of perversion to be a moral one. The voyeur wants to look but is not concerned with what the other person's response might be or he or she desires not to be seen.

But Nagel's criterion of mutual responsiveness, as we have already noted, also contains a considerable degree of ego-involvement and thus bears within it the same potentially sinister overtones as Sartre's system of mutual caresses that can eventuate in sadism. To speak of each person's responding to the other's desires and recognizing the desire of each as something good and worthy of being responded to does, to be sure, sound like something beautifully humane. But could it not be a desire for mutual possession as well? Because both partners desire the same thing—recognition and endorsement of one's desires—it certainly does not follow that the situation can be described as altruistic, even if both persons eventually gratify each other in the deepest sort of way. Sexual acts can perhaps be altruistic, but this demand for the recognition of and response to "my" desire—as expressed in Nagel's theory at least—leaves one confused as to what the central motivation is: mutual respect or sheer narcissism. (There is no such demand, for example, on the part of those who prefer that their partners be coolly controlled.)

Indeed, as we noted earlier, at one point in the paper Nagel claims that such mutual recognition "involves a desire that one's partner be aroused by the recognition of one's desire that he or she be aroused." Here a demand is being made that suggests the pressure placed on females in the back seat of cars in the nation's "lover's lanes." Nagel himself at one point compared his concept of arousing one's partner to the expression of anger, in which the latter is an attempt at "*domination* of the object's feeling" (p. 254).

Even more ominous is the section of his paper that seems to reveal the ultimate goal to be fulfilled by his two criteria for a natural or "complete" sex act:

> These reactions are perceived and the perception of them is perceived, and that perception is in turn perceived; at each step the domination of the person by his body is reinforced, and the sexual partner becomes more possessible by physical contact, penetration, and envelopment. Desire is therefore not merely the perception of a preexisting embodiment that in turn enhances the original subject's sense of himself. This explains why it is important that the partner be aroused, and not merely aroused, but aroused by the awareness of one's desire. It also explains the sense in which desire has unity and possession as its object: physical possession must eventuate in the creation of the sexual object in the image of one's desire, and not merely in the object's recognition of that desire or in his or her own private arousal (pp. 255–56).

Those readers who recall Sartre's theory of sex described earlier will see a curious resemblance between it and what Nagel says here. For Sartre the goal of sex is to possess one's partner by trapping or incarnating his or her freedom in the flesh. And Nagel says virtually the same thing: "The domination of the person by his body is reinforced and the sexual partner becomes more possessible by physical contact, penetration, and envelopment." When Nagel adds that physical possession must eventuate in the creation of the sexual object in the image of one's own desire, the sadistic overtones of possession become even more apparent.

Indeed, since Nagel's theory requires that the one who possesses also become embodied, that is, controlled by lust such that his responses become virtually involuntary, then how is he going to be in a position to possess the other person or be able to create the sexual object in the image of his desire? He thus faces the same difficulty that Sartre describes when he shows why attempts at possession end in failure. Each partner becomes lost in his own private sensations and is no longer capable of or interested in relating to the other as possessor to possessed. But since Nagel seems to be fascinated by possession and the creation of the sexual object in the image of his desire, such things require control of one's partner. It would then seem that Nagel would have to resist becoming embodied and resort to manipulative techniques to maintain possession and control. But then he himself would become a pervert by violating his own criterion of total embodiment.

A final difficulty with Nagel's theory is suggested by the type of example he uses to illustrate the mutual feedback he defends: two people in a nightclub, who embody each other by a series of mutually interacting stares. They thus seem to fulfill his criteria for a complete sexual act, even though they never touch. Here Nagel should have at least drawn a distinction between a sexual experience and a sexual act, for even though they may have had a sexual experience they certainly did not perform a sexual act. It would seem, therefore, that Nagel's two criteria do not define a complete sex act, but perhaps only sexual arousal and seduction.

Furthermore, if there is as much narcissism in the demands for mutual recognition of each other's desires as mentioned above, then one wonders why Nagel's couple should go home and perform a sexual act at all. For if one's desire for recognition can be achieved in a nightclub, why bother to go home? Indeed, the orgasm would only bring to an end the deliciously aroused state of lustful embodiment, as well as ending the ego-fulfilling process of progressively arousing each other in the way Nagel describes. (Perhaps Nagel has inadvertently explained why so many people leave discotheques alone or only with a crowd of friends. Have the seductive nightclub stares Nagel speaks of become ends in themselves?)

Furthermore, if the goal of sex is possession, as Nagel indicates, then many would find their desire to possess satisfied by simply bringing someone under one's control by the nightclub stares. This explains why so many people in such places like to flirt and then lose interest as soon as they have "hooked" their victims. They then move on to seduce someone else in an endless ritual of seduction. To go home and allow one's partner to have an orgasm would only end the partner's helpless state of embodiment and she or he would no longer be possessible. (It is significant that Nagel never mentions orgasm in his paper.)

Nagel's philosophy of sex, therefore, runs the serious risk of not being a description of a complete sex act, as he claims, but rather simply a theory of seduction, whose goal is a form of possession with distinctly sadistic overtones.

In summary, it would seem that Nagel's highly ingenious attempt to prove that some acts are perverted has not succeeded. If he feels that his criteria for non-perverted acts describe what most people do sexually, it is highly doubtful that this is so. If, on the other hand, Nagel feels he has proved that there is some ideal of naturalness, such that sexual acts falling short of this ideal are perverted, then he has failed to answer the familiar liberal claim that there are many ideals and many natures of a sexual kind.

8
Robert Solomon's Theory of Sexual Perversion

One final theory of perversion will be examined—that of Robert Solomon in his article "Sex and Perversion."[13] Solomon's theory opens with an attack on the common view that the central purpose of sex is the release of sexual tension or the yielding of orgasmic pleasure. If the central purpose of sex were the simple release of physical tension, he thinks that masturbation would be all that we would ever need. He writes: "If sex is pure enjoyment, why is sexual activity between persons far more satisfying than masturbation, where, if we accept recent physiological studies, orgasm is at its highest intensity and the post-coital period is cleansed of its interpersonal hassles and arguments?"[14]

Furthermore, many persons regard masturbation as but a substitute for failure to have sex with another human being. Why should this be so? Solomon might have noted that it is not just that masturbation is lonely; one could, after all, invite someone else into one's room and let that person masturbate also. But this person still would not satisfy the desire most people feel to have sexual intercourse with another person. Why is it so common, Solomon might have asked in this connection, that prominent businessmen in strange cities so often seek out prostitutes and thus risk ruining their reputation and personal well-being when they could just as well stay in the hotel room and masturbate?

Although Solomon believes that sex has a natural purpose, he does not think it is either procreation or sexual pleasure. He views pleasure, for example, as merely an accompaniment to gratifying sexual activity. Solomon might have argued, in defense of this view, that if a pill were invented which gave us a unique kind of orgasmic thrill that could never be achieved by conventional sexual intercourse, we would still not be satisfied. There is something else, he claims, that we aim for in sexual activity. But what is this goal?

Solomon's own theory is that the real aim of sex is interpersonal communication, in which sex is a kind of body language in which the partners communicate by gestures (the bodily equivalent of a sentence) certain feelings and attitudes that cannot be conveyed by words alone. Solomon thinks that Sartre held essentially the same theory, but that he unduly restricted it to the

---

13. In *Philosophy and Sex*, pp. 268–87. An earlier statement of Solomon's theory is found in his paper "Sexual Paradigms," *Journal of Philosophy* 71 (1974): 336–45.

14. "Sexual Paradigms," p. 343.

communication of degradation. For Solomon the entire range of feelings and attitudes may be communicated, including tenderness and trust, mutual recognition, "being with," hatred, indifference, jealousy, conflict, shyness, fear, lack of confidence, embarrassment, shame, domination, submissiveness, dependence, possessiveness, and passivity. Sex that is based on sheer lust without the communication of one or more of these bodily messages, is, for Solomon, a joyless, mechanical ritual. A love bite or a caress, he argues, only acquires significance in terms of the message it conveys.

If, however, the essential goal of sex is communication of such feelings and attitudes, what happens to lust in Solomon's theory? Like Nagel, Solomon has clearly been heavily influenced by Sartre's theory of sex as communication. Sartre, for example, argued that concentration on sexual pleasure and becoming overwhelmed by lust interfered with the communication of the one particular attitude a person wanted to communicate: possession. It is thus not surprising to find that Solomon, while not wishing to defend Sartre's theory of sex as concerned solely with possession, nevertheless takes the same dim view Sartre does toward sensual pleasure: "That is why the liberal mythology has been so disastrous, for it has rendered unconscious the expressive functions of sex in its stress on enjoyment . . . It is thus understandable why sex is so utterly important in our lives, and why it is typically so unsatisfactory" (p. 345).

Solomon's defense of his attack on sex as pure enjoyment focuses on his disdain for our obsession with achieving orgasm, which can, of course, just as easily be achieved by masturbation. He writes: "No one would deny that sex is enjoyable, but it does not follow that sexuality is the activity of pure enjoyment, and that gratification or purely physical pleasure, that is, orgasm, is its end" (p. 341). For Solomon, orgasm should at most end the act, but not be its "end" or goal. To be obsessed with orgasm means that one is going to rush through the act like a sailor who hasn't had sex for six months, consequently neglecting any communication of feeling whatsoever.

This sort of criticism of sex as based on pleasure is surely unfair, however. For not all persons who engage in sex for pleasure view sex, to use Solomon's words, as a "two-minute emissionary missionary male-superior ejaculation service." Many such persons view the sex as an evening spent in a variety of sophisticated forms of mutual epidermal stimulation. Such persons, rather than being obsessed with orgasm, view the orgasm as Solomon does, that is, as the end but not the goal of the act. For Solomon to assume that the only alternative to his sexual theory is sex as a quick release of pent-up tensions (or "evacuation lust," as he calls it) is simply not justified.

What would a sex act be like for Solomon? Since he says that sex is essentially a form of language and that the bodily equivalent of a sentence is the gesture, the concept of gesture would seem to mean that he has the caress in mind. Certainly caresses can communicate feelings, but couples who caress each other are hardly going to fail to become sexually aroused eventually.

Solomon himself does, of course, have to grant that sexual feelings must play some role in the act; for otherwise one would not be able to distinguish a caress from a body massage. But he wants to keep sexual pleasure a strictly secondary consideration so that it will not become such an obsession that communication of bodily messages becomes impossible because one is overwhelmed by or imprisoned in one's own lustful sensations. But once sexual feelings enter into the act, it is like the camel who puts his nose under the tent; eventually he is going to enter and take over the entire tent. One can, of course, try to hold back one's increasing sexual arousal, but for those who are sensually oriented, this would be quite frustrating. Solomon's couple would perhaps not mind restraining their sexual impulses, for being more sensuous than sensual, they would find that the joy in communicating feelings by sensuous caresses would more than compensate for having to suppress a movement toward total sensual abandon. But not all persons are sufficiently refined to be able or want to sublimate their sexual arousal in this way.

Solomon, with his obvious disdain for sensualists, would then ask them why they don't just masturbate rather than seek out a partner. But Solomon ignores the fact that there are many other reasons besides communication of feelings that explains why so many prefer sexual intercourse to masturbation. With a sexual partner, one may enjoy a variety of sexual techniques, positions, and forms of mutual sensory stimulation and kinesthetic (muscular) sensations that one cannot have alone. Solomon might reply that a robot could also provide these forms of stimulation but that we would not be satisfied with such a partner even if the robot could be made to feel warm and fleshlike and could be programmed to respond to one's signal for a change in sexual techniques or positions. But wouldn't the sensualist be dissatisfied because the robot couldn't communicate feelings? Yet it is not clear that the sensualist would be distressed because nothing is being communicated; all that is apparent is that he would find it highly unusual to have sex with a machine.

Indeed, we know that many people find immense gratification from prostitutes, who may vary little from machines or plastic dolls in communicating anything. They must, of course, be sexually responsive, but this does not mean that they are communicating anything from within, least of all inner feelings of lustful desire. The most that Solomon could say is that the prostitute's patron pretends that something is being communicated as to his sexual desirability, or allows himself to be deceived or actually believes the prostitute is communicating her enchantment at his virility. But whether all patrons seek this confirmation of their self-worth or whether some are simply seeking a little variety in their sex lives or unusual sexual thrills is open to question. (I am inclined to think that the latter considerations more often provide the motive.)

In summary, Solomon's downgrading of sensual pleasure would be a sore point of dispute with those who view sexual intercourse in much simpler terms than Solomon does and who think that purely lustful intercourse can provide a unique kind of sexual pleasure that masturbation cannot give. Such persons reserve their communication messages (if any) for foreplay or afterplay. The sex act itself, they would argue, is complex enough without introducing additional worries as to whether one is communicating successfully. The only communication that is necessary is that each partner be able to respond to the other's sexual desires and perhaps communicate feelings of lust. And this distinctive kind of purely lustful communication where each partner feels not only his own sensual pleasure, but that of his partner as well, could explain why so many people prefer intercourse to masturbation. One would then not be driven to Solomon's type of communication as the sole basis for explaining why most persons prefer intercourse.

Furthermore, in Solomon's theory penile-vaginal penetration would not seem to be of great importance. One could always communicate Solomon's bodily messages by caresses and skip the orgasm. As I noted earlier, this might be satisfying for those who are more sensuously than sexually oriented, but it would hardly do for the latter. Indeed, it is not at all clear what a penis thrusting inside in a vagina communicates in Solomon's sense of the word. If a man does it slowly, does he communicate love or is he merely relaxing a little? If he does it rapidly, must he be expressing dominance or is he simply highly aroused? Certainly if he thinks his partner, a female liberationist, thinks he is expressing male dominance or power, he might be hesitant to proceed. But she need not think he is communicating anything at all; she may simply lie back and enjoy the pleasurable stimulation her vagina and its surrounding organs are receiving.

Furthermore, when one is highly aroused or has an orgasm, it is far from clear that one will be able to communicate Solomon's bodily messages at all. If this is true then Solomon's theory will have to reject not just, as he says, obsession with orgasms but orgasms completely. But using Solomon's language-model for sex, a sensualist would consider this analogous to a suitor who says things that lead his beloved to think he is about to ask her to marry him, and then does not ask her. She would feel as frustrated as the female who is sexually aroused but whose partner makes no attempt to perform in such a way that she can have an orgasm.

If, on the other hand, one feels that one can communicate Solomon's messages when one is highly aroused or when one has an orgasm, then the sensualist would hold that such communication (dominance, for example) is desirable only because it heightens and enriches the lustful arousal of both partners. Thus, rather than downgrading sensual pleasure and using sex as a means to an end—that is, for communication of Solomon's bodily messages— the sensualist would reverse Solomon's approach and use Solomon's type of communication as a means to heightened sexual arousal of himself and his mate. The sensualist's priorities would seem to be the more valid if one respects sex for sex's sake rather than using sex primarily as a tool for communicating messages. For it is surely sexual feelings that define an act as being distinctly sexual, whereas Solomon's messages could just as well be communicated non-sexually.

Let us now turn to how Solomon would define criteria for perversion in terms of his body-language theory of sex. The difficulty with presenting his theory is that he seems to be very much at odds with himself as to whether he wants to defend such a concept. At one point he writes: "Perversion is an insidious concept. It presents itself as a straightforward descriptive term, but carries with it an undeniable connotation of moral censure . . . what I should like to argue, perhaps perversely, is that the very idea of sexual perversion is itself perverse."[15]

However, Solomon goes on to develop a theory of perversion based on his language model of sex. If sex is a form of language for the communication of emotions, then there could, Solomon argues, be two kinds of perversion based on the communication model. One would be a deviance of form, that is, a breakdown or absence of communication. The other would be a deviance of content, when what is communicated is morally wrong. This would include the verbal equivalent of lying, that is, pretended tenderness or some other form of deception.

Using the first criterion of an absence or breakdown of communication, Solomon would ask how one could communicate with a sheep or a shoe or a dead body or the one whom one is peeping at through the window. Such activities would be perversions for Solomon because there is no communication. The obvious difficulty with this criterion is that a perfectly normal heterosexual couple may suffer a breakdown of communication if they both want to express dominance or if one wants to communicate dominance and the other wants him to communicate tenderness. But surely they are not perverted, even though there is a breakdown of communication. Similarly, if a man is trying to communicate something to his sexual partner that she misinterprets, or if he fails to get through to her at all, then he might be a poor performer (using Solomon's definition of the goal of sex), but he could hardly be called a pervert. But if such a breakdown of communication as this fails to prove that such an act could be perverted, then Solomon's first criterion could not be used against the voyeur, shoe fetishist, and so forth, either.

Solomon himself seems to agree with this point in one instance. He writes:

As a language sexuality admits of breaches in comprehension, and it is here that we can locate what little is left of our concept of "sexual perversion." It should now be clear that it is not a moral term but more of a logical category, a breach of comprehensibility. Accordingly it would be advisable to drop the notion of perversion altogether and content ourselves with "sexual incompatibility" or "sexual misunderstanding" (p. 282).

But then he adds:

It is not always clear what is to count as a literal expression, a metaphorical usage, an imaginative expression, a pun, a solecism, or a bad joke. And so what might be taken as incomprehensibility and perversion by a sexual conservative would be taken as poetry or a pun by

---

15. "Sex and Perversion," p. 269.

someone else. *Perversion, then, is a communication breakdown;* it may have general guidelines but ultimately rests in the context of the bodily mutual understanding of the people involved (pp. 282–83). [Italics mine]

Solomon thus seems to be very suspicious of a word like *perversion,* yet he somehow wants to continue using it. He apparently feels that he has disinfected the term of its overtones of immorality by calling it a "logical category" or a "breach of comprehensibility," so perhaps he thinks it would be harmless to continue using it in the way described. Yet, as we shall soon see, he introduces the term in a moral context as well.

In the case of rape Solomon argues that such an act also involves a communication breakdown, on the grounds that the two parties are incompatible. Of course, he can no longer use this criterion since we have already shown that it applies equally well to consenting heterosexuals as well. Even if a breakdown of communication were a valid criterion for perversion, is this really why rape is a perverted act? Indeed, in one sense they are communicating perfectly, for the rapist communicates aggression and his victim communicates feelings of horror or surrender or humiliation or agony, and each understands what the other is communicating quite well. There is, of course, no voluntary communication on the part of one person; thus the perversion in rape, if it *is* a perversion, is that the woman is being forced to respond contrary to her will. But voluntariness or the lack of it has no clear connection with the concept of a breakdown of communication, only with the will to communicate freely. One who is tortured into revealing a military secret is communicating, albeit unwillingly.

Surely the link between rape and a violation of the language model lies in its being analogous to a perverted use of language, such as attempting to dominate another person by using language to hypnotize or brainwash someone against his will. But since Solomon has already listed dominance as one of the ways in which sex can communicate emotion and thus raise sex above the level of mere lust, the rapist then would ask why, if a little dominance can enrich the sex act, a lot more dominance would not enrich it further. If Solomon's goal is to enrich the sex act by communication, what basis does he have for saying that the rapist can't enrich it even more by total dominance?

Solomon's reply might be that it violates the language model in the way I described, that is, that rape is analogous to using language to brainwash another person against his will. Yet in the previous quotation he said that perversion is not a moral term at all. Or if he does want to reintroduce perversion as a moral term when one forces one's will on another, then someone like de Sade would say that consent is precisely the point at issue. As we noted in an earlier section de Sade and his fellow sadists can develop an elaborate rationale (or rationalization, depending on one's point of view) for violating the moral claim that all sex must involve mutual consent of both partners. And there is nothing in Solomon's language theory of sex that answers their arguments.

We must now turn to Solomon's treatment of masturbation, a phenomenon that is so common that it poses a serious challenge to both Solomon and

Nagel, whose entire theories rest on the concept that sex is essentially a form of communication between two partners. Utilizing his language theory of sex, Solomon holds that masturbation is not a perversion but rather a deviation, on the grounds that it is, he claims, essentially a sexual way of speaking to oneself. But why is that not a valid form of communication? Solomon argues that language is primarily a form of communication between persons, and that speaking to oneself is a derivative, secondary use of language, analogous to a soliloquy. He writes: "Masturbation is not self-abuse, as we were once taught, but it is in an important sense self-denial. It represents an inability or refusal to say what one wants to say, going through the effort of expression without an audience, like writing a letter to someone and then putting it in a drawer" (p. 283).

However, while it might be true that talking to oneself is a deviant use of speech, surely language is not just speech. For language also includes writing, and writing a diary that is meant for oneself alone because it contains many thoughts one doesn't want to share with others is surely a valid and not a deviant use of language. Thus masturbation could be considered, on the language model, as a form of self-expression analogous to writing a diary that is meant for oneself alone, and this would be a perfectly valid, rather than a deviant, form of expression.

Furthermore, if masturbation is deviant on the grounds that it is a refusal to communicate, one could just as well hold that a person who refuses to have sex with anyone but his wife is deviant also. Using Solomon's speech model of language, such a person would be analogous to someone who goes through life refusing to speak to anyone except one other individual. But while it would be clearly odd to spend one's life speaking only to one person, it is not clear that it is odd to have sex with only one person. Sex with only one person might mean having to repeat the same sexual messages over and over and thus lead to boredom; but sex with only one person is surely not deviant behavior, however undesirable it may be in other ways.

Finally, the masturbator can mention that his or her sexual preference avoids a significant problem that Solomon's communication theory can so often lead to: a breakdown of communication and the subsequent frustration and disappointment that both partners suffer. Indeed, couples who prefer a relatively simple form of sex based primarily on sexual pleasure rather than communicating emotion are far less likely to suffer such a communication breakdown. For such couples know precisely what they want before they enter the bedroom, that is, sexual pleasure, and, assuming that they agree on sexual techniques, there will be no conflict. Even if they happen to disagree on sexual techniques, each one can with time learn to enjoy the sexual techniques the other partner enjoys.

However, when one enters Solomon's complex word of people who focus on communicating emotions, the problem of incompatibility is severely increased. For moods are often unpredictable, and one partner may be in the mood for dominance, while the other may feel like expressing tenderness. Partners can train each other to agree on sexual techniques, but one cannot train one's partner to invariably feel the same way one feels. Thus, if Solomon feels that perversion is a breakdown of communication of emotions, then his communication theory could vastly increase the amount of perversion (or at least disappointment and frustration) in the world of sex.[16] Let us now turn to Solomon's second form of perversion that is a deviation in terms of what is communicated. He writes:

> There is, however, still room for a concept of sexual perversion. It does not involve any deviation of "sexual aim or object," as Freud insisted, nor does it involve any special deviation in sexual activity, peculiar parts of the body, special techniques, or personality quirks. As a language, sex has at least one possible perversion: the nonverbal equivalent of lying, or *insincerity*.
>
> And, as an art, sex has a possible expression in vulgarity. [He gives blatant sexual propositions and subway exhibitionists as examples of the latter.] Given the conception of sexuality as the art of body language I have defended, we are forced to see the brutal perverseness of our conception of sexuality in which insincerity and vulgarity, artificial sexual "roles" and "how to" technology still play such an essential and generally accepted part.[17]

Solomon spells out his concept of insincerity more fully in the earlier paper:

> It seems to me that the more problematic perversions are the semantic deviations, of which the most serious are those involving insincerity, the bodily equivalent of the lie. Entertaining private fantasies and neglecting one's real sexual partner is thus an innocent semantic perversion, while pretended tenderness and affection that reverses itself is a potentially vicious perversion.[18]

In surveying Solomon's new criteria for perversion, it is not clear that any of them can serve as a basis for calling an act sexually perverted. For one

---

16. If, on the other hand, one finds a partner who is predictable in terms of some one message he or she invariably communicates, then one has solved the problem of incompatibility at the price of eventual boredom. Indeed, Solomon argues that his communication theory works best with strangers. He writes: "This (communication) model also makes it evident why Nagel chose as his example a couple of strangers; one has far more to say, for one can freely express one's fantasies as well as the truth, to a stranger. A husband and wife of seven years have probably been repeating the same messages for years, and their sexual activity now is probably no more than an abbreviated ritual incantation of the lengthy conversations they had years ago ("Sexual Paradigms," p. 344).

But if Solomon's theory is meant to apply to strangers, then the problem of finding a stranger who shares one's ideas as to what emotions to communicate is vastly increased. On the other hand, those strangers who want only a rather straightforward act based on purely sexual pleasure encounter no such problems.

17. "Sex and Perversion," p. 285.

18. "Sexual Paradigms," p. 345.

thing, they rest on moral considerations, and, as we have seen even in the odious offense of rape, it is difficult to offer a philosophical proof that rape is always immoral. Solomon, for example, speaks of vulgarity, but this is largely an aesthetic concept that exists primarily in the eye of the beholder, and is hardly serious enough an offense to merit the label "perversion." Someone who finds the subway exhibitionist vulgar may find oral sex vulgar; such persons only reveal their own narrow-mindedness about the naked body or certain sexual practices.

Solomon's key criterion for perversion is that of insincerity. Insofar as he links it with artificial sexual roles, how-to technology and fantasizing, this would mean that one is refusing to surrender oneself fully to one's partner or to sexual embodiment; but while this may be superficial sex, it surely is not perverted sex.

If, on the other hand, insincerity means pretended affection and tenderness that disappears or reverses itself after the sex act is over, one's partner may very well feel deceived and disappointed. But it is not clear that this is a serious enough offense to merit the label of perversion. The partner who was deceived did, after all, perhaps enjoy a thrilling sexual experience, and the subsequent disappointment may be the price he or she has to pay for engaging in sexual acts where one knows that pretended tenderness is most likely to occur. A more serious case of deception occurs when a homicidal maniac pretends to be sexually interested in women and lures them to his home with promises of sexual thrills. He then kills them when he has reduced them to a helpless state of lust in the bedroom. But while this is a perverted use of sex, the correct label is not "sexual pervert," for his motives were not sexual at all.

In summary, it is clear that, from a strictly philosophical viewpoint, a certain subtle kind of moralizing or set of value judgments about the true purpose of sex has been reintroduced by Solomon and, indeed, by Nagel as well. Traditional theorists based their concept of perversion on a value judgment: Procreation was elevated as the one valid goal of sex, and all else was condemned as perverse, despite the fact that sex can have many purposes. In Nagel and Solomon, however, the concept of perversion has been shifted from condemning physical acts themselves to depicting the ways in which partners fail to communicate with each other in certain psychological ways. One assumption such theories make is that the only really valid sex is that involving two partners; but this is itself a value judgment that someone who prefers masturbation would reject.

Furthermore, theories like that of Solomon and Nagel, which make so much of the psychological communication of feeling or desire, could be accused of downgrading the more sensual, orgasmic aspects of sex so many prefer. Solomon is quite frank in his disdain for sensual pleasure, because he thinks it takes one's attention away from the communication of feelings and attitudes; and although Nagel speaks highly of lustful "embodiment," his example of Romeo and Juliet staring at each other with desire in a nightclub results in their becoming embodied without ever touching or having an orgasm.[19] Indeed, Solomon's own body-language theory of sex does not require that the two partners touch. A frown, a certain kind of gesture, a smile, a stare, or the movement of one's body can all communicate feelings and attitudes without one's making bodily contact. If touching were necessary, it would still not be required that it have any sexual significance.

Even Sartre is a communication theorist in the same mold as Nagel and Solomon, except that he feels that sex basically attempts to communicate degradation. Sensuality for Sartre is clearly secondary, and, in his view, obstructs the goal of attempting to possess the partner's freedom. Thus, someone of a more sensual nature, who cares about lust and orgasm, would argue that a kind of neo-Puritanism has crept into these three communication theories that make so little of the sheer sensual aspects of sex. It would seem that neither Solomon, Nagel, nor Sartre gives a value-free account of human sexuality that would allow one to derive a similarly value-free theory of perversion. The so-called pervert would then say that he or she is given this label simply because his or her set of values happens to conflict with the values of others.

Finally, one wonders if the theories of Sartre, Solomon, and Nagel either try to solve or build into sex some of the tensions and conflicts and lack of communication one finds in contemporary society. Sartre's theory of sex as mutual attempts at possession seems merely to reflect the "get them before they get you" aspect of competitive societies; sex, instead of becoming a momentary release from such viciousness, is now seen as bringing into the bedroom the very things one finds in society. (That this is often true one need not deny, but need it be so? Certainly Sartre should not portray this sexual mirror of society as if it were the essential function of sex.)

Similarly, our society's inability to communicate in a sensitive, emotionally moving way on the verbal level might be what is behind Solomon's demand that sex satisfy this need. And in Nagel's theory the confirmation of each other's worth could also be a substitute gratification for the need for recognition in an alienated society. None of these theorists go into matters of this sort, but in failing to do so they may be unwittingly placing a burden on sex that it cannot satisfy, at least in any permanent way. And if sex fails to satisfy these deeper needs, the demands that such theorists place on sex could backfire into a disenchantment with sex that they did not intend.[20]

---

19. At the conclusion of his article, Nagel makes the following brief remark about sexual pleasure: "It is not clear that unperverted sex is necessarily *preferable* to the perversions. It may be that sex which receives the highest marks for perfection *as sex* is less enjoyable than certain perversions, and if enjoyment is considered very important, that might outweigh considerations of sexual perfection in determining rational preference" (p. 259). Here it is clear that he has defined sexual perfection largely independently of sexual pleasure. Indeed, how could sex be "perfect," and yet sometimes yield less pleasure than what Nagel regards as imperfect or perverted forms of sex? And his phrase "if enjoyment is considered very important" is certainly a very lame way of referring to sexual pleasure; for such a phrase suggests that sexual enjoyment need not be considered important, which is surely false. These considerations further reinforce my view that Nagel's theory is fundamentally like Sartre's: that the goal of sex is not pleasure but possession for possession's sake.

20. I am not, of course, speaking of Sartre, who already thinks sex is a failure for reasons of his own.

Three

What Is "Good Sex"?

Some Difficulties with "Transcendent" Orgasms:
Reichian and Tantric Sex Compared

In this chapter I wish to consider a number of claims about what is said to be essential for having good sex, including a number of the more exotic sexual systems, such as those of Wilhelm Reich and the espousers of Tantric sex, which have acquired a virtually sacred status among their followers.

Let us begin by examining two commonly practiced but radically divergent approaches to what is considered necessary for a fulfilling sex act. To some people, sex should involve no foreplay at all, but should be a relatively brief act in which the male mounts the female, inserts the penis in her vagina, and with a rapid series of powerfully thrusting motions ejaculates as quickly as possible. Such males regard foreplay as a complicated set of techniques that only frustrates their attempt to achieve orgasm as rapidly as possible. And both partners may regard such things as oral sex as either perverted or a distraction from the simple type of sex they desire.

Robert Solomon, of course regards such an act as being a crude "two-minute emissionary missionary male-superior ejaculation service." Feminists scorn such sex as being primarily concerned with the male's orgasm. The male usually fails to arouse the female adequately, and when his orgasm is finished, the act is finished and the female is bereft of any chance of orgasmic fulfillment. Oddly enough, however, there are millions of couples in the world who are perfectly content with such a simple act, and who spend their lives with one partner repeating the same act. The thought of trying something new, either in the way of a new partner or experimenting with new sexual techniques or positions, never occurs to them. Unlike the writers of sex manuals, they simply are not oriented toward curiosity and novelty. And the female who is attracted to such a male would respond to the feminist by saying that she is not concerned with orgasm at all; she receives her joy from submitting to and pleasing a dominant male. Indeed, even sexual sophisticates may prefer this type of sex when both partners are already highly aroused before they reach the bedroom; they skip the preliminaries and get into the act as rapidly as possible.

Is it possible to evaluate this type of sex without being accused of looking down on simple souls who may be enjoying what to them is fantastic sex? My own impression is that such persons, rather than being simple souls, actually are heavily conditioned to view sex as a ritual that must be finished as rapidly as possible. In regarding sex this way, they seem to come from an environment where sex is viewed as an ugly business that is to be completed quickly. And how could the female know whether or not she is really achieving maximum sexual fulfillment if, as so often happens in such relationships, she has never experienced orgasm at all? Furthermore, just as in the dining room even the person of very simple dietary tastes eventually becomes bored with nothing but hamburgers, one would think that such couples would eventually come to view the sexual act as a mechanical ritual. Even if they don't view the act this way and are contented, it still does not follow that they have reached the heights of ecstasy of which they are perhaps capable. There are persons who are content to live in Buffalo, New York, or Peoria, Illinois, throughout their lives and who never leave the city to sample the delights of Paris or New York City; but contentment is not the same thing as expanding one's horizons and living life to its fullest.

The sexual philosophy that diverges the most from the one just described is that of sensuous eroticism. Such persons are highly sophisticated in the use of elaborate forms of sexual techniques and positions and novel forms of sensory stimulation. Such sensuous persons may even spend a long evening doing nothing but kissing, caressing, fondling each other's erogenous zones, or indulging in such things as mutual oral sex or even whipping each other. Some sensuous erotics regard these things as sufficient and do not even bother to finish the act by engaging in penile-vaginal intercourse. For the sensuous erotic, the orgasm, if any, is the end of the act and not the goal of the act. And the orgasm would often be achieved by oral sex or mutual masturbation. The male might even regard the orgasm with scorn because it could leave him feeling exhausted and unable to continue with any enthusiasm the mutual epidermal stimulation such erotics find so delightful. For the female, the orgasm would commonly be achieved by her mate's massaging the clitoris; in her case the clitoral orgasms could continue at length without her feeling exhausted or depleted.

The advantage of sensuous eroticism is that it is highly imaginative and unpredictable, and both the male and female are regarded as equals in terms of sexual satisfaction. One possible disadvantage is that the male must restrain himself from ejaculating for a considerable length of time, since sensuous erotics often like to spend an entire evening indulging in what others would regard as foreplay.

Clearly both philosophies we have examined would be rejected by many people. Yet each of these philosophies, could, under certain conditions, be valid sexual experiences. As I noted earlier, when both partners are already highly aroused they would be annoyed by foreplay and the use of elaborate sexual techniques. They would prefer a relatively simple, lustful type of act that provides a quick orgasm. The difficulty with such a philosophy is when it is the sole sexual method and the only one used under all circumstances. In the case of sensuous eroticism, such a philosophy would be ideal for those who are oriented towards novelty and experimentation and who are more sensuous than sensual. Since it does not require penile-vaginal penetration, it would, for example, be ideal for unwed couples who fear pregnancy, for lesbians, and for older persons who prefer a more relaxed form of sex.

Let us now turn to the philosophy of Wilhelm Reich and his leading exponent, Alexander Lowen.[1] Reich's theory of human sexuality is especially interesting for a philosopher, since he claims to have developed the *ideal* sex act which is the only one that can produce what he describes as a "total orgasm." For Reich, a total orgasm gives a person a complete sense of oneness with one's partner and provides a quasi-mystical form of ecstasy in which one feels lifted, as it were, outside of oneself into a sense of oneness with the cosmos.

Before examining Reich's techniques for producing such an orgasm, we should note that Reich and his followers claim to reject totally the two sexual philosophies we have already explored. The first philosophy, that of the quick orgasmic release preceded by little or no foreplay, he rejects as being a sadistic attempt of the male to dominate the female. Reich claims that such men are so concerned with dominance that they are unable to reach a point of complete surrender to the sexual energy within them; such men, he argues, feel that total surrender and abandon to one's sexual impulses is somehow feminine. He writes:

> It took me more than two years of experience to rid myself completely of this cultivated reserve and to realize that people confuse "fucking" with the loving embrace. . . . Most disturbed of all were those men who liked to boast and make a big show of their masculinity, men who possessed and conquered as many women as possible. . . . It became quite clear that, though they were erectively very potent, such men experienced no or very little pleasure at the moment of ejaculation, or they experienced the exact opposite, disgust and unpleasure. The precise analysis of fantasies during the sexual act revealed that the men usually had sadistic

---

1. See Reich, *The Function of the Orgasm* (New York: Farrar, Straus & Giroux, 1973), pp. 95–104; Lowen, *Love and Orgasm* (New York: New American Library, 1965), pp. 175–207.

or conceited attitudes and that the women were afraid, inhibited, or imagined themselves to be men. . . . In none of these cases is there the slightest trace of involuntary behavior or loss of conscious activity in the act (p. 100).

While Reich's analysis may very well be true of most of those who confine themselves to a quick release of sexual tension, it is not clear that this is true in all cases. Some men are simply often very highly aroused and want to release their tensions as quickly as possible. And many of them are so highly aroused that I suspect that their act does become involuntary and involve the loss of ego-control that Reich demands.

The Reichians reserve their most scathing condemnation, however, for the sensuous erotic. Lowen, for example, argues that the sensuous erotics limit themselves to what he calls superficial epidermal stimulation totally devoid of any emotional depth. Furthermore, sensuous erotics are so concerned with sexual technique that they are unable to lose ego-control and surrender completely either to each other or to being controlled by lust. And by confining themselves to the most superficial aspect of sex, that is, stimulation for stimulation's sake, Lowen claims that they are driven to constantly try to find new techniques and sexual partners to avoid the boredom to which he claims their brand of sex inevitably leads.

Lowen's major complaint, however, is that sensuous erotics are somehow neurotically afraid of penile-vaginal penetration, which for the Reichians is the sole way to achieve total orgasmic release. Lowen argues that stimulation for stimulation's sake leaves both partners utterly frustrated, and that if the male does finally penetrate the female, he will either be so highly aroused from the prolonged foreplay that he will ejaculate prematurely or else he will be so exhausted from hours of sensuous activity that his orgasmic energies will be depleted and he will have only a weak orgasm. In the case of the female, the emphasis on achieving clitoral orgasms by massaging the vulval area is also rejected by the Reichians. Lowen claims that his female patients report that clitoral orgasms do not leave them with any satisfying release of sexual energies, and that only vaginal orgasms (those produced deep within the vagina by the vigorous thrusting of the penis) provide any true gratification. And he would argue that her sensuous male partner will either be too sexually exhausted or will ejaculate prematurely and thus will not be able to provide the lengthy and vigorous penile thrusting necessary to produce the vaginal orgasm.

This sweeping indictment of sensuous eroticism, while valid in some respects, clearly goes too far. The sensuous erotic would argue that his philosophy is being rejected mainly because the Reichians are obsessed with their special brand of orgasm and are using sex primarily as a means to this one end. Nor need sensuous eroticism be merely superficial epidermal stimulation devoid of the love and tenderness that the Reichians demand. (Reichians make the familiar claim that only those who love each other can fully surrender to each other and to their sexual energies, a view I criticized in the first chapter.)

Indeed, if sex can express emotions at all, the sensuous caressing of each other's body would be a far more feasible way of doing this than the involuntary surrender to animal urges the Reichians defend. (Lowen writes at one point: "In love we are human; in sexuality we are animal." How he proposes to combine love with the animalistic or make the animalistic an expression of love is unclear.)

Lowen's other attacks on the sensuous erotic are equally dubious. An erotic who has mastered sexual techniques so that he or she can use them in a spontaneous way is not hampered by reducing himself or herself to a deeply lustful state. Nor is it clear that a sensuous erotic who has an orgasm by oral means necessarily has a less satisfying orgasm than the one achieved by the Reichian philosophy. And some females may prefer the clitoral orgasm because it is far more intense than the vaginal orgasm and because they can have a multiplicity of such orgasms with no diminution of sexual energy. Finally, the sensuous erotic would hold that the Reichians, like Freud, view the sexual act primarily as a means of arousing oneself to peak of excitation for the sake of enjoying the thrill that accompanies the release of these tensions. But does such a philosophy really respect sex for sex's sake, any more than does the man who indulges in the two-minute quick form of sex the Reichians condemn? The sensuous erotic would note that the Reichian orgasm brings the act to a sudden end, while he prefers to enjoy an entire evening of a more relaxed approach to sex that is to him more satisfying.

Let us now examine the steps Reich and his followers claim are necessary to achieve total orgasm. They would first note that one must space one's acts in the proper way. Too long a period of abstinence leads to a premature ejaculation and engaging in sex acts too frequently prevents the build-up of sexual energy necessary for their orgasm. (Promiscuous persons, they would argue, never really have a satisfying orgasm for the latter reason; such persons are driven to try to make up in quantity what they lack in quality of orgasmic fulfillment.)

A further requirement for the Reichian act is that both partners must be able to totally surrender to each other and to the unimpeded flow of sexual energy that unites them. One must be totally at ease with one's own body and that of one's partner. (Masturbation would be admissable only as a means of coming to know one's body and of being at ease with it in preparation for the Reichian act.) There must be no reservations or inhibitions; one must be free of psychological and bodily rigidities that are the product of an authoritarian upbringing. Finally, one must not fear experiences where there is a temporary loss of ego-control and where one's sexual energy assumes complete control of one's movements.

In terms of the act itself, there should be just enough foreplay to bring the couple to an emotional peak where there is a desire to penetrate the female and for the female to desire to be penetrated. To prolong foreplay is, for the Reichian, a sign of fear of orgasmic release and a sign of a lack of complete surrender to each other and to being controlled by sexual energy. On the other hand, no foreplay at all amounts to jumping on top of the woman without her being properly aroused; to Reich this is sadistic.

At a certain point during foreplay the male will feel the urge to penetrate the woman's vagina. At the moment of penetration, Lowen notes that there will be a momentary relaxation of sexual intensity. It is as if the male had symbolically returned home to the womb from which he came. When the male withdraws after orgasm, he will feel, as it were, born again. During the first stage of penetration the couple will proceed in a slow, relaxed manner and retain voluntary control over their act, using whatever sexual techniques that allow one to be aroused to a point where the body begins to act on its own and lust takes command over consciousness. For the Reichian it is especially important that one's entire body move in a relaxed, rhythmic way so that one may enjoy the kinesthetic sensations that are essential to the act. The Reichians lay great emphasis, for example, on allowing the pelvis to freely move up and down. Lowen suggests that active partner dig his or her feet into the mattress and allow the entire body to move up and down in a unitary rhythmic way analogous to the tensing and relaxing of a bow.

After the voluntary stage, one will find oneself so highly aroused that one's movements will proceed at a much faster rate. The bodily sexual energy aroused by foreplay will start to flow to the genitals, the primary focus of concentration at this state. As one's movements go faster, one's actions should gradually cease to be voluntary. There should be a total surrender of will, intellect, and consciousness to direction by the sexual energy that is the essence of one's animal nature.

Finally, once the bodily movements have become involuntary, the climactic orgasm should involve the convulsing of the entire bodily musculature in rhythmic waves, including the arms, legs, and head. The orgasms that most people have are jerky, spasmodic, or hysterical and, for the Reichian, reveal a fear of surrendering totally to the sexual act. The Reichians claim that the "total" orgasm provides a peak experience of overcoming one's isolation and of being lifted outside of oneself, with an accompanying sense of total oneness with one's partner and the primal energies of the cosmos. This experience will be further heightened if the orgasms are simultaneous. Lowen writes:

At the acme there tends to occur a loss of ego consciousness. This is a temporary eclipse of the ego and is not to be confused with a feeling of abandonment. One doesn't become unconscious in the process of orgasm. It would be more correct to say that the individual tends to lose consciousness of the self. The self disappears in fusion with the love object: love has achieved its final goal. There is not only a feeling of complete unity and merger with the partner, but also a feeling of being part of the total pulsating universe. This latter feeling supports Reich's idea that in orgasm, man finds his identification with cosmic processes (p. 198).

The final stage of the Reichian act is that of resolution. After orgasm the sex energy concentrated in the genitals flows back into the entire body, giving it a glow of sweaty warmth and a total release of sexual energy. One then feels a deep urge to sleep. Other forms of penile-vaginal intercourse that do not fulfill the Reichian procedures are said to produce, at best, only a partial release of sexual energy and fail to reach the transcendent heights of ecstasy of the Reichian orgasm. The Reichians argue that those who do not reach orgasm by penile-vaginal intercourse but by some other means are all neurotically afraid of such intercourse; and neurotics, Reich claims, enjoy no satisfying release at all. They are said to be left feeling hot, tense, and disturbed after the orgasm. These are very sweeping and dubious generalizations, indeed.

Is this the one, true, ideal sexual act as the Reichians claim? It seems to be only a highly sophisticated version of the philosophy that a sex act is largely a means to releasing pent-up sexual tensions by orgasmic release. By being so obsessed with the end result of the act, one wonders if the Reichians really care any more for what proceeds the orgasm than does the man who masturbates simply in order to relax and to be able to sleep better.

One or two final criticisms are in order. Reich's involuntary state involving a total surrender of consciousness to lust is, of course, the embodiment of consciousness discussed by Sartre and Nagel. Sartre argued that when one becomes embodied, one becomes so lost in one's own sensations and movements that one ceases to relate entirely to one's partner. Yet the Reichians insist that such embodiment must involve the two partners feeling as if they were in a state of total unity with each other. This, of course, requires that their movements be precisely synchronized and that each partner want precisely what the other partner wants throughout the act. It also assumes that each partner will view the act in the same way. But what if the female views the act more as an expression of tenderness or some other emotion? Will the male's surrendering himself to involuntary movements directed solely by animal lust be compatible with tenderness and love?

Furthermore, since orgasm is of such overriding importance in the Reichian act, the unity of the two partners would seem to require simultaneous orgasms. But simultaneous orgasms are extremely rare. And since the female's orgasm usually takes longer to achieve than that of the male, this means the male is going to have to pay close attention to the state of arousal of the female and postpone ejaculation until she is clearly ready to have an orgasm. But how is the Reichian male going to be able to do these things if he is proceeding in a completely involuntary, animal-like way with his consciousness overwhelmed by lust? If he does have to pay attention to his partner's state of arousal, then the Reichian requirement of utterly spontaneous abandon to animal urges is violated. And if he does not note carefully his partner's degree of arousal, then he may very well ejaculate first. He is then, within Reich's philosophy, utterly drained of sexual energy and is confronted with the sight of a partner moving involuntarily in the throes of animal lust whom he is not going to be able to bring to climax with the required Reichian vaginal orgasm.

Finally, the claim that the Reichian orgasm is the best there is and that a totally satisfying orgasm must involve rhythmic convulsions of one's entire body is highly doubtful. For example, one would think that the most fulfilling orgasm would involve a unity of thought, emotion, and lust rather than Reich's neoprimitivistic, purely sensual release of sexual energy. And while Reich and his fellow psychoanalysts would regard, say, shoe fetishists as hopelessly neurotic, there is no reason to think that their orgasms are any less satisfying to them than are those of Reich. Indeed, those whose acts do not involve the requirement of total unity with a sex partner might be able to achieve a far greater spontaneous abandon since they do not encounter the difficulties of having simultaneous orgasms or matching their needs to those of their partner. There is, to be sure, great joy to be had in satisfying a sexual partner; but a price has to be paid in terms that violate Reich's philosophy of total abandonment to sensuality.

Let us now turn to an even more exotic form of sexual philosophy, that of Tantric sex. The theories of Wilhelm Reich and that of Tantric sex come, of course, from very different traditions. Reich represents to an extreme degree the Western world's preoccupation with orgasm, whereas Tantra is the sexual expression of certain Eastern religions and ways of life in which meditation and relaxation and total surrender to and identification with the cosmic harmonies of the universe are central.

Both Reichian and Tantric philosophies believe that our bodies are permeated by something called sexual energy; for Reich the term would be orgasmic energy. And both philosophies seem to hold that this sexual energy is somehow akin to or identical in its very essence with the underlying cosmic energies that direct the universe. It is this belief that allows the exponents of each philosophy to claim that "their" sexual act enables one to feel at one with the universe. For Reich, this is achieved by the arousal and total discharge of sexual energy, whereas for Tantra the sexual energy is retained and sublimated to produce a state of consciousness where one becomes at one with what Tantrics believe to be the divine forces of the universe. For Tantra sexual energy (as in semen) is the source of creation of life, and to retain the semen rather than to ejaculate it puts one on a plane where one becomes at one with what is believed to be the ultimate source of all creation, that is, the divine creative forces of the universe.

Furthermore, both Reich and Tantra hold that the act should eventuate in a total surrender to the flow of this sexual energy and that the act should be ultimately disengaged from control by the rational intellect or consciousness. Finally, both philosophies believe that the conclusion of the act results in a total oneness with one's partner and with the universe, that it leads to a sense of being lifted outside the barriers of our individual existence and of being outside of space and time. In both philosophies it is claimed that the partners feel utterly blissful and in some way reborn at the conclusion of the act. Lowen compares the state the male feels when he withdraws the penis the vagina to a kind of rebirth. Tantra practitioners, on the other hand, believe that each partner emerges from the act reborn as an incarnated version of the Divine.

Here, however, the resemblances end. For a Tantric yoga, sex is not practiced for the sake of orgasm. Rather sex is the starting point for a progressive sublimation of sexual energy that is ultimately claimed to yield a kind of ecstatic mystical union with one's partner and ultimately with the divine forces or ultimate sources of creative energy that underlie the universe. Since its goal is an ecstatic experience of what the Tantrics believe to be the boundless, timeless Infinite, it is clearly not sex for sex's sake or sex for orgasm's sake. The latter, for Tantra, would be mere carnal lust. In achieving this mystical union with the divine forces of the universe, Tantrics feel that they are lifted out of the boundaries of the finite ego, lustful desires, and the rational intellect. One feels completely relaxed and at one with all things. One thinks neither of the present nor the future, for one is totally absorbed in a deep state of meditation in the present moment.

For Tantra, the Western preoccupation with the rational intellect is scorned because it is always concerned with trying to analyze or calculate or "figure things out" and reduce them to tidy formulas or laws; it does not allow one to relax in things just as they are in themselves. Furthermore, the rational intellect is concerned with the future, with ambition that compels us to make plans for the future that cause anxiety and tension lest such plans be unfulfilled. Anxiety and tension are relieved only when we are capable of a meditative acceptance of the present and union with the wholeness of things as they are in themselves. Tantra therefore uses sexual energy to arouse and awaken the deeper, freer levels of the subconscious mind where we are free of the restrictions the conscious intellect imposes upon us.

Furthermore, the Tantric philosopher views Western man as constantly having his rational intellect interfere with the spontaneity of the sexual act, what with his obsession with orgasm. The Westerner's mind is bothered by such questions as: Do I know all the latest sexual techniques for producing the best orgasm? Will I be able to hold my erection? Will I ejaculate prematurely? Will I be able to give my mate a good orgasm? Can we synchronize our act so that we will have a simultaneous orgasm? Tantra would thus view Reich's obsession with total orgasm and his insistence on surrendering the rational, conscious ego to the direction of the body by sheer sexual energy as contradictory ideals.

For Tantrics, the solution to the problem of being obsessed with orgasms (so that one is thereby able to make the entire act one of meditation and relaxation) is to reject the concept of the orgasm completely. In the typical Western sexual act, the partners progressively arouse each other's body to a point where they have a brief, peak experience of an orgasmic release of tension. They are then, according to Tantric philosophy, left exhausted and drained of sexual energy, and are unable to proceed further. But since Tantric philosophy seems to reject the idea of ejaculating semen, the Tantric couple can continue the act for hours, after which they claim to feel revitalized and refreshed rather than exhausted and depleted.

The question of whether Tantrics allow the ejaculation of semen and precisely what is the Tantric concept of orgasm is, however, most difficult to ascertain from my sources. In an article entitled "Tantric Sex: Going All the Way" by Bhagwan Shree Rajneesh, one of India's leading Tantric gurus, the author rejects the idea of ejaculating semen altogether. Instead of the peak orgasm people in the West experience, he refers to a "valley orgasm," which describes the way Tantrics feel when they are in a state of total relaxation and communion with divine cosmic energies of the universe. Omar Garrison, on the other hand, reports that a curious kind of orgastic phenomenon occurs in the Tantric act that resembles the Reichian orgasm, although it is not stated whether ejaculation of semen occurs:

> According to Pandit Chatterjeel, among Western students practicing the *sadhana,* a sudden acme of sensation occurs at some point between the twenty-eight and thirty-second minute of practice. This abrupt exultation, unlike anything ever experienced before, results in orgasmic and involuntary contraction to the total body's musculature.[2]

Philip Rawson does not seem to think that Tantric sex excludes orgasm entirely, although he does not make clear whether such orgasms involve an ejaculation of semen:

> In the higher reaches of Indian erotics orgasm becomes merely a punctuation in, and incentive for, the state of continuous intense physical and emotional radiance which lovers evoke in each other. Sex is not regarded as a sensation, but as feeling; attraction is not appetite, but the meeting of eyes; love is not a reaction, but a carefully nurtured creation. Its meaning is a prolonged ecstasy of mind and body, whose fires are continually blown by prolonged engagement and stimulation of the sexual organs, not mutual relief. . . . The self-abnegation it demands of both partners in prolonging intercourse and studying each others' needs has no place in European cultural attitudes.[3]

At another point, in describing Hindu Tantra, Rawson writes:

> All the concrete enjoyments and imagery are supposed to awaken dormant energies, especially the energy which normally finds its outlet in sexual intercourse. The energy, once aroused, is harnessed to rituals, meditation, and yoga, turned back up *(paravritta)* within the human energy mechanism, and is used to propel the consciousness towards blissful enlightenment. Orgasm is in a sense an irrelevance, lost in the

2. Garrison, *Tantra: The Yoga of Sex* (New York: Causeway Books, 1964), p. 114.

3. Rawson, *The Art of Tantra* (Greenwich, Conn.: New York Graphic Society, 1973), pp. 78-79.

sustained and vastly enhanced inward condition of nervous vibration in which the energies of man and world are felt to be consummated, their infinite possibilities realized virtually on the astronomical scale of time and space (p. 32).

In the next paragraph, however, Rawson writes: "Much Hindu Tantra in fact welcomes orgasm, provided it is recognized as being the analogue to ancient Hindu sacrifice" (p. 32).

In general it seems safe to say that in Tantra there is either no orgasm at all as we understand the term, or else if there is an ejaculation of semen it plays only a minor role or must have some symbolic significance within the Tantric religion. In no case is orgasm permitted for orgasm's sake. The reason most Tantrics totally reject the idea of ejaculating semen is that they think it would deplete one's sexual energies rather than allow them to energize one's body and subconscious mind and thus develop the special state of consciousness that allows the Tantric to feel that he is at one with the divine forces of the cosmos.

Let us now briefly describe a Tantric ritual as presented by Omar Garrison. The act is preceded by elaborate breathing exercises, the eating of certain foods such as fish, which have symbolic significance, and the drinking of wine or sometimes using drugs to relax tensions. Bhagwan Shree Rajneesh suggests that couples who are already highly aroused sexually should avoid the act altogether since they will only be frustrated by the prolonged Tantric ritual.

To put oneself in the proper frame of mind is vital in the Tantric ritual. The texts suggest that one should get as far away from any distractions as possible, such as going to a country retreat where total relaxation and absorption in the act can be attained. Garrison suggests the use of a dimly lit room where a violet light is focused on the body of the nude female. The male, he says, must gaze upon her with admiration and awe, as one pondering the mystery of creation and the unfathomable secret of being. He must view her as "extremely subtle, the awakener of pure knowledge, the embodiment of all bliss." She is the "unsullied treasure house of beauty, the shining protoplast, the begetter of all that is, that inscrutably becomes, dies, and is born again." Garrison cautions that unless the male can so visualize his partner as a virtually sacred or spiritual being rather than an object of lustful desire, the act will be merely a carnal one and he is advised to proceed no further (p. 112). Although there are doubtlessly many sexual positions used by Tantrics, Rajneesh suggests that the female mount the male and insert his erect penis in her vagina. His reasoning is that the female will be passive and the male who is beneath the female will be in no position to be his usual aggressive self. With both partners being in a passive state, the act will be able to proceed in a relaxed way for hours if the couple so desires. At no stage in the act is there the normal thrusting movement of Western intercourse.

How does such an act lead to an identification with what the Tantrics believe to be the divine forces that underlie the universe? In Tantric philosophy these divine forces are essentially androgynous in nature; that is, such forces are a harmony of opposites of the masculine and the feminine poles. In the Buddhist and Tibetan Tantric philosophies, the masculine pole is described as being positive, kinetic or active, and electric. The feminine pole is negative, passive or inert, and magnetic in attracting energy to itself. In the Hindu Tantric system, however, the dynamic pole is ascribed to the feminine side, and the static pole is ascribed to the masculine. The concept that there is a natural attraction of opposites and that the opposing masculine and feminine poles can only achieve true completeness when they are united in harmony is central to Tantric thought.

In the Tantric sexual act the goal is for each partner to become just such a harmony of opposites of the masculine and feminine poles. In doing so, each will thereby become a living embodiment of the divine androgynous forces that permeate the universe. When this is accomplished, each partner will, as it were, become at one with the divine forces of the universe by taking on the androgynous nature of the Divine. Garrison writes: "It is the ultimate destiny of the soul to achieve that completion through the union of polar opposites within his own body. Thus reborn as the divine androgyne, the offspring of Shiva (the masculine principle) and Shakti (the feminine principle), the soul will inhabit only the higher *lokas* or planes of existence" (p. 10). But how does a sexual act achieve such a difficult goal?

The Tantrics seem to believe that in their sexual act there is a gradual interchange of sexual energy between the two partners. The male partakes of the female's feminine pole which, united with his own masculine pole, produces an androguous state or a harmony of the masculine and feminine forces within him. And the same occurs within the female: her feminine energy pole is united with the male's masculine energy pole and she becomes a harmony of the opposites within herself also. These energy forces are then thought to rise through the spinal column and affect the subconscious mind in a way that leads to a sublime and blissful state of consciousness wherein the Tantrics claim to be at one with the divine forces of the universe by each partner's having taken on the androgynous nature of the Divine. This mystical form of sexual union with the Divine is, therefore, a route to spiritual perfection and knowledge for the Tantric couple.

June Singer writes glowingly of how the Tantric couple must feel:

We can imagine what it must be like to sit immobilized, in sexual union with the god. How still one must be, to feel within oneself the shape and form of Divinity, to know with that deep inner knowledge that encompasses the totality of oneself, body as well as psyche—undivided, that there is an immortal presence within, around, and flowing through oneself. Experience it as Sakti-Prana if you will; the air you breathe is charged with it. Being in touch with that immortal body means being able to be alone and yet not be alone. It means reunion with that Primordial Androgyne that is the womb of God, the ancestor of the psyche. . .[4]

Finally, I should like to warn the reader that there are many varieties of Tantric philosophy, and I do not pretend to have done justice to them all. The doctrine, bathed as it is in mystic rituals, is impossible to set forth in words that adequately describe its essence. The way in which the Tantric act produces a harmony of opposites in each partner can, for example, be interpreted in a variety of ways. Indeed, Garrison describes the Tantric ritual as if the female were already a kind of divine being even before she enters the act.

The importance of the female consort in Tantric practices stem from the fact that, according to Shastra, every woman is a *shakti*; that is, she embodies the secret, fundamental forces that control the universe. By correctly joining himself (in the Tantric sexual ritual) to this line of force, pouring forth from the supreme Absolute, the yogi experiences the bliss of divine union (p. xxii).

How can a philosopher hope to evaluate such a complex doctrine as Tantra? Some might feel that the ultimate Tantric state of otherworldly ecstasy is a form of escapism. One would think those who seek the Reichian or Tantric transcendent experiences would find it a terrible letdown to return to the real world, and would come to view everyday existence as terribly mundane once they see how it contrasts with the sublime bliss they claim to have experienced.

Yet the Tantrics resolutely deny that they (unlike traditional Eastern religions) denigrate the material world and seek a permanent state of Nirvana. The Tantric act is, for example, performed only once a month as a religious rite. Can the Tantric act still be criticized for being a grueling ritual involving the suppression of desire for orgasmic release? To the Western mind it would seem terribly frustrating to sit for thirty minutes or more with one's erect penis in the vagina of a woman and do nothing. How is meditation, relaxation, and total surrender of the rational ego to sexual energy possible when one must be on the alert to maintain one's self-control?

Yet the Tantric would insist that he enjoys the act from beginning to end, and that such criticisms as these merely reflect the Western mind's addiction to orgasm. Once one has mastered the Tantric techniques of self-control, one no longer has to exert any conscious effort to prevent orgasm nor does one suffer feelings of frustration. And the Tantric would argue that the sublimating of sexual energy and the transcendent, blissful state of mind this produces is a far

4. Singer, *Androgyny: Toward a New Theory of Sexuality* (Garden City, N.Y., Doubleday, 1977), pp. 182–83. Ms. Singer notes that it is not essential that one ascribe the feminine and masculine poles to the female and male respectively in the Tantric act. The act would work just as well if the male were feminine and the female were masculine. What counts is not who is masculine and who is feminine, but that there arise a harmonious union of the opposing feminine and masculine principles in both partners.

richer and longer-lasting experience than that produced by the conventional Western act aimed at a quick orgasmic release of sexual tensions.

What would a follower of Reich think of Tantra? A Reichian would probably argue that the Eastern approach reflects a fundamentally passive form of sensuality where the partners are neurotically afraid of orgasm. Lowen, although not directly attacking Tantric sex, reveals these attitudes in his attack on the sensualist:

> The sensualist lacks the aggressive drive to do things for himself, and he lacks the aggressive concept necessary to achieve satisfaction. The absence of this aggressive component forces him into a sensual way of life. . . . Sexuality demands maturity of mind and body. The sexual individual as opposed to the sensual individual . . . is a person who stands on his own feet and acts aggressively to obtain the satisfaction of his needs. His life is oriented to achievement and fulfillment to mobilize his aggression in the service of desire (*Love and Orgasm,* p. 187).

This quotation illustrates beautifully the clash between the more passive Eastern approach to sex and to life, and that of our own male-oriented, aggressive Western philosophy. And although the Reichians would condemn rape, the passage from Lowen perhaps reveals why rape is so common in our culture: rape is simply aggression pushed to its ultimate expression.

Let me conclude with a few criticisms of my own of Tantric sex. To someone who defends sex for sex's sake, that is, sex that aims at producing sexual feelings which can be had in no other way, the Tantric act could be accused of denigrating the physical aspect of sex and of using sex primarily as a means to a mystical experience. And whereas sex alone can produce uniquely sexual feelings, it has been shown that the use of certain drugs can affect the subconscious mind and produce a state virtually identical to the mystic's feeling of oneness with the universe. Apparently the suppression of sexual energy that is common among religious mystics, coupled with an overpowering belief in and a desire to know God, affects their subconscious minds in ways analogous to those produced by the use of hallucinogenic drugs. The major difference between the religious mystic and the user of drugs is that the former might be more likely to be obsessed with a belief in divine powers and thus think he or she has actually communicated with a deity.

In summary, this section has surveyed four different types of sexual philosophy. Is it possible to say which one is ideal? A sexual pluralist would argue that there is no one ideal sexual act, and that what is ideal for one person may produce utter frustration for someone else. In a later chapter I shall, however, defend my own sexual ideal: sex for sex's sake.

2
Moulton's Feminist Critique of Conventional Sexual Intercourse

Some of the most interesting recent controversy about orgasm has occurred over the nature of female orgasm and the research about the frequency of their occurrence. Kinsey's statistics, for example, showed that fewer than 14 percent of women had orgasms a major portion of the time, while over 56 percent had never had an orgasm during coitus. On the other hand, Mary Jane Scherfey has argued that the capacity of females to have one orgasm after another is virtually unlimited.[5] Why this wide discrepancy?

Let us turn to a philosophical paper on the subject, Janice Moulton's "Sex and Reference," and outline her central thesis:[6]

First, she argues that the usual form of male-female intercourse involving penile-vaginal penetration is primarily for males; that this sort of intercourse could never provide equal satisfaction for the female, no matter how many new techniques one might add to it (for example, more foreplay); that it embodies a conceptual confusion about what the real goal of such intercourse is: Male satisfaction is its primary aim. "[F]emale arousal and satisfaction, although they may be concomitant events occasionally, are not even constituents of sexual intercourse" (p. 35).

Second, to attempt to solve this problem by new techniques of female arousal of the Masters-Johnson variety only creates, for Moulton, even greater problems. She notes that Kinsey holds that "the average female is no slower in response than the average male *when she is sufficiently stimulated and when she is not inhibited in her activity.*"[7] But for Moulton the key words are *sufficiently stimulated*; she feels that the introduction of new techniques to stimulate the female would turn sexual activity as ordinarily practiced into a "complicated and difficult skill, something to be mastered and not enjoyed" (p. 35).[8] Examples of such techniques would be trying to reprogram the male so he can prolong intercourse or trying to increase foreplay. And she notes that direct stimulation of the female usually ceases when intercourse begins.

Third, Moulton notes that the language that we use in polite intercourse is "symmetric"; if a man has intercourse with a woman then it follows she has had intercourse with him. But such polite discourse about sexual intercourse leads people to think that the male and female really do enjoy equal gratification. However, when one turns to the more vulgar expressions, which connote deceit and injury, the language is asymmetrical and reveals male dominance

---

5. Mary Jane Scherfey, *The Nature and Evolution of Female Sexuality* (New York: Random House, 1972), pp. 134-35.

6. In *Philosophy and Sex* (Buffalo, N.Y.: Prometheus Books, 1975), pp. 34-44.

7. Alfred Kinsey et al., *Sexual Behaviour in the Human Female* (Philadelphia: W. R. Saunders, 1953), p. 163.

8. An example of this would be the Masters and Johnson recommended technique of having the female squeeze the male's penis when he is about to ejaculate too soon. This would certainly interfere with the spontaneity of the act and with the male's "embodiment."

and an absence of equal participation in the act by both male and female. One says he has fucked or screwed her, but one does not say she has fucked or screwed him. We are then deceived into thinking that if sex does not involve deceit or injury, that if the female had "sexual intercourse" rather than being "screwed," then it must have been equally pleasurable for both. This Moulton denies.

Fourth, Ms. Moulton's next argument must be quoted to bring out its full impact:

> Thus, although there are exceptions, sexual intercourse is widely accepted as a process that is brought to a conclusion by the male orgasm. Thus, any discussion of the female orgasm during sexual intercourse is actually a discussion of the female orgasm before or during the male orgasm. Once the male orgasm occurs, sexual intercourse ends. This puts an arbitrary restriction on the period during which female orgasm may occur. In addition, sexual intercourse formally begins when the primary focus for sexual stimulation in the male (the penis) is inserted in a container particularly well suited to bring about the male orgasm (the vaginal orifice). Although Webster's dictionary merely says that sexual intercourse "involves" this insertion, anything prior to this insertion is termed "foreplay" or "preliminaries"; the real thing does not begin until the insertion occurs.
>
> The important point to notice is that this activity, which is (politely) described by verbs that are logically symmetrical, is in fact *defined* exclusively in terms of *male* stimulation by contact with the female, leading to (or at least aiming at) *male* orgasm. Thus discussions of the female orgasm during sexual intercourse amount to discussions of the female orgasm after the source of *male* stimulation is placed in its container and before or during the *male* orgasm. The female locus of stimulation [which for Moulton is the clitoris] and the female orgasm are not even part of the definition of sexual intercourse (p. 37).

Fifth, Moulton grants that pleasing the man may be of great psychological significance, but she also insists that there must be direct stimulation of the clitoral area, which "produces more intense and rapid orgasms."[9] But this would involve redefining sex for the woman as something more akin to masturbation than to the traditional form of penile-vaginal thrusting. She seems to suggest having the man massage the clitoris when she says:

9. Moulton's claim that clitoral orgasms are superior because they are more "intense and rapid" is highly controversial; there are many other aspects to an orgasm besides intensity and rapidity. The psychoanalyst Robert Robertiello writes: "There are two easily distinguishable kinds of orgasms as they are subjectively experienced. The clitoral orgasm, which is so-called because in most women it can be elicited by manually stroking the clitoris, is a very intense, rather short-lasting response which builds to a rapid crescendo and falls just as rapidly. It is closer to the usual sexual response of the male. The so-called vaginal response is one that is more frequently reached during sexual intercourse and arises more slowly, does not reach such a sharp peak, lasts much longer, falls off much more slowly and usually gives a deeper and fuller feeling of satisfaction. To women who

But if a woman spends the time and energy to produce someone else's orgasm, with the understanding she is engaging in a mutual activity, it is only fair that her partner do the same for her. If she has to be satisfied with sympathy and understanding alone, then so should her partner (p. 42).[10]

Perhaps, however, Moulton does not have masturbation in mind. Does she think that a man could somehow change his mode of penile thrusting to bring it into closer contact with the clitoris and thus produce a clitoral orgasm? Or would this violate her earlier claim that new techniques of female arousal introduce additional complexities that would disturb the spontaneity of the act? It is not clear just what solution Moulton is recommending. Indeed, stimulation of the woman after the man's climax is hardly going to be a spontaneous act for him; he is usually so spent that stimulating his partner would become a mechanical, duty-ridden process that the woman could not help noticing.

A reader of Moulton's paper might argue that she is "hung up" on orgasms and fails to see that they are not a necessary condition for a valid sexual experience. Yet if the man is getting both psychological and physiological gratification, it does not seem unreasonable to insist that the woman have both types of satisfaction as well.

Indeed, it seems reasonable to assume that a woman who is not interested in orgasm is also someone who does not particularly care for the more lustful and physiological aspects of sex either. This, however, would hardly please a man who does not want his mate to simply lie there like an inert object and passively take what he does to her. If the desire for orgasm and active physiological contribution to the sex act regularly go together, then it would seem natural that a man would want a woman who desires orgasm and would try to satisfy her.

---

have both kinds of orgasm, the distinction is very clear. The vaginal one is usually preferred although there is considerable satisfaction in the clitoral orgasm as well. Many women experience no orgasm at all. Many more women experience only clitoral orgasms. A small percentage of women experience both kinds of orgasm." Robertiello bases his thesis on years of experience discussing the female response with many women. (See Robertiello, "The 'Clitoral versus Vaginal Orgasm' Controversy and Some of Its Ramifications," *Journal of Sexual Research* 6 (1970): 307–11.) For an excellent survey of the clitoral-vaginal controversy written by a philosopher, see Irving Singer, *The Goals of Human Sexuality* (New York: Schocken Books, 1974), Chapters 3 and 4. Singer himself thinks that vaginal orgasms do have a physiological basis and are not just imaginary or psychological phenomena based on the female's masochistic joy in submitting to the male. He argues on page 97 of his book that the vaginal response results from peritoneal stimulation when the women's viscera are jostled by the penis.

10. At one point Ms. Moulton seems to suggest that females avoid intercourse entirely if they wish to be assured of orgasmic fulfillment. She writes, "If there were no conceptual confusion, then those who were only concerned with male satisfaction in sexual activity between males and females could restrict that activity to intercourse, while those concerned with female satisfaction as well would not be so restricted" (p. 40). But where would females turn for satisfaction? Ms. Moulton, in describing an analogy of sexual behavior with feeding, mentions the following hypothetical society. She writes: "Other women relied on self-feeding to survive but this was frowned on by the whole community as perverted antisocial behavior. The influence of custom was so strong that few believed that women in the kitchen might feed each other. It was commonly believed that women who fed each other did so only because they could not get men to feed. No one ever thought (or realized) that they did it to get food" (p. 41). Is Ms. Moulton, in her feeding analogy, recommending masturbation or lesbianism as possible routes for the satisfaction women cannot obtain in conventional heterosexual intercourse? This is not clear.

Many of my male students report that giving their partner an orgasm is vitally important to their own sense of manhood and virility. (Whether they also do it for the sake of the woman's satisfaction is not clear.) Such young men, however, often report that they must "endure" prolonged foreplay and consciously restrain themselves from ejaculating as soon as they would like so that the woman will become sufficiently aroused. Sex for them becomes either a self-sacrificial act to please their partner or else a means to prove their own ability to provide the woman with an orgasm. Spontaneity and sex for its own sake as a pleasurable experience is ruined for such a man.

Do these considerations mean that heterosexual intercourse is doomed to please either the man or the woman, but not both at once? One reply would be that not all males care for a "two-minute quickie"; many prefer sensuous eroticism. Sensuous erotics do not regard foreplay techniques as difficult to master, but engage in them in a pleasurable, spontaneous way, believing that the resulting orgasms will be more powerful. They also enjoy prolonged penile-vaginal thrusting for its own sake and do not become obsessed with instant orgasms. Would a sensuous-erotic male be the answer to Moulton's criticism of conventional sexual intercourse with its lack of stimulation for the female? Certainly a sensuous-erotic female is far more likely to have orgasms. However, recent research shows that females who have such partners still fall well below the rate of orgasmic success for males. (See Chapter 6 of *Beyond the Male Myth* by Anthony Pietropinto and Jacqueline Simenauer.) What is wrong now?

Perhaps to obtain the answer we must first recall Moulton's quote from Kinsey: "Data show that the female is no slower in response than the average male when she is sufficiently stimulated and *when she is not inhibited in her activity.*" (Italics mine.) Moulton says that the key words are "sufficiently stimulated," and holds that the main difficulty for women is that they are not getting enough stimulation. Yet the women mentioned above are getting plenty of stimulation but still do not match the male's orgasmic rate of success.

What Moulton has overlooked is Kinsey's other point about the necessity of the woman's not being *inhibited* in her activity. Would she enjoy parity with the male if she were not inhibited? Sexologists have often noted that women have been the victims of a sexual value system that teaches them that sex is not for sensual pleasure but is solely for procreation or the emotional satisfaction of pleasing the male. If she *is* the victim of such inhibitions, then one cannot blame penile-vaginal intercourse alone for being unstimulating and non-orgasmic for the female. If such inhibitions could be prevented or removed, then perhaps women could enjoy both physiological and psychological satisfaction, and one would not have to mouth the old physiology-psychology dichotomy that has traditionally been used to differentiate male-female sexual satisfaction.

3
On "Sex for Sex's Sake"

We have already noted in preceding sections of this book that many things that are thought to be necessary conditions for good sex are not really so at all: at least not for all people. A sex act can be performed to express love or to produce babies; it may be "natural" or "moral" or sophisticated in its techniques. Nevertheless, the act itself as a sexual experience may be utterly unfulfilling to many even when it has the preceding results or characteristics. Nor does it seem to be true that foreplay, penile-vaginal penetration, or even orgasm are necessary in all sexual philosophies. And such familiar claims to the effect that an act must involve interpersonal bodily communication or mutually responsive partners would not hold true for shoe fetishists or voyeurs. Those who say that the latter forms of sex are not "good" or are perverted are actually passing a kind of moral judgment on the act rather than admitting that it may be a good sexual experience *qua* sex for the person who enjoys it. And those who use terms like "embodiment" to put down those who like to make considerable use of their intellect in performing a sexual act (such as those who delight in inventing new sexual games with their partners) fail to see that any aspect of our being can, for some people, be charged with sexual significance and arousal, including, of all things, the intellect.

A central difficulty with many of the traditional "necessary" conditions for good sex is that sex is viewed as a means to something else rather than sex for sex's sake, that is, sex as an experience of sexual pleasure that is anticipated with joy rather than frustration and is followed by a sense of happy fulfillment rather than a feeling of postorgasmic depletion and "let-down." Some instances of using sex as a means to an end include:

(a) Sex used for procreation.

(b) Sex used to prove one's love, to win a lover, or to hold on to a lover, or even to convey feelings of love.

(c) Sex used like a tranquilizer pill to relieve tensions and frustrations, including sexual ones. Such persons rush to the orgasm the way one rushes to the toilet for a bowel movement. And such persons commonly view the sex act itself with about as much respect as they do a bowel movement.

(d) Sex used to prove that one is liberated or that one is still potent or that one is skilled in the use of the latest techniques.

(e) Sex used to prove to oneself that one can possess or master another person, either by causing pain or by overwhelming one's partner with pleasure and finding joy in seeing one's partner reduced to a lust-controlled object that one can manipulate at will.

(f) Sex used as a means of revenge: revenge against oneself for guilt feelings or to hurt one's lover whom one suspects of infidelity.

(g) Sex used to overcome loneliness, alienation, boredom, feelings of meaninglessness by losing oneself in an experience that seems to transport oneself outside of space and time, or by losing oneself in another's body in order to absorb his happiness or other qualities one lacks into one's own being.

(h) Sex used as a means to attain an experience of the divine, to become at one with the harmonies of the universe (Tantric sex).

(i) Sex used primarily as a mode of communicating emotions.

One difficulty with each of these instrumental uses of sex is that each is perfectly compatible with a disdain of the sex act itself, at least in its physical sense. This does not always happen, to be sure; but it is quite possible that such sex need no more be enjoyed in itself than the bitter pill one takes as a means of relieving pain. As I noted earlier, those who use sex primarily for non-sexual purposes remind one of those who pour gobs of cream and sugar in their coffee; they don't really like coffee at all: it's just an excuse to enjoy the cream and sugar.

A further difficulty is that when sex is done primarily as a means of achieving something else, sexual pleasure and spontaneity is diminished. For the possibility always lurks in one's mind that one will at any moment fail to achieve one's purpose, and one will have to concentrate all the harder on the extrinsic goal to see that one does not fail. Sex that is used to prove that one is potent, for example, invites impotency; for one is so worried that one will be found impotent that one will not be able to function.

Furthermore, sex that is viewed in instrumental terms often requires that one perform the act in one particular way. Those who use sex as a means of achieving transcendental experiences, such as Reichian and Tantric sex, must adhere to a prescribed sexual ritual. And those who use sex primarily as a means of expressing love must confine themselves to sexual methods that communicate tenderness and trust. For many persons, love has built into it a set of moral requirements: trust, care, respect, and so forth. And such moral considerations may positively impede experimenting with some new technique for fear that one will violate these moral criteria. Actually such a new sexual approach may make the act more fulfilling on the sexual level for both part-ners, and could even come to be viewed as a novel way of expressing love. In the case of reproduction, I have been informed by a gynecologist that the best way to be certain that the male sperm reaches the female ovum is the tradi-tional man-on-top sexual position.

A final difficulty is that the things sex is often viewed as a means of achiev-ing could just as well be achieved by non-sexual means, and in many cases in a better and more permanent way. Sacrificing in order to buy a beautiful home for one's beloved may be a far better and more permanent way of expressing one's love than sex could ever provide. Sex that is used to overcome loneliness, boredom, and alienation provides only a brief respite from such difficulties. Alienation and loneliness are problems that are far better resolved by friend-ship than by sex. For those who wish to master others, using the rabble-rousing techniques of a dictator would achieve one's purposes on a far greater scale than sex. Indeed, perhaps the reason why sex has been viewed with con-tempt down through the ages by so many is that they used sex for such ulterior purposes and then turned against sex when it did not satisfy their needs in any permanent way.

One might argue that these criticisms could just as well be applied to the view of sex for sex's sake, that is, sex for pleasure. For example, it might be argued one can invent a pill that would give one pleasurable sexual sensations, and that sex would be unnecessary to fulfill the goal of sexual pleasure. However, such a pill could never be a substitute for the sensations that are enriched by bodily movements and contact. Or it might be argued that sex used to produce pleasure is also compatible with contempt for the sex act that produces this pleasure; but sex could hardly be a pleasurable experience if one viewed the sex act itself with contempt.

Indeed, in sex for sex's sake the sexual act and sexual pleasure and even sexual techniques form an organic whole in which all are pleasurable and there is no means-to-an-end attitude whatever if the act is performed in a spontaneous, carefree way. Those who are obsessed with sexual pleasure or who are worried about whether the act will be sexually fulfilling will, of course, often find that their obsession or their worries will make sexual pleasure impossible. There is the old claim that a watched pot never boils; and those who are on the alert to see that the sex act is fulfilling their expectations of pleasure may be disappointed. Indeed, for such persons sexual pleasure is commonly used as a means for compensating for a lack of excitement in other areas of their life. None of these things are compatible with enjoying sex just for sex's sake.

At this point a critic might argue that a sex act can be fulfilling even if one is not motivated by a desire for sexual pleasure. One might imagine a couple who, for some reason, have no sexual interest in each other at all. Yet they engage in a sex act solely because they want to have a child. Wouldn't the joy of knowing that the act is going to produce a human being be sufficient to make it a valid sexual experience, even though they derived no sexual pleasure from the act at all? Indeed, in the film *Summer of '42* a fifteen-year-old boy who is infatuated with a woman twice his age goes to her home and learns that her soldier-husband has been killed in action. The woman is overcome by grief and invites the boy to perform a sexual act with her. The boy, wishing to console his beloved, obliges. Wasn't this a valid sexual experience, even though the act was motivated not by a desire for sexual pleasure but was rather an expression of grief and sorrow?

I should like to argue, however, that even though such persons doubtlessly had interesting and important experiences that in some way involved the use of the sexual organs, they nevertheless did not engage in acts that had any sexual significance. A prostitute, for example, uses sex as a means to an end in ways analogous to the couples mentioned above, albeit in ways perhaps not as noble as theirs. Yet for her the act doubtlessly has no sexual significance even though she (like the couples mentioned above) experiences certain feelings, which in her case is the thrill of making money. The reason she feels that the act is of no sexual significance is surely that she is not motivated by considerations of sexual pleasure at all. Simply because an act involves the use of the sexual organs in, say, certain characteristic penile-vaginal thrusting motions, does not necessarily make the act sexual or mean that the experience connected with the act was sexual. The claim that the couple in the film mentioned above had a kind of sexual experience seems to rest on the assumption that because the couple's expression of sorrow involved the use of the penis and the vagina, their act was sexual and therefore could be said to have yielded a sexual experience. I think this interpretation of such an act is entirely mistaken for reasons that I will now develop.

In extending my thesis that the essence of sex is certain uniquely sexual feelings, I should like to argue that an act is sexual or has sexual significance precisely to the extent that it is motivated by a desire for or yields such feelings. On this view, an act which was motivated by a desire for sexual pleasure, but which yielded no pleasure was still sexual because of the intent behind it; it would merely be an unsuccessful sexual act. And an act that was neither motivated by a desire for sexual feelings nor yielded any such feelings would not be sexual at all. (If I were ever to defend a concept of sexual perversion, it would be to use sex as a means to ends which inhibit rather than enrich the specifically sexual feelings I have in mind.)

Given this theory of what is meant by an act's being sexual, an act of sexual *intercourse* would require that both partners be motivated by desires for sexual pleasure. In the case of rape or prostitution, the act may have sexual significance for one partner but none at all for the other. This is why it is advisable to describe, say, rape as being not an act of sexual intercourse, but rather the act of the male's forcibly masturbating in the woman's vagina.

A critic of this view would, however, argue that the intent behind the act, successfully fulfilled or not, has nothing to do with whether the act was sexual. He would say that the only thing that is required for an act's being sexual is that it involves the sexual organs in certain characteristic movements, such as penile-vaginal intercourse.

Furthermore, such a critic would argue that I am presupposing that a sex act can have only one purpose, the production of sexual feelings, or else it is not sexual. But can't sex have many purposes, including procreation or expressing love or making money or degrading another person, and aren't all these acts sexual even if they were not motivated by a desire for sexual feelings or did not yield sexual feelings? One can wave one's arm for many purposes, such as flagging down a car or greeting someone. Yet these are both acts of waving one's arm, regardless of their motive. However, the example of waving one's arm is analogous only to the sheer thrusting of a penis in a vagina. But when does this bit of physical exercise of parts of one's body become a sexual phenomenon? Surely the intent behind the act is of vital importance as to how we are describing it in ways that transcend a description of sheer physical movements. The waving of one's arm in order to flag down a car is no longer merely the movement of an arm. It is now an act of flagging down a car and has become, as it were, a flagging phenomenon because of the intent behind the act. But don't penile-vaginal motions become sexual phenomena because they are motivated by a desire for or produce sexual feelings?

One might, however, argue that penile-vaginal intercourse could also be called a sexual phenomenon when it is motivated solely by a desire to reproduce. But if no sexual feelings were involved, such penile-vaginal intercourse should actually be called a reproductive act and nothing more. If humans had been born with no desire for or ability to have sexual feelings, but only with a desire to procreate, the terms *sexual organ* and *sexual act* would surely never have arisen. We would have spoken only of reproductive organs or reproductive acts. It is, therefore, the desire for or the presence of sexual sensations that makes an act distinctly *sexual,* as opposed to its being merely a reproductive act, an expression of love, and the like. Furthermore, someone who enjoys sexual feelings to their utmost is surely a fully sexual being even if he or she never reproduces. A woman, for example, who can no longer reproduce hardly ceases to be a sexual being; and the reason is surely that she continues to enjoy sexual feelings.

A final reply to the claim that the criterion for acts being sexual would be that my concept of a sexual experience presupposes the concept of a sexual act or a sexual organ rather than the reverse. But this is surely not true: a sexual experience does not presuppose a sexual organ, for eunuchs have sexual desires also. Nor need one engage in a sexual act in order to produce a sexual experience. A man who looks at a beautiful nude woman has a unique sexual thrill even if he performs no sexual act. He did, of course, have to perform an act, that is, the act of looking at a nude woman in order to have his sexual experience. But the criterion for saying that any act of looking at an attractive person has sexual significance is that it was motivated by a desire for or produced sexual feelings. (Indeed, one need not perform any kind of act at all in order to be able to claim that one had a sexual experience. A young boy reaching puberty may experience sexual arousal, yet he may have no idea as to what sort of act such feelings should lead to.)

In summary, I should like to note that my concept of sex for sex's sake does not commit me to reducing sex to merely an experience of raw sensations. For sensations can in some cases be enhanced and enriched rather than diminished by certain emotions and thoughts. A woman once told me, for example, that the best orgasm she ever had was the one that occurred when she felt that the sex act she engaged in was going to produce a child. But such thoughts or emotions acquire sexual significance only when they heighten rather than diminish sexual feelings.

4

A New Theory of Sexual Immorality

I now wish to consider the question of good sex not so much in terms of how good it is as a purely sexual experience but how good it is in the moral sense of the term. It should be noted that there is not necessarily a connection between a sex act's being moral and its being good simply *qua* sex. Indeed, in the theory I am about to examine, we may discover an example of how different the two concepts can be.

I have avoided discussing the usual pros and cons of such vast subjects as abortion, incest, adultery, promiscuity and premarital sex. Discussions of the morality of such issues have by now become so complex that it would take a book to handle each of them (for example, abortion); or else some of them seem, at least to me, so simple to resolve that they warrant little extended philosophical treatment. A promiscuous person, for example, seems to be simply someone who is partaking of so much sex that it has become a bore to him; such a person is more like an overindulgent eater than a sinner, and he might be encouraged to go on a sexual diet out of simple self-interest.

The theory that I have selected is a relatively new one. It adheres closely to the actual interrelationship of two sexual partners in the sexual acts they perform or in the proposals they make for such acts. It is thus in tune with what has been the central emphasis of this book. The theory, by Bernard Baumrin, is set forth in his paper, "Sexual Immorality Delineated."[11]

Let us begin by outlining the central feature of Baumrin's position: Baumrin opens his paper with an attack on the traditional romantic-idealist position that sex (or at least the best sex) is a perfectly altruistic relation between two persons who do not want to manipulate or use each other and who claim they want to please each other in every way as a spontaneous expression of their feelings for each other. For Baumrin, sex is a kind of *mutual manipulation,* where each partner agrees to allow himself or herself to be used as a means to the other's ends. Baumrin does seem to be at least partly on solid grounds here; for even within altruistic presuppositions, how could one *give* to another if both partners had the view they wanted to give pleasure without getting anything in return? Between two such partners there would be no point in giving if neither expected any satisfaction for himself from the other but only wanted to "give".

When Baumrin speaks of the conscious manipulation of one's partner, he is clearly rejecting the concept of the total surrender of one's ego to lustful feelings, that is, the embodiment theory of sexuality defended by Nagel and Reich. He writes:

> Perhaps no one has ever had a perfectly spontaneous interaction with another, but everyone has spoken to cajole, shifted eyes to charm, acquiesced to trick, clothed to attract. . . . We use our own emotions sexually to change the emotions of others. We seek to know the inner psyche of our partners at least to enhance for ourselves our interaction with them. We want to know their physical responsiveness, their likes and

---

11. In *Philosophy and Sex,* ed. R. Baker and F. Elliston (Buffalo: Prometheus Books, 1975), pp. 116–128.

dislikes, for our use now or in the future . . . who supposes that our interest in such information is sought solely by us to benefit our partner? Is it not patent that even if we wish to benefit a sexual partner, we seek such knowledge at least also for our own benefit, and possibly only for our own benefit? (p. 118)

Thus, for Baumrin, "Sexual interaction is a bundle of disparate activities we try to manage, devoting to it a great deal of energy, foresight, and care" (p. 118).

He further writes: "The intellectual picture of sexuality we have had for quite some time applauds the natural, the pastoral, the uninhibited, the silent communion of souls; it treats the contrived, the cultured, the controlled, and the merely carnal as contemptible. This legacy of romanticism has endured in our thinking about sex, while all the intellectual paraphernalia that supported it has long been swept away by clear thinking and rational criticism" (pp. 122–23). He further condemns the romantic view that sexual interaction is a "romance between feelings, where feelings have been elevated to a sacrosanct position" (p. 122). Thus he would reject Solomon's theory of sex as a bodily communication of feelings and attitudes, as well.

There are, however, some disturbing features in the quotations mentioned above. For example, when he writes that "even if we wish to benefit a sexual partner, we seek such knowledge at least for our own benefit, and possibly only for our own benefit," this suggests a highly egoistic way of viewing the sexual act. And when he speaks of sex as a kind of mutual manipulation, it would then seem clear that one is allowing oneself to be manipulated solely in order to enjoy the self-gratification of manipulating someone else. Viewing the other person as a kind of instrument of one's gratification suggests that one is cynically using the other person strictly as a means to an end. For Baumrin, the sexual act is one which is "contrived" and "controlled," with apparently no communication of feeling or surrender to one's partner. How, then, is Baumrin going to develop any kind of theory of sexual morality that will have any application to his self-interested manipulators of each others' bodies?

Indeed, given what Baumrin has said thus far, why should such egoistic persons allow themselves to be manipulated as well or allow the other person to have any sexual gratification? Baumrin insists that there be mutual manipulation, but how does he exclude the sexist male (or even the rapist) who is a classic example of someone who manipulates another without providing any satisfaction in turn? At one point Baumrin makes the following moral claim:

If it is immoral to propose to use someone else as a sexual instrument without at the same time being prepared to be used by them as their instrument, then it is also immoral to use someone as a sexual instrument without permitting oneself to be used. While the immorality of the unilateral proposal is derived from intending to use someone only as a means, the immorality of the behaviour is derived from the actual depersonalization of the other (p. 121).

Yet it ill behooves Baumrin to condemn the depersonalization of another when his entire theory of sexual interaction rests on the idea of each partner's being viewed as a kind of "instrument" of the other's gratification. The concept of a sexual act which is manipulative, contrived and controlled and from which feelings are virtually absent would seem to be the ultimate depersonalization of human sexuality.

At the end of his paper Baumrin suggests a possible way of defending himself against the charge of sheer egoism. He argues that one cannot expect to get anything from the act unless he also gives what his partner expects. For, short of rape, the other person can simply refuse to continue with the act in the way the one desires (or even abandon one entirely) if one's partner is not fulfilled as well. In short, the egoist cannot get his fair share unless he also gives his partner her fair share. Furthermore, Baumrin might argue that someone who gets a reputation for not providing any satisfaction will be unable to attract any further sexual partners at all.

This sort of reply, however, will certainly not work in all cases. What of the man who enjoys a one-night stand in a strange city or sex with a stranger? He takes his orgasm, only to abandon his partner without giving her an orgasm as well. He has obtained what he wants without giving anything in return, and his reputation is not endangered because he simply selects a new city or a new partner who is unfamiliar with his selfish practices. Thus, despite the fact that Baumrin thinks he can avoid egoism in its most blatant form, it seems that such egoism could return to haunt him on the basis of what he has said thus far. Indeed, even if in the more common cases one does give in order to get as Baumrin suggests, this is only a form of enlightened egoism, more subtle to be sure, but still a form of egoism. And if such basically egoistic persons have to give something in order to get something, it is far from clear that they will do anything more than the bare minimum to keep their partner satisfied. Nor would their giving pleasure necessarily be done with any enthusiasm, something which would make the act into a mechanical ritual which neither partner would enjoy. Indeed, one of the great joys of sex would be missing, that is, the thought that one's partner is sincerely interested in giving one sexual pleasure without calculating the benefits he or she is going to get in return.

Let us now examine in detail Baumrin's concept of sexual morality. Here he introduces the notion of certain duties that the sexual partners owe to each other, such that each is obligated to respond in certain ways if he or she has agreed to do so. He thus seems to be moving toward something far more idealistic and moral in the traditional sense than his earlier comments about sex as mutual manipulation on a strict quid pro quo basis of mutual self-interest. He now says that each person somehow has a right to expect to receive sexual gratification in turn and not be used exclusively as a means to one's own gratification, as does the playboy who "loves and leaves them" utterly unfulfilled.

He then outlines the conditions of his "sexual contract": the first three are general criteria that are not unique to the sexual realm, while the latter three define uniquely sexual duties:

1. The persons involved must in some positive respect treat each other as a non-means. (This is meant to exclude the playboy mentioned above who treats his mates solely as a means to his own gratification without providing any gratification in turn.)

2. Each person properly expects some such treatment.

3. That expectation is based on the apparently voluntary choice of the other to engage in this kind of behavior, that is, sexual interaction.

4. If a person makes a proposal to engage in a certain form of sexual behavior, then he has created in himself a duty to perform (or at least try to perform) that type of sexual act if the other accepts his proposal.

5. The acceptance of such a proposal creates a similar duty in the person accepting the proposal to perform the act he has agreed to perform. If he wishes to perform some other type of act that the initiating agent does not care for, then he has no right to expect the initiating agent to satisfy him and the latter is discharged of his duty to perform. For example, if the one who makes the proposal wishes to engage in penile-vaginal intercourse and the person who accepts his proposal also wishes to engage in oral sex, then the one who made the original proposal is not bound by duty to carry out his proposal if oral sex offends him. On the other hand, if the one who makes the proposal agrees to engage in oral sex, then he is bound by duty to satisfy his partner's desire for oral sex if his partner has satisfied his desire for penile-vaginal intercourse. Thus, if John knows that Mary wishes to engage in oral sex and if he has agreed to do so, then if Mary does what John wants but John does not do what he knows Mary wants, then John is immoral on Baumrin's criterion.

6. Finally, Baumrin argues that the initiating agent implicitly makes the following proposal which guarantees the mutuality and voluntariness of the act. He writes:

> *I wish to use you as an instrument for my sexual purposes and therefore undertake to make myself an instrument of your sexual purposes to the extent that you agree to my proposal.* Thus, on this view the crucial elements in creating specifically sexual rights and duties is the desire to use another as a means for a certain kind of end and the willingness to offer oneself to that person as an inducement to perform a voluntary arrangement. What one is offering is to make oneself the other's means for the satisfaction of their desires. Otherwise one would not be making an offer at all, or at least not a sexual one, since one would merely be behaving in a peculiar way or forcing one's attentions on another (p. 120).

As an example of a blatant violation of this sexual contract, Baumrin mentions the following situation: A approaches B and suggests charmingly to B that due to B's attractive characteristics, A would like to make love to B. In response, B invites A to B's home. On arrival A shakes B's hand and leaves.

As we noted earlier, Baumrin argues that without offering to make oneself a means to the other's gratification, one is immoral because one intends to use the other only as a means, and one is thereby depersonalizing the other person. But Baumrin's whole view of sexual interaction as constituting two partners who view each other as a kind of instrument to their own personal gratification, as well as his view that sex is something manipulative, contrived, controlled and virtually without feeling, all suggest the very kind of depersonalization he wants to avoid. And if his theory of sexual interaction fosters depersonalization, how can he expect his mutual manipulators to carry out the duties he puts before them? One's concept of sexual morality should be derived from or have some connection with one's view of what sex is like; in Baumrin's case this does not seem to be true at all. (Indeed, his criterion that each partner must in some positive respect treat each other as a *non-means* seems clearly at odds with his view that each partner views the other solely or primarily as a means to his or her own gratification.)

Furthermore, one might argue that if other theories of sexuality have overemphasized the expression of feeling at the expense of the sheer sensual aspects of sex, Baumrin's theory of a sexual contract between two partners delineating all sorts of previously agreed upon rights and duties has made sex too cold and calculating. To be sure, one might argue that his criteria for mutual rights and obligations could serve as a check on unpredictable feelings and states of utter abandonment to lust that can as easily lead to a disappointing sex act as they can to an ecstatic one. (I have already noted how a partner's totally surrendering himself to lust can lead to a loss of all sense of his partner's needs.) On the other hand, one might argue that Baumrin's contractual rights create an utterly non-sexual state of mind in which each partner is constantly on the alert to see that he or she is getting his or her fair share of pleasure as set forth by their sexual contract. In such an act there would seem to be no spontaneity at all. (The problem of combining spontaneity with the presence of mind needed to pay attention to one's partner's needs is, of course, one that faces all theories of sexual intercourse. This is doubtlessly why so many people prefer masturbation.) And given Baumrin's view that sex is essentially egoistic, no one would go beyond the contract to provide any extra measure of enjoyment that the contract did not provide for.

Furthermore, Baumrin argues that a "flirt" who gives every appearance of wanting sex, but who does not actually intend to allow himself to be the other's source of sexual gratification, is nevertheless bound by duty to perform a sex act since his apparent offer creates a right in the other to use him if the other could have reasonable grounds for viewing, say, his flirtatious wink as a sincere offer. And, as we have already noted, feeling does not play any central role in Baumrin's theory. If someone's feelings change in the middle of the sex act and he no longer feels that he wants to gratify the other person even though he has previously agreed to do so, then he is, for Baumrin, still duty-bound to complete the act so long as his partner holds up her end of the bargain as well.

However, one wonders if one would really want to insist on one's rights to go through with the act if the other partner was merely flirting or playing eye games in the first place, or if one's partner's feelings change in the middle of the act and he does not wish to fulfill his end of the bargain. For who would want to perform an act if the other person's heart were not really in it, except, of course, for those who do not mind prostitutes who only do it for money and whose internal feelings are irrelevant to her partner. Some may of course, say, "You agreed to do it and it's your *duty* to do it whether you now feel like it or not." But then the mutual fulfillment of a contract becomes very different from mutual responsiveness in the fullest sense of the word, which would include the feelings Baumrin considers to be of exaggerated significance.

In summary, the nature of Baumrin's sexual contract (allowing each to use the other as an object to be manipulated) and the nature of the parties involved as Baumrin depicts them (persons highly concerned with their own gratification) contains within it elements that virtually guarantee the breakdown of the contract in terms of equal gratification for both. For if we are as calculating and self-interested as Baumrin suggested earlier in his paper, then the mere fact that we must fulfill others' interests in order to fulfill our own does not offer much hope that each party is really going to try to benefit each other equally.

Will not each one try to get as much as he or she can and give only what is necessary so that his partner will not become so disgusted that he or she will simply abandon the act altogether? Baumrin tries valiantly to overcome this problem by imposing on his mutual manipulators a set of strict contractual agreements; he ignores the fact, however, that self-interested persons in the final analysis view themselves as having duties and commitments only to themselves and that "duties to others" is only a euphemism for doing the minimum necessary to be sure that they are not left utterly without gratification from their partner. To be sure, one would hope that an enlightened egoist would come to see that the more one puts into the sexual act, the more one is likely to gain from it. A highly aroused partner is surely more likely to provide one with more satisfaction than one who thinks he or she is simply being exploited.

5
Sex and Privacy

Is there a necessary connection between good sex and sex that is conducted in private? If *good* is taken to mean moral, there has been such a connection traditionally between morality and closed doors. But what could be said to someone who claimed that public sex, as sex, could be as good or even better than sex conducted in private? Of course, most people do not engage in public acts of sex because they consider them shockingly immoral or because they know such acts are illegal. But morals change, and the day may come when it will no longer be considered immoral (or even illegal) to perform public sex acts. Here a critic might argue that a public display would still be avoided because there is a necessary connection between intimacy and truly fulfilling sex; to make it public would, he might claim, destroy its very meaning. (This view is sometimes defended by the sophisticated critic of pornographic films and theatrical performances containing simulated sex acts.)

What is the reason for keeping sex behind closed doors? A cynic might argue that this is because man is not prone to share things like sex. When he finds someone who is attracted to him, he wants to keep her to himself, like a dog selfishly guarding his bone. He treats his sexual relationship like an exclusive club in which only one other person is admitted; others aren't allowed to participate at any level, including the visual one. Such a person might defend his actions by saying that he shows his genitals only to those who are special, just as he brings out his best wine only for certain guests. Sex that is performed in public would, he might claim, lose its status as a special gift to the partner. Furthermore, to make it public could destroy its mystique and reduce it to the everyday level of sharing a hamburger.

Attempts to defend sexual privacy because it makes sex a "special gift" to one's partner or because it preserves some kind of mystique overlook the fact that these same arguments were used years ago to condemn kissing in public. Yet hardly anyone who publicly kisses his beloved in a crowd of people feels that its status as a special gift is being destroyed. For one thing, he is not kissing the crowd, but only his beloved; for another, in their *psychological* space they are completely alone, even though they occupy a public space.

One difficulty with the sex and privacy theory may be that it reveals that we still view sex as something dirty and thus to be hidden from public view. Sophisticated persons would, however, insist that just because they do not perform sex in public does not mean that they feel it is obscene or shameful. Yet some might argue that such persons at least feel unconsciously guilty about sex. (Even those who participate in orgies do not conduct them in public. A multiplicity of couples does, of course, mean that the couples can witness each other's actions. But an orgy is simply a sex act with more than two persons involved, and there is apparently no concern about being viewed by others so long as one is part of the sex act.)

St. Augustine is the philosopher most famous for developing a theory about the connection between sex, shame, and privacy. In Augustine's view the Garden of Eden was originally a paradise in which man had complete control over his body. For example, Augustine claims that man had complete control over his genitals by the use of his free will and reason. If he willed an erection, his penis would become erect; if he forbade his penis from becoming aroused, it would obey his command. Then came man's sin of eating the forbidden fruit, and thereafter, as punishment, God decreed that Adam's sexual organs would no longer be obedient to his will. When he desired an erection, the penis would not necessarily obey his will; and when he did not desire an erection, he might find himself in just such a state. Since this would clearly be an embarrassing situation for a nude man, Augustine claims that Adam began to wear a fig leaf to hide his shame at not being able to control himself. This shame, Augustine claims, was carried over into the sex act itself:

Lust requires for its consummation darkness, secrecy; and this not only when unlawful intercourse is desired, but even such fornication as the earthly city has legalized. When there is no such fear of punishment, these permitted pleasures still shrink from the public eye. Even where provision is made for this lust, secrecy is also provided, and while lust found it easy to remove the prohibitions of law, shamelessness found it impossible to lay aside the veil of retirement. For even shameless men call this shameful; and though they love the pleasure, dare not display it. What! Does not even conjugal intercourse, sanctioned as it may be by law for the propagation of children, legitimate and honorable though it may be, does it not seek retirement from every eye?[12]

Even Sartre, hardly a Christian philosopher, argues that nudity would make one completely a "being for others" and would be a source of utter shame. Clothing, for Sartre, is in a symbolic way one's attempt to retain some degree of one's own subjectivity and not to stand utterly exposed as a mere object or thing for the gaze of others.

It might, however, be argued that shame and public embarrassment really have very little to do with why sex should remain private. For example, one might hold that sex is a form of communication or is an expression of some emotion such as love. It would then be argued that what one wishes to communicate is directed to one person only and not to a crowd of viewers. The sex as communication theory, however, would seem to be valid for only certain kinds of sex or for certain parts of the sex act, such as foreplay. When a couple is in the throes of lust it might be asked just what is being communicated when a penis is going up and down in a vagina. The two partners have "become their bodies," so to speak, and the additional attempt to communicate feelings would only seem to decrease the spontaneity of the act.

Indeed, even if the two partners were communicating, it is not clear that an audience which did not blatantly disrupt their acts would inhibit the process of communication. Couples often kiss in public, for example, and as long as they are psychologically alone, there is no problem of communication. Such couples are so involved in each others' feelings that the public is tuned out of the proceedings entirely.

A second argument against sex in public could be the claim that the spontaneity and focus of the act would be destroyed. Instead of surrendering to one's partner, one would be engaging in a "performance" for others, who would be judging one's sexual prowess. Furthermore, we are all reasonably competent in kissing and eating, but our sexual competencies vary; and those who are unsure of themselves would suffer greatly if they knew they were being viewed in a judgmental way. One difficulty with this argument is the

---

12. St. Augustine, *The City of God* (New York, Hafner Publishing Co., 1948), Vol. 2, p. 38. One suspects, however, that St. Augustine's elaborate theory was not the original reason why sexual partners performed their acts in private. To perform an act in public where both partners are on the ground and lost in a helpless state of lust would surely leave them vulnerable to attack from outsiders.

fact that in a conventional sexual act one is already being viewed and perhaps judged by someone: one's partner. (The only really private act is masturbation.) To becomes secure in one's performance with one's partner sometimes takes time and practice; but then the same could be said about a public sexual act. You could arrive at a point where you could say, "I don't care what they think." It would seem that one could ignore the audience and focus on one's partner, just as we do in a private act.

A critic of the preceding reply might ask: If one is going to end up tuning out the audience, what is the point in having an audience to begin with, other than possibly to satisfy one's benevolent desire that others share at least visually in one's good fortune? Rather than taking the trouble to accustom oneself to a public performance, why not take a simpler route and continue to perform sex in private (unless, of course, private facilities are unavailable)?

To answer this objection, one might argue that what a secure sexual performer eliminates is his concern about being judged. But might he not still want the *stare* of others in some way? For Sartre, the answer would still be no, since he views sex as a means of capturing the freedom of one's partner by reducing the partner to a helpless, lust-filled body through one's caresses. Clearly one would feel shame about trying to capture another's freedom by imprisoning it in the flesh, and would therefore not want an audience present. Indeed, if the gaze of the third party captured one's subjectivity and reduced one to a helpless thing or object (like a jury staring at a rapist), then one's ability to control the situation in a Sartrean way would be destroyed.

Suppose, however, that we reject Sartre's theory of sexual motivation. If we are not concerned about capturing the freedom of our partner by lustful arousal, we might engage in sex in order to "become our body" through the caresses of another. The purpose would be to surrender ourselves to the direction of our movements by sheer lust, and thus have a respite from a mind-directed, rational existence.

Could the stare of others in any way facilitate and heighten this goal of becoming one's body? Of course, if the stare were in any way judgmental or accusatory, then one's self-consciousness would only be heightened, and the goal of surrendering one's consciousness to direction by the body would be impeded. One would be obsessed with the question, "What are they thinking of what I am doing?" But if the audience is not judgmental and is aroused by what one is doing, and if one senses this, then it would seem that one could be further aroused by its arousal rather than merely being aroused by one's partner. And the more one is aroused by the audience, the more the audience is aroused in turn. Thus a feedback loop would have been established between the observers and the observed leading to ever increasing degrees of arousal on both sides. One would not be aroused merely by sensing one's partner's arousal; one would be aroused by sensing the arousal of an entire audience as they view one's sex act. This would surely produce a far deeper level of sexual arousal than could be produced by one's partner alone. (This is perhaps the motivation for group sex in our own time.)

To become the object of an audience's gaze would deepen the feeling that one is being turned into an object or thing or body directed by lust. The sexual partners would come to see themselves as others see them: as bodies that arouse lust, a perception that deepens their own sense of embodiment. (The sense of being seen doing something forbidden could also heighten their sexual arousal.)

One difficulty with this enhanced means of reaching a state of embodiment is that in the initial stages of the act one would be responding primarily to an audience rather than to the partner's needs. Indeed, if being stared at by several people could produce an even deeper level of embodiment than could be attained with one's partner alone, it might seem as if the partner had become superfluous; one could simply masturbate and if this aroused the audience, one would still have the feedback loop.

Nor does the problem of relating to one's partner end here: ultimately as we sink deeper into being identified with our own body, our awareness of the audience and the world around us will disappear. But part of the world includes our partner. Unless lust has some kind of wisdom of its own that permits each partner to continue to be able to sense the other's changing moods and needs as the act progresses, they might very well find themselves two isolated individuals, each one much like the lonely subway exhibitionist opening his raincoat.

Furthermore, if doing something forbidden before an audience helps increase one's arousal, there would be no such sense of forbiddenness in a world where public sex was an everyday thing. Indeed, in a world where such sex was commonplace, probably no one would stop to stare at all, and whatever advantages there were to being stared at would be lost.

In summary, it would seem that if a couple really wants to focus on each other (whether or not this means communicating feelings), the two have to be able to create for themselves a psychological space, at least, in which they are alone. And clearly it is easier to create such a space when they are physically alone, although it is not impossible to do so in public. On the other hand if they want feedback from the public to enhance their sexual arousal, either they might not get such feedback if public sex became commonplace, or, if they do get such feedback, initially they would be viewing themselves as being for "the others" rather than for each other. And if the ultimate state of embodiment could be produced by the gazing audience, there is still the danger that each partner would come to be a being for himself or herself alone.

6
Can Masturbation Be "Good Sex"?

Must all good sex—or at least the best sex—be sexual intercourse?

It is commonly believed that only sex between two partners is the real thing and that masturbation is a second-rate substitution for interpersonal sex. But is our concept of what constitutes the real thing perhaps only a value judgment that we have never sufficiently questioned? Although studies by Masters and Johnson showed that masturbation produces the most intense orgasm (physiologically), most people would probably claim that the orgasm they receive from intercourse is far more psychologically satisfying. Is this because the joys of shared intimacy between partners is more emotionally gratifying, while masturbation seems lonely, selfish, and ego-deflating because one feels one has not been able to attract a partner? Perhaps, however, those who masturbate have been conditioned to think that they are indulging in an inferior form of sex, so that their feelings of dissatisfaction arise because they have been taught this is the way they will and must feel if they masturbate. If masturbation were viewed as a valid form of sex in its own right—merely a different kind of sex—and not a dismal substitute for the real thing, might it not then become psychologically, as well as physiologically, gratifying?

Traditionally, philosophers themselves have fallen victim to the view that the only valid sex is sexual intercourse, that sex is somehow in its very essence a relation to another person. One even finds philosophers who defend the dignity of plain sex, that is, sex divorced from procreation or love nevertheless championing interpersonal sex. One would have thought that sex for its own sake is any delight in sensual pleasure, however produced. Alan Goldman, for example, defines plain sex as the "desire for contact with another person's body and for the pleasure which such contact produces."[13] As for masturbation: "Voyeurism or viewing a pornographic movie qualifies as a sexual activity, but only as an imaginative substitute for the real thing. . . . The same is true of masturbation as a sexual activity without a partner" (p. 270).

But Goldman is not the only philosopher still tied to question-begging value judgments as to what the real thing is. Consider the following quotation from Robert Solomon. (Solomon, as we noted earlier, defines sex as a kind of body language in which one communicates thoughts and emotions to another that can be expressed better physically than verbally.)

If sexuality is essentially a language, it follows that masturbation, while not a perversion, is a deviation and not, as Freud thought, the primary case. Masturbation is essentially speaking to oneself. But not only do children, lunatics, and hermits speak to themselves; so do poets and philosophers. And so masturbation might, in different contexts, count as wholly different extensions of language. With Freud, we would have to distinguish masturbation as autoeroticism from masturbation as narcissism— the first being more like muttering to oneself, the latter more like self-praise; the first being innocent and childlike, the latter potentially either pathetic or selfish or self-indulgent. Masturbation is not "self-abuse," as we were once taught, but it is, in an important sense self-denial. It represents an inability or refusal to say what one wants to say, going

---

13. Goldman, "Plain Sex," *Philosophy and Public Affairs* 6 (1977): 268. Alan Soble of Southern Methodist University takes issue with Goldman in an unpublished paper "Sexual Desire and Sexual Objects."

through the effort of expression without an audience, like writing a letter to an audience and then putting the letter in the drawer. If sexuality is a language, then it is primarily communicative. Autoeroticism, therefore, along with Freud's primary processes, is not primary at all, but conceptually secondary or derivative, similar to a child's early attempts at language, which can be interpreted as phonemes only within the context of the language his parents already speak. But any language, once learned, can be spoken privately. Masturbation is this secondary, private use of sexual language, minimal rather than primary . . . essential as intimate retreat, but empty and without content. Masturbation is the sexual equivalent of a Cartesian soliloquy.[14]

Solomon's analysis, however, is valid only to the extent that his "language" theory of love is valid; we have already noted the deficiencies of such a theory. Furthermore, Solomon has a curious contempt for the loner, for one who may prefer the self-expression of private diaries, journals, or poetry even though he or she does not care to communicate them to others.[15] Could masturbation also be a valid form of self-expression of one's emotions, even if no communication is involved?

Furthermore, is it really true, as Solomon argues, that masturbation is somehow parasitic on sexual intercourse, that the "language" of sex is used only after it has been learned from others? Or is masturbation actually the original form of sex, in which we first learn about our own bodies and their sexual possibilities from the masturbation that is so common with otherwise inexperienced adolescents? George Groddeck, for example, writes:

I should like to call attention to a strange distortion of the facts of which men otherwise sensible are found guilty. They call masturbation a substitute for the normal sex act. Ah, what might not be written about the word "normal" sex act! But here I am dealing only with the idea of "substitute". . . . In one form or another onanism (masturbation) accompanies man throughout his life, while normal sex activity only begins at a particular age, and often ceases at a time when onanism takes on again the childish form of a conscious playing with the sexual organs. How can the one process be regarded as a substitute for another which only starts fifteen to twenty years later?[16]

14. Solomon, "Sex and Perversion," p. 283.

15. Alan Soble makes a similar point in an excellent unpublished paper, "Sexuality and the Binary Framework."

16. Groddeck, *The Book of the It* (New York: Vintage, 1961), p. 45. I am grateful to Jacqueline Kinderlehrer's unpublished paper "Masturbation and Women's Sexuality," read as an address to the Society for Love and Sex, for bringing this quotation to my attention. For Ms. Kinderlehrer, masturbation provides a unique route to knowledge of one's own sexuality.

Another philosopher who clearly disapproves of masturbation is Sartre. He distinguishes an "honest" masturbator, one who masturbates only because a partner is unavailable, from a "dishonest" masturbator, who actually prefers masturbation to intercourse. Of the latter he writes:

He asks only to be slightly distanced from his own body, only for there to be a light coating of otherness over his flesh and over his thoughts. His personae are melting sweets. . . . The masturbator is enchanted at never being able to feel himself sufficiently another, and at producing for himself alone the diabolic appearance of a couple that fades away when one touches it. . . . Masturbation is the de-realization of the world and of the masturbator himself.[17]

We must recall, however, that Sartre thinks that sex is essentially a way of relating to others, in which one attempts to capture the other person's freedom in the flesh. What would be the point, Sartre would ask, of trying to "possess" oneself?

One must remember, however, Sartre's original (and rather curious) motive for trying to possess another's freedom: It is an attempt to recapture one's subjectivity that Sartre thinks has been stolen by the inscrutable "stare" (that is, judgments) of others, which we can never penetrate and which reduce us to objects. But since one masturbates alone and away from the threatening stare of others, it would seem that the Sartrean motivation for possessive sex would disappear and masturbation could be enjoyed simply for the pleasure it gives. One can, after all, feel sexual desire whether the Sartrean "other" is present or not. (Sartre feels that we are still tormented by thoughts of others' judgments even when we are alone; but then it would seem that masturbation would provide relief or escape from such obsessions.)

Those who condemn masturbation commonly argue that it is self-centered and narcissistic. But this need not be true: Not all masturbators are the sort of persons who delight in staring at themselves in the mirror for hours on end. Furthermore, some might argue that even sexual intercourse is determined by egoistic motives: the desire to prove that one can appeal to or attract another person, the desire for possession, aggression, or the need to prove one's sexuality by being able to give another a good orgasm. Even the apparent desire to feel lovingly toward another, to feel that person's pleasure as well as one's own, could really be a desire to double one's own pleasure by making the other an extension of one's self.

Furthermore, since simultaneous orgasms are rare, it might be argued that each partner (like the masturbator) is essentially alone in the privacy of his own ultimate sensation at the moment of orgasm—a case of total self-absorption. Indeed, an egoist would deny that an aroused penis or vagina or clitoris is in any way an altruistic organ, whether one is alone or with a partner. What lust demands, they would claim, is its own satisfaction or release.

17. Sartre, *Saint Genet* (New York: George Braziller, 1963), pp. 367–68.

One need not, of course, concur with such cynical generalizations about the motives for sex between persons. Persons, and not just penises and vaginas, engage in sex acts, and there is no reason to think that everyone's motives are so selfish. But the egoist's arguments are clearly valid in many cases, such that one must proceed very carefully in drawing superficial comparisons between masturbation as necessarily egoistic and intercourse as necessarily altruistic. Indeed, to call masturbation egoistic because it is done alone hardly causes it to deserve such a label; one does not, after all, really "owe" anyone else sex in the way that one owes care to the sick, the hungry, and the poor. For if someone really needs sex, that person can always masturbate or else pay for it. To deny others sex and to masturbate alone thus need not be considered egoistic at all, for no duties to others are being neglected. Nor do all masturbators fail at all times to gratify others sexually; it is simply that there are some occasions when one wishes to do something for oneself (such as meditating) without having to gratify or communicate with others.

If one still insists that masturbation is essentially narcissistic and that intercourse is altruistic, there is yet another criticism of intercourse as it is performed in our society. Could it be that even intercourse is essentially masturbation, albeit a mutual one? A critic of our society might argue (1) that a capitalistic system is composed of self-seeking, essentially isolated individuals engaged in dog-eat-dog competition for money, status, and power, and that these self-seeking traits extend even to the bedroom; and (2) that in a sexist society men are incapable of true interaction with a partner they (perhaps subconsciously) look down on. If these two propositions are true, then intercourse is a "vaginal onanism," a case of selfishly masturbating in a woman's vagina, rather than being a true interaction between self-giving partners. In such circumstances the woman may not have an orgasm and will demand that at least her clitoris be masturbated (something she may very well have to do for herself).

Therefore, the resulting orgasms in such a society will be essentially the product of a kind of masturbation by both partners, and "intercourse" would not be a true alternative to masturbation at all. Such masturbatory "intercourse" would be less lonely perhaps, but the gap between what one expected and what one actually got could be far more devastating psychologically than simply masturbating alone, where one has no such expectations of true intimacy. Indeed, mutual masturbation in a self-seeking society would actually be morally inferior to masturbating alone, since in the latter case at least no one is being exploited.

There is yet another argument that our society would be better off if we were all self-sufficient sexual beings, dependent on no one else at all. One feminist critic, Ti-Grace Atkinson, goes so far as to claim that male-female sexual relationships will eventually disappear once women realize the way men (she thinks) have been using the reproductive function of sex to exploit a woman's relative weakness and dependency during pregnancy and to keep them confined to the home for purposes of child-rearing. But if extrauterine reproduction and incubation were possible, then women would, she argues, be free of pregnancy and of dependence on men for sex and child support.

Indeed, Ms. Atkinson thinks sex is not a natural urge at all, and will disappear once the reproductive function is no longer necessary and once women realize the way such a function has been used as a political ploy to keep women in an inferior status. But even if sex were divorced from reproduction, would the sexual urge disappear? Ms. Atkinson might then argue that women have been conditioned to think they need sex in order to keep them dependent on men, be it for reproduction or pleasure. But why give up sexual pleasure, even if one must depend on a man?

Here one must look at the possible source of this pleasure, and ask if what produces it makes it really worth pursuing. One might, for example, argue that the thrill of the vaginal orgasm actually comes from the woman's masochistic urge to please her male master, and that the man's sexual thrill comes from his sense of mastering what he regards as an inferior being. But in a society where men and women truly respected themselves and regarded each other as equal, independent beings, the master-slave relationship would disappear and so would the supposed sexual "needs" that are engendered by and dependent on such relationships. If (as Ms. Atkinson believes) the master-slave relationship were the only motivation for sexual intercourse, then relations between the sexes would utterly disappear. (Ms. Atkinson thinks love is motivated by the same considerations and would also disappear since independent, self-respecting beings would resist any dependency relationship.)

But even if all these highly speculative assumptions were true, and if master-slave relationships did disappear, what if people continued to have sexual desires? Here the defender of masturbation would claim he has the perfect solution: the masturbator would be the paradigm of a sexually self-sufficient being who is able to gratify his or her urges in an utterly non-dependent way. This would be the new breed of sexual being who has transcended all master-slave relationships. But is the picture of a society of isolated masturbators really any better than the capitalistic and sexist society? Could there be a dependency relationship between sexual partners that is not sexist and exploitative? The reader is invited to think through these questions for herself or himself.

One further criticism of masturbation must be considered. It is commonly argued that masturbation can be shown to be a substitute for the real thing on the grounds that it is commonly accompanied by fantasies. This is taken to indicate that the masturbator would prefer to be with the partner he or she is fantasizing about. Furthermore, critics of masturbation think that fantasies somehow make the sexual experience unreal. Jacqueline Kinderlehrer, a defender of masturbation, writes:

> Laing and Sartre agree with Kant; they object to masturbation because when there is fantasy that is part of the experience, it seems absurd to them that there is *real* bodily excitement, *real* orgasm, *real* relaxation. A food fantasy when you are hungry will not produce a *real* feeling of

having feasted. Laing especially worries that the fantasy might become a substitute for reality or even become confused with reality.[18]

Clearly, however, one cannot compare the fantasy of a feast with the fantasy of masturbation. A feast fantasy is only a fantasy, while masturbation involves doing something with one's sexual organ, not just fantasizing. Furthermore, not all masturbators needs fantasies, especially if they are already highly aroused. (One woman in *The Hite Report* states that she achieves orgasm by having a strong stream of water massage her clitoris to orgasm. In such a case it is highly doubtful that fantasies are needed.)

But even if one does fantasize, does this mean masturbation is really only a pale substitute for the intercourse one's fantasies are about? This is not at all clear. Fantasies are often preferred to reality because one is shy, one prefers to be alone, or one does not want to endure the hassles of attracting partners or submitting to their unpredictable whims. But it still might be argued that the masturbator would *prefer* a partner, if only whatever obstacles there are could be overcome. But this is not necessarily true. It is possible, for example, for a man or a woman to enjoy a fantasy that he or she is president of the United States for the momentary sense of power it conveys; yet if that person were told he or she could actually be president, the fantasizer might not want the job at all because of the enormous and burdensome responsibilities.

Furthermore, masturbatory fantasies not only provide an infinite variety of sexual images of partners that one could never hope to find in reality; such fantasies also allow one to have the unique sensation of being the lover and the beloved simultaneously. One can also, in a sense, feel the fantasy partner's pleasure as well as one's own, and one's pleasure is thus doubled just as it is in actual intercourse.

There are, finally, further advantages of masturbation that should be noted. We have already seen that it can be an expression of emotions when one does not care to communicate these emotions to others. Furthermore, it can be a learning experience about one's body and feelings and about sex itself. And if one holds that we cannot love others unless we love ourselves, then it could be argued that we could not love and satisfy another's body until we are able to love and satisfy our own body through masturbation. As one respondent in *The Hite Report* commented:

Masturbation is one of the sacred rituals that women can enjoy among themselves. I say it is 'sacred' because it is *self*-initiated, *self*-controlled and *self*-gratifying—coming from a position of strength. It is not only about a physical or emotional (they are inseparable) closeness to one's own body, but a conquest of all the fears that families and men have instilled in women about their bodies and sexual dependencies.[19]

18. Kinderlehrer, "Masturbation and Women's Sexuality," p. 6.

19. Shere Hite, *The Hite Report.* (New York: Dell Publishing Co., 1976), p. 69.

Four

Types of Sexual Philosophy: A Summary

In the realm of sex I have attempted to show that sex without love can be just as fulfilling an experience as sex with love; indeed, it may be even more so. But first let us place those arguments in a somewhat broader context. Sexual philosophies can be classified roughly into three categories: I shall call them the conservative, the liberal, and the radical positions. First let us examine the conservative viewpoint.

1
The Conservative Point of View

For the conservative sex for sex's sake is held to be not only immoral but also bad simply as sex. For him or her sex is moral and fulfilling only if it is linked to such things as love, procreation, and marriage.

Why would one call this position "conservative," other than the fact that it defends an ancient tradition? The main reason is that the conservative is essentially concerned with the sense of security that he or she thinks love and marriage bring. It is a commonplace that people desire a life of both security and excitement and adventure. But perhaps sensing that a life that combines both security and adventure in perpetual harmony is impossible to fulfill, the conservative opts for security. Conservative treatises typically defend their philosophy as containing all the good things one could hope for in the realm of sex. Yet they carefully avoid mentioning what they have sacrificed in the name of security: adventure, novelty, variety, and experimentation. But surely the quest for security is no proof of the superiority of their brand of sex, either in moral terms or simply as good sex. What the need for security does reveal is the choice of a certain life-style that in turn reveals more about the conservatives' psychological needs than it does any alleged "proofs" as to the inherent superiority of sex combined with love and marriage.

Not all conservatives, of course, require all three of the traditional requirements to sanctify what is considered, by itself, to be degrading. Many young couples, for example, are willing to sacrifice procreation and marriage. But they will then utter the familiar proclamation that sex before marriage is all right *only* so long as there is a "loving commitment" between the two partners. Such couples generally consider themselves to be liberated from old-fashioned norms. Yet lurking behind their view is the traditional notion that sex without love is a dirty business; and the insistence on a "loving commitment" reveals the same quest for security that traditional conservatives seek.

Even if we grant that the conservative position is somehow "moral," is it really the case that the conservative enjoys good sex as sex? If one must sugarcoat a bitter pill to make it taste good, does one enjoy the pill or only the sugar? If one must "make love" rather than "have sex," is one really enjoying the sex or is the sex only an excuse to—or a mere means to—enjoy the real goal, that of being loved? It is interesting to note that in the phrase *making love* the term *sex* has mysteriously disappeared. To be sure, "making love" is often a mere euphemism for "having sex," but in its strict sense as used by lovers the absence of any reference to sex makes it clear that the real focus of their act is elsewhere. The pill that is sugarcoated is still bitter in itself; and those who insist that sex must be sugarcoated with love are still going to consider the physical aspect of their lovemaking a bitter pill to swallow. Indeed, someone who enjoys sex for its own sake is surely going to be disappointed with the inhibited sexual responses of such a conservative. If love and marriage are a quest for security, as I have argued, those who seek security are not, to put it mildly, going to be the most exciting sexual partners in the world.

A critic of the preceding argument might reply that some lovers are not obsessed with security and do have a healthy respect for sex. But if this is true, the focus of their foreplay probably will not be on communicating love but rather on arousing sexual desire; and as they sink more deeply into a state of lust, thoughts of love will disappear altogether. Indeed, it is not within the power of a penis or vagina to communicate love at all. But if these things are true, then sex between lovers of this kind and sex between non-lovers is going to be virtually identical, and the fact that one of the couples is in love is not going to prove the superiority of sex with someone who also happens to be one's lover.

2

The Liberal Point of View

The second major sexual philosophy I will call the liberal point of view. For the liberal, sex is primarily for pleasure, yet he or she does not believe in gratification without some limits. From a moral point of view the liberal holds that sex must be between consenting adults or at least between those who are mature enough to know what they are doing without harming themselves; that sex must not harm others; and that it must be done in private. Such things as bisexuality, premarital sex, sex without love, homosexuality, adultery (so long as it does not psychologically damage one's spouse), and experimentation with unusual sexual techniques are quite permissable if they do not violate these norms. Unlike the conservative who thinks anything not involving love, procreation, and marriage is perverted, the liberal restricts his use of the term only to those who molest children or force their will on others and cause psychological or physiological suffering. Many liberals summarize their concept of perversion by saying that it is simply any act that exploits or degrades others.

A critic of the liberal position might ask, however, just how a pleasure-seeking philosophy can provide any rationale for the concept of respecting the rights of others. If we believe that pleasure-seeking is essentially based on self-interest, why should we respect the rights of others and not simply seek pleasure wherever and however we can find it, regardless of whom it hurts? To be sure, one might reply by noting that many pleasure-seekers find their greatest pleasure in giving pleasure to others; and even self-interest dictates that one who harms others will ordinarily (but not always) destroy his chances of finding another partner. But the critic will reply that even if these things are true, still pleasure-seeking does not entail any moral obligation to respect the rights of others. The critic of the liberal would argue that all one has to rely on is that, hopefully, such a pleasure-seeker will find it in his own best interest to want to give pleasure to others and to avoid harming them. But this is no logical guarantee that these things will happen in all cases.

Could the liberal defend himself or herself against this attack? He would first want to point out that he is not just any kind of pleasure-seeker; he is also a liberal. And to be liberal means to him that he is in some sense liberated and that to be liberated means to be free. He is then free to impose restrictions on himself and not be the mere victim of whatever lustful desires may tempt him, particularly when these desires involve harming others. The critic would reply that if the liberal is free to impose restrictions on himself, is he not also free to ignore all restrictions? But this is a misunderstanding of what it means to be liberal; in politics, for example, a liberal does not wish to destroy his society but only to reject those outmoded norms that needlessly restrict human fulfillment and violate human dignity. If the sexual liberal wished to destroy all norms, then he would be a sexual radical as defined below.

But while the critic of the liberal might admit that this is a correct definition of what it is to be liberal, there is still lacking a philosophical rationale to justify the limits he places on himself. To this the liberal would reply that while pleasure-seeking does not in and of itself entail any moral obligations, there is nevertheless an intimate connection between pleasure and moral limitations. The liberal holds, for example, that sex with or without love is a "beautiful thing," and for it to involve degradation would only leave both partners disgusted with what had occurred; this would be a clear violation of the pleasure principle. Even if the one who harmed his partner had no feelings of remorse, he or she would still have missed one crucial element: the ability to feel not only pleasure but, through empathy, to feel the partner's pleasure as well. But to have missed this double-edged pleasure would violate a cardinal tenet of hedonism: the maximization of pleasure. In these ways the liberal would argue that pleasure-seeking and respecting certain moral limits go hand in hand, even if they do not strictly entail each other.

Another familiar criticism of the liberal pleasure-seeker can now also be answered. The conservative critic commonly charges that he or she is a mere vulgar hedonist, whose desires are so overwhelming that he or she is driven to promiscuity and to the subsequent denial of a uniquely human freedom and rationality. But a liberated man or woman is free and is thus quite in control of his or her higher faculties. Indeed, his reason will tell him that promiscuity only leads to boredom with sex and the ultimate destruction of the sexual pleasure he seeks. Furthermore, a phrase like *vulgar hedonism* or even *pleasure* hardly does justice to the ecstatic state of bliss one enjoys in a really good sex act. One feels transported out of one's finite ego into a state of oneness with the partner and the universe, a state that borders on the experiences mystics say they feel. To refer to this experience as vulgar pleasure or a mere sensation in the groin is surely unjustified.

Another important advantage of the liberal position is the willingness to experiment with a variety of sexual possibilities, something that horrifies the conservative. A liberated person will want to say that before he can claim that he prefers a certain type of sex over another, or that he has made an informed choice as to what is the best sex for him, he must have experimented with several possibilities, subject only to the moral limits he has placed on himself. For example, no one can say that he prefers heterosexuality to homosexuality unless he has tried both.

A critic might reply that you don't have to cut your arm to know that you are not going to like it, and that one doesn't have to try homosexuality to know that one isn't going to like it. But the fact that one will bleed is a universal experience that one will know will happen to oneself as soon as he sees it happen to others. Sexual tastes, however, vary, and observing the sexual experience of others is not necessarily going to reveal how one will feel about a particular sexual act. A further example will illustrate my point: If someone places a piece of apple pie and a piece of cherry pie in front of me and asks me which one I prefer, how could I possibly say that I prefer cherry unless I had also tasted apple and compared the two. Clearly no informed choice between the two can be made unless I have tried both. And no one can claim he is liberated or free unless he has freely chosen his own sexual life-style. An informed choice is impossible unless there are alternative possibilities that one has tried with an open mind and from which one has made a selection. Otherwise one's so-called sexual preferences will merely be the product of social conditioning and not one's own at all.

A critic of this position might, however, argue that freedom of choice is really impossible and that our sexual preferences are completely determined by either social conditioning or natural instinct. But neither of these are impossible to transcend: revolutionaries and rebels are able to reject their society's teachings, and the natural instinct for self-preservation has been transcended by those who sacrifice their life for others. Indeed, I know several heavily conditioned people who were heterosexual for years but who experimented with homosexuality and who then chose the latter over the former, or discovered that they like both equally.

Many persons would, however, still argue that experimentation is unnecessary because their feelings of disgust with alternative sexual views tell them in advance they are not going to enjoy anything other than what they prefer now. But consider the following example: I recently asked someone if he would enjoy sex with a black person, something he had never experienced. He replied that he "knew" he would be disgusted by such an act, and that experimenting with interracial sex to see if he would like it was thus quite unnecessary. But this person was raised in a small Southern town. Could he really say that his feelings were his own even though they were "in" him? Actually these feelings had been engendered in him during his childhood by others, and it could be said that they were not truly his own. His claim that the feelings were truly his own is merely due to the fact that he forgot their origins. Thus, consulting one's "feelings" is no basis for making a judgment as to what kind of sex is best for oneself.

A final argument against experimentation has a much more serious implication for the liberal position. If one has to experiment to discover what is the best sexual life-style for oneself, one is going to have to try everything, including rape. But such things as rape clearly violate the liberal's moral position. Yet the liberal could reply that all choices are subject to certain limitations due to such things as lack of time or opportunity. When we choose a city to reside in or a profession to pursue, we cannot sample them all. Yet an informed choice is possible if we sample at least a variety of cities or professions but not necessarily every one. Indeed, the possible forms of sexual gratification are virtually infinite, and if one engaged in the endless pursuit of trying every one, it would be impossible to settle on a final choice at all. A person who relentlessly tries every form of sexual gratification would become so enslaved to sex that he or she could hardly be called a free agent who could make a free choice of any kind.

One final question must be raised regarding the liberal position: Where does he or she stand with regard to love? Many liberals would reject love because they regard the claim that love provides superior sex as an illusion. Lovers often claim that they know each other's needs best, but to many liberals this would mean that what happens during the sex act is going to be predictable. Predictability often means that the sex act is going to become a boring routine. With sex with a stranger, however, one does not always know what to expect, and this lends a sense of adventure and excitement to the act. In addition, one may also discover new possibilities for heightening sexual pleasure.

It is also often argued that a lover is more forgiving of one's failings; yet to fail in the presence of a lover (as opposed to a stranger whom one will never see again) is a devastating blow, no matter how forgiving the lover is. One is also hurt by the thought that one's lover may suffer the feeling that he or she has been the cause of one's failure, perhaps because the lover erroneously thinks his or her sex appeal is gone. Furthermore, it is far from clear that lovers are in fact more forgiving of one's failings, as the prevalence of divorce, adultery, and prostitution would seem to indicate.

Another argument for sex with love is that such sex is readily available and easily obtainable. But this destroys any sense of challenge; and it is a commonplace that that which is readily available becomes devalued, is taken for granted, and ultimately becomes a boring routine. Lovers are also commonly said to give more of themselves in the act because they are thought to be much more eager than strangers to please one another. But there are millions of loving husbands who leave their wives orgasmically unfulfilled with a quickly completed act designed only to relieve their own tensions.

Furthermore, if the beloved considers it her duty to please her lover, the lover may be haunted always by the question: Is she really having sex with me because she wants to or is she merely doing it out of a sense of duty when she is tired or not in the mood? Non-lovers who seek pleasure, on the other hand, have sex only because they want to; they have no duties to fulfill when they are not in the mood. The non-lover, then, has the perpetual satisfaction of knowing that his partner really wants sex with him and is enjoying it, rather than simply going through the motions, as many tired housewives do in order to keep their husbands happy.

It should also be noted that just because one falls in love does not mean that one suddenly acquires a whole range of splendid virtues. Many lovers are egocentric, cantankerous souls or insecure clinging vines whose lack of self-confidence makes them a failure in the bedroom. Nor is it true, as many lovers assume, that if someone isn't in love he is going to exploit his partner. Many non-lovers find their greatest joy in being able to provide their partner with a loving—that is, a considerate and fulfilling—sex act. The only "love" that they want is that one *love* having sex with them; this is all they need to have the most fulfilling sexual experience.

For these reasons many liberals would eschew sex with love. Even if they happened to believe that sex with love provides more pleasure, they might want to avoid love, because to surrender one's heart to another and become dependent for one's happiness on the unpredictable emotions of another human being is hardly compatible with being a liberated, free person.

But what of those liberals who, although they enjoy sex with a non-lover, nevertheless claim that sex with love provides them with the most ecstatic experience they have ever known? Such liberals do not prize love as an end in itself, but only as a means of heightening sexual pleasure. But does this claim really prove that, at least in all cases, sex with love is superior? One must, I think, ask just what this ecstatic sensation derives from. Is it from the addition of love to sex, or from some other source?

In pondering the answer, consider the following example: Suppose someone drives what has been called the world's most prestigious automobile. Yet it is commonly agreed by automotive authorities that this particular automobile actually performs, rides, and handles no better than any other car, and is indeed inferior to many others in these respects. Yet the person who drives this car will insist that it provides an ecstatic experience and that its performance, ride, and handling are like no other car he has driven. His claims for its superiority are clearly an illusion, however. But why did he experience the car this way? The reason is obvious to any psychologist: The driver had been conditioned by advertising to believe that this was the world's finest automobile; therefore he experienced it that way.

Could the same be true of those who claim that sex with love is an ecstatic experience? It would not be love itself that produced the ecstasy, but rather the conditioning that taught the partners to believe that sex with love is superior.[1]

One does not have to resort to the concept of social conditioning to explain the same phenomenon. A couple anticipating their wedding night will desperately want and expect it to be the most thrilling sexual experience of their lives. And if it does seem to be the most ecstatic sexual experience they have ever had, they will conclude that sex with love is truly the best sex there is. But did love contribute to the ecstasy, or was it because they desperately wanted it to be an ecstatic experience and thus experienced it this way? Once the honeymoon is over, they will start to view their experience in a more realistic way. They may then find that the partner's sexual abilities are quite ordinary and in no way superior to that of a non-lover, a fact that love cannot hide forever. If they continue to insist that they prefer sex with a lover, it will not be because they are really having a superior *sexual* experience; rather it will be because they prefer the experience of feeling that they are *loved.*

---

1. A similar explanation can explain why so many claim that sex without love is unfulfilling and degrading. The young female especially has been so conditioned to believe that sex without love is vicious and dirty, that she experiences it as being vicious and dirty when it may not have been so. Her experience of degradation is the result of a self-fulfilling prophecy. And perhaps the young man has been conditioned in the same way when he says: "I don't love her, so this means that I am going to have to exploit her, for this is what society expects to happen with someone you don't love." But if he had not been conditioned to view sex without love as animalistic and selfish in the first place, perhaps his unselfish side could assert itself naturally so that he could provide her with a "loving act" even though he wasn't romantically involved with her.

3
The Radical Point of View

The final type of sexual philosophy I shall dub the radical point of view, with its foremost exponent being the Marquis de Sade. Like the liberal, the radical thinks the goal of sex is pleasure, but unlike the liberal he or she believes that to be truly liberated sexually one must observe no limits whatsoever to experimenting with new kinds of techniques or sexual partners. Indeed, the radical would claim that the more bizarre the sex act, the greater the sexual pleasure. This increased pleasure derives in part from the challenge of exploring the unknown and also from the knowledge that one is taking great risks in violating society's most cherished norms. Any object or type of partner can be the object of sexual interest, if one can overcome narrow-minded social conditioning. To those who think the radical is perverted or practicing "unnatural" acts, de Sade replied that everything that we can do is natural. If Nature had not intended us to do certain things, she would never have given us the imagination to conceive of them or the desire and ability to carry them out and enjoy them. Those who don't use their imagination or feel no desire for bizarre sexual acts have had their natural instincts repressed by social conditioning.

This sort of argument, if valid, would then mean that such things as exhibitionism (exposing oneself to others), sadomasochism between consenting partners, voyeurism (the peeping Tom), bestiality (sex with animals), and necrophilia (sex with the dead) are all natural and permissible. If someone replies by saying these acts are disgusting, the radical would reply that feelings of disgust only reveal one's social conditioning and constitute no counterargument.

A critic might also argue that the radical has reduced himself or herself to an animal and is so obsessed by sex that his higher, distinctly human faculties of freedom and reason are destroyed. Indeed, if one did feel sexual interest in every object, it is hard to see how one could avoid being in a perpetual state of lust and think of nothing but sex. But the radical would argue that he is not an animal, since animals do not experiment with a wide range of sexual techniques; they are limited to a fairly narrow routine prescribed by instinct in order to preserve the species. Furthermore, he would argue that his higher human faculties have not been destroyed, for does he not use his distinctly human imagination to conceive ever new forms of sexual delight? To the argument that he is obsessed with sex, he would reply that many people are obsessed with what they are doing and can think of nothing else; an artist or a writer may be obsessed with his or her creative work but they are praised for what they do. Why should the sexual libertine be condemned for being obsessed with his equally creative sexual philosophy? To continue to condemn him after hearing these lines of defense would only reveal one's prejudice against sexual experimentation.

But what of sex in which one forces one's will on others or harms others? Since the radical believes there should be no limits to sexual pleasure, he or she will have to grant that even pedophilia and rape are acceptable. Indeed, de Sade thought that hearing the screams and cries of a victim of torture or rape was the greatest sexual thrill imaginable. He defended the shocking proposition that the most immoral sex of all is also the best sex.

But how, the liberal would ask, can one justify harming others, or forcing one's will on others? Setting aside de Sade's argument about the naturalness of all things, a radical would reply that society itself condones harming others (as in self-defense) if there is a good reason for doing so. Governments regularly force young men to go to war and perhaps be greatly harmed or even killed, but this is deemed justifiable since there is a "good" reason for forcing men to do these things: the defense of one's country. The sadist would then claim that he is equally justified in forcing his will on others and perhaps harming them because there is, in his eyes, also a good reason for doing so, namely, his own sexual ecstasy.

But if one feels, as I do, that this is not a sufficiently good reason to justify or defend such acts, the radical will reply that the concept of good reasons is simply a value judgment and that all value judgments are ultimately matters of personal opinion. Good and evil are not tangible things like water (which we all agree is wet) or stones (which all agree are hard). Not only are good and evil not things one can see or taste or feel; there is also no universal agreement as to what the terms apply to. Can one think of any moral argument to which there has been universal assent? The amoralist then concludes that the notions good and evil are merely reports of how one feels about certain things; thus, if one feels like committing rape, there is no objective moral standard that can prove one is wrong.

Suppose, however, that society prevents the amoralist from doing what he or she feels like doing. Won't he then claim that his rights to his personal convictions have been violated? But from whence come rights in the amoral universe devoid of any objective standards of good and evil or any concept of moral rights? If the amoralist insists that he has a right to do as he pleases, then one could argue that someone else would have the right not to be molested. And, as we noted in the earlier section on sadism, there is every reason to believe that the right not to be molested takes precedence over the so-called right to rape.

Now that we have briefly examined all three types of sexual philosophy, we must ask the ultimate philosophical question. Can one say which is the "best" philosophy and provide philosophical proof that one is best? Or must we say that each is merely an account of varying life-styles, and that one life-style is as valid as another, so long as those leading these life-styles are happy with what they are doing? (Of course, because someone is happy with what he is doing doesn't necessarily mean that this is the best philosophy for him; for he might be far happier if he tried some other philosophy.)

The conservative sexual philosophy must, I think, be rejected because it assumes that sex by itself is something degrading and immoral and that love, procreation, and marriage must be added before it can have any claim to dignity. Furthermore, the claim that sex with love provides a superior sexual experience cannot be sustained if one holds that sex, by itself, is disgusting. For although one can sugarcoat a bitter pill and make it taste good, one cannot sugarcoat sex with love and hope to make it taste good.

Indeed, both the sexual conservative and the sexual radical are really brothers under the skin in a way, for both seem to feel that sex is basically disgusting and degrading. The difference is that the conservative tries to rescue sex from its supposed ugliness by using it as a tool to express love or procreate. On the other hand the radical says: "Sex is disgusting and degrading, so let us make it precisely what it is supposed to be by engaging in the most degrading forms of sex possible, especially those acts that degrade others."

The sexual liberal, on the other hand, seems to be the only one who can really respect and enjoy sex for its own sake. Although he or she can enjoy sex with love, he or she can equally well enjoy sex without love. He does not need love to overcome any feelings of disgust with sex itself or to overcome any feelings of insecurity. Unlike the conservative, he feels free to explore new types of sexual experience; but unlike the radical, he sets standards of human decency as to how far his experimentation goes. My own view, then, is that the liberal position is the best of the three, although I leave it to the reader to decide for himself whether I have proved my case or whether I have merely revealed my own life-style.

Part Two

THE PHILOSOPHY OF LOVE

One

Erotic Love:
Is It a Viable Concept?

1
Some Preliminary Difficulties

Before analyzing some various attempts to define love,[1] let us first see if it is a viable, internally coherent concept. Or does it suffer from certain fatal contradictions? It may, of course, be true that any such contradictions (as well as possible difficulties in defining it) will only enhance love's potency, mystique, and charm. But internal conflicts can also be a source of disappointment and even tragedy, if one ignores or resolves them in some superficial way.

There is also the question of whether erotic love is a natural phenomenon, and there is the question of whether this sort of love is a desirable thing. One can, for example, cite certain societies in which erotic love is unheard of; they seem to be none the worse for lacking such a concept. One might then argue that erotic love arises primarily in industrial societies where the ugliness, drabness, and alienation is so overwhelming that erotic love develops and serves as a kind of escapist fantasy. But whether love is natural or unnatural is difficult to settle either way, for the societies in which it does not exist may simply have suppressed it for certain reasons.

Furthermore, certain writers would argue that there is no such thing as love at all. Consider this opinion from Proust:

1. In this section I will once again be speaking of the ordinary affiliative love between Joe and Mary, which may or may not lead to marriage; I shall not be concerned with sibling love, parental love, or love of God, country, or abstract ideals.

The bonds that unite another person with ourselves exist only in our minds. Memory as it grows fainter relaxes them, and notwithstanding the illusion by which we would fain be cheated and which, out of love, friendship, politeness, deference, duty, we cheat other people, we exist alone. Man is the creature that cannot emerge from himself, that knows his fellows only in himself; when he asserts the contrary he is lying.[2]

Furthermore, the sociologist Sidney Greenfield has argued that erotic love is undesirable for the reason that it maintains the status quo of our social system, which is based on the consumption of goods and services.[3] Love, he thinks, is the primary motive for marriage, which in turn requires the setting up of households that consume goods and require husbands to enter and support the system that sustains the family. Others would argue that a truly unselfish form of love cannot arise in our capitalistic system at all. Capitalism, they would argue, breeds a society of self-centered individuals engaged in a constant competitive struggle for jobs, money, and power. And those seeking love must make themselves into attractive packages of erotic goods that will be saleable in the marketplace of love. Love thus becomes like capitalism with its competitiveness; those who win enjoy its riches and those who lose live in love's slums.

One might ask such a critic, however, just how it is that there are apparently so many enduring, seemingly loving relationships in our capitalist society. One answer he might give is that up until the present it is the male who has been in the capitalistic marketplace and who has taken on its aggressive characteristics. The family has endured, he might argue, simply because the female has been sheltered from the marketplace and has remained passive. She submits to the husband's dominance in order to keep peace in the family and hold it together.

But what happens when the female becomes liberated from confinement to the home and enters the capitalistic world of work? Will she not then take on the same aggressive, competitive traits as her husband? If capitalism breeds egoism and aggression, a critic might ask how two equally aggressive, egoistic individuals are going to be capable of unselfish love or an enduring relationship. If both partners are equally aggressive, how are they going to resolve a situation where there is a conflict of interests that cannot be settled by compromise? The critic would then argue that capitalistic love and marriage seem to be faced with a fatal contradiction: either one must cling to the sexist view that the woman remain submissive and meek and stay at home in order to avoid such conflicts and hold the marriage together; or, if she does achieve equality with the male in climbing the capitalistic ladder of success, society will have two equally aggressive individuals unable to compromise their differences

2. Marcel Proust, "The Sweet Cheat Gone," Chapter One, *Remembrance of Things Past,* trans. C. K. Scott-Moncrieff (New York: Random House, 1932).

3. Greenfield, "On the Critique of Romantic Love: Some Sociological Consequences of Proposed Alternatives," *Symposium on Love,* ed. Mary Ellen Curtin (New York: Behavioral Publications, 1973), pp. 60–61.

in situations where no compromise is possible. (In the case of abortion, for example, no compromise is possible; one either gets an abortion or one doesn't.)

Feminist critics of our society offer another reason for thinking that a truly loving relationship between equals is impossible: the endemic presence of sexism and male dominance, and the damaging effects this has had on both the male and female psyche. Such feminists would argue, for example, that in a sexist society the female's love for the male is really a kind of pathological dependency on her mate. Having been conditioned by a sexist society to believe that she is an inferior being, she seeks to resolve her feelings of inferiority by identifying herself with what she has been conditioned to believe is the stronger sex. Rather than developing her own powers, she feels that she can gain a sense of strength by becoming one with the male and vicariously partaking of what she believes to be his superior powers. Or one might even argue that she unites with a man in order to recapture, as it were, the identity that has been stolen from her by the male sex. The male, on the other hand, is attracted to the female because, feeling that he is the dominant sex, he must therefore find someone to dominate. If a couple insisted that their love was not prompted by any such considerations, the feminist would hold that this dominance-submission syndrome perhaps exists largely on the subconscious level. Thus, what one feels on the conscious level to be one's motives for entering into a heterosexual love relationship are not necessarily the real motives.

Can there be a healthy dependency relationship between males and females once sexism is eliminated? Shulamith Firestone, in *The Dialectic of Sex: The Case for Feminist Revolution* (New York: William Morrow and Company, 1970), argues that there could be a healthy relationship in the future when the sexes respect each other as equals. Ti-Grace Atkinson, on the other hand, adopts the more radical view that all human dependency relationships are destructive, and that the only healthy, truly liberated being is one who is self-sufficient and independent. (The contrasting views of Ms. Firestone and Atkinson are developed in Elizabeth Rapaport's paper "On the Future of Love: Rousseau and the Radical Feminists," cited earlier in the text.)

A defender of erotic love might, however, argue that such criticisms as these prove nothing against erotic love itself; they are only criticisms of the conditions under which erotic love cannot thrive and be the beautiful thing it really can be. But regardless of the society in which erotic love is found, could it not be that erotic love suffers from certain fatal contradictions within itself? The following section will explore such a possibility.

2
Is Erotic Love a Contradictory Ideal?

I now present some of the claims that love suffers from certain contradictions. The reader is encouraged to ponder each to decide whether the contradiction is only apparent or whether it is a fatal one for love.

A. *Ecstasy vs. Endurance.* Love seeks to be long lasting (some would say that it seeks eternity); or it at least seeks more than a brief "fling." But for many love also seeks the heights of romantic ecstasy. To combine these things is an impossible goal. Those who have long-lasting relationships, it might be argued, usually live to see them develop into a kind of unexciting, non-ecstatic companionship. The man becomes the "good provider" and the woman develops into a "housewife." Such couples often describe their relationships as deepening as the years go by, but the deepening is more that of familiarity and habit and an unhealthy state of mutual dependency than it is of romantic ecstasy and passion. And those who have been able to taste the sublime bliss that romantic passion can give, also know that it is like a Roman candle: its beauty is momentary and can never last except in memory. Thus, it might seem that Romeo is doomed to choose either Juliet or else a housewife, but that he cannot expect to have both in the same person. One might, of course, have a series of romantic affairs outside of marriage, but to return to reality (be it to the "good-provider" husband or the housewife) after tasting romance, intrigue, mystery, and so forth, would be a painfully obvious comedown to both wife and husband if each still expects the other to be something more than a faithful, predictable companion.

B. *Altruism vs. Self-Interest.* Love is said to be unselfish, and the person in love to be concerned with the other person as a *person* and not someone adored merely because of certain qualities that are self-gratifying. But while such a claim is often made for erotic love, the truth does not seem to be like this at all. The erotic lover is ordinarily quite selective, choosing for a mate one who has attractive qualities that stir the emotions and gratify the lover's own needs and self-interest. Millions of people who have few exceptionally appealing qualities never find such love, even though they desperately seek it and think they need it. The more intense and passionate the erotic love is and the more one feels lifted out of oneself to become virtually a part of the beloved, the more possessive it becomes as well. (When a lover says, "You can go out with whomever you wish; it won't hurt me in the least," this is ordinarily taken as a sign that the lover is on the verge of breaking off the relationship rather than as a sign of generosity.)

There is, however, another kind of love, non-erotic in nature, called agapic love. Agapic love would find the selectivity, exclusiveness, and possessiveness of erotic love utterly revolting. For the agapist, love must be love of the total person for his or her sake alone, and must therefore be utterly unselfish and non-discriminating. For if one loves persons *as persons,* one must love all mankind equally, since every human being is a person. Furthermore, if one loves another as a person, one's love should never die, for one does not cease to be a person until death. (Erotic lovers, however, are haunted by the question, "Will you still love me tomorrow?") Furthermore, the agapist is rescued from the possibility of being jealous or deceived or rejected, since agapic love does not depend on reciprocity. It does not "give in order to get," and the agapist may sacrifice his own happiness and even his life to help those most in need.

Agapic love has not been without its critics, however. Nietzsche argued that such charity love is really a disguised and selfish attempt to make others dependent on oneself. And Freud argued that the agapist is merely someone who so fears being rejected that he develops an agapist philosophy that does not depend on reciprocity as a kind of defense mechanism to overcome his fears of rejection. And others have argued that such a self-sacrificial person is really motivated by a kind of masochistic pleasure he receives from sacrificing his own happiness for others. Indeed, if the agapist has no concern for his own interests, could he really be said to love or respect himself at all? But one who is filled with masochistic self-hate could hardly love others, since he would only project his own self-hate onto others.

Whatever one thinks of these rather cynical views of the agapist's motives, the agapist's thesis that if one claims to love persons *as persons* then one should love all mankind equally and eternally is surely valid. But this is certainly a telling blow against erotic lovers, who commonly claim they love each other unselfishly and for their own sake alone. As we have already noted, in erotic love one is selective, taking one and rejecting others who may need one's love far more than the one to whom it is given. In erotic love, not to be selective is ordinarily taken as a pride-destroying sign that one is in no position to be selective. A person views himself in such circumstances as being forced to settle for someone he wouldn't otherwise choose were he more handsome or powerful or rich.

Furthermore, the loved one would ordinarily be distressed to think her lover would give his love to just anybody. Nor would she ordinarily accept a love given out of purely altruistic considerations, that is, someone who gives his love to whomever he sees as needing love, regardless of other qualities. Not only does one feel demeaned by a love that is given as a purely charitable act; one also wants to feel that he or she is something more than some kind of abstract entity called a "person," but is an individual uniquely defined by and chosen for his or her own distinctive qualities. But if one wishes to be loved as an individual, then our original question of selectivity arises. If, say, a female is selected for her charming qualities, isn't she being selected because the man finds these qualities valuable in satisfying his own needs for beauty, intelligence, wit, and so forth?[4]

Of course, selectivity is perfectly innocent insofar as one must select someone with whom one is compatible or someone who is honest and

---

4. By using a term like *select,* I do not mean to imply that the choice of a lover is necessarily a rational one. A phrase like "is attracted to" would be a more apt description of the way erotic lovers come together. Except for those who view love primarily as companionship and who, as it were, proceed to go shopping for a mate in a cold and calculating way, the choice of a partner is heavily determined by emotional and other non-rational considerations. The need that one seeks to satisfy (such as the need for a father-figure) may, for example, be largely subconscious. This explains why some people are surprised to find themselves attracted to someone who does not at all match what they were, on the conscious level, searching for. One sometimes hears someone say, "I found myself falling in love with him even though I knew the relationship was going to harm me." Once again, this is because the person to whom one is attracted may fulfill certain needs and interests of which one is not even conscious.

considerate. But the selectivity of erotic love (as opposed to that in mere companionship) is usually much more "picky" than these minimal requirements. One need only think of all the people with whom one is compatible but whom one does not love. Indeed, it is not just those who lack appealing qualities who are never loved in an erotic way; many people who are extremely beautiful or intelligent never find a lover because others feel that their own qualities would suffer by comparison.

Thus the beloved faces a fatal contradiction: she wants to be chosen for her own intrinsic worth as a person and not just as a means of satisfying her lover's needs. But one cannot separate pure "personhood" from the qualities that are its manifestation and that give it its individuality.[5] But selectivity seems to be based on selecting someone whose qualities best suit the lover's needs. She herself, of course, also wants to be selected for her own unique qualities and not be viewed as just another abstract being. Furthermore, her pride dictates that she merit love by having those qualities that win the heart of another; she does not want to be loved out of sheer charity. But then how does she avoid being picked as someone who has those qualities that the lover's self-interest requires? For as soon as she loses those qualities, the lover will lose interest in her.

Could one say in reply that the selective aspect of love does not imply sheer self-interest, but rather that we select each other on the basis of those qualities we can share, whether they be ones that are like our own or ones that are different but could still mutually enrich each partner? Thus, one might say that selectivity involves getting and giving; and the view that we cynically give solely in order to get what the other has is just an unproved egoistic way of interpreting the matter.

The problem this latter answer faces is why it is that erotic love so often comes to an end. Certainly two of the most significant reasons are that either the beloved has lost the qualities that made her so appealing in the first place or one has simply become bored with her qualities even if they do not change. But don't these reasons suggest a "give in order to get" self-interest interpretation of erotic love? When the beloved is no longer interesting or useful to the lover, he or she says goodbye.

What, however, of those cases in which one spouse sacrifices his or her own happiness to care for a bed-ridden partner, who may have lost not only attractive physical qualities but a beautiful personality as well? Wouldn't this indicate unselfish love after all?

An answer was suggested to me years ago by a man who was sacrificing his own happiness to care for a bed-ridden wife. He was, perhaps, acting out of charitable love, but was he acting out of erotic love? This man confessed to

---

5. Philosophies of love are particularly prone to speak of a "person" or "human center" that somehow lies behind the qualities or which contingently possesses certain qualities. But many philosophers have argued that they find no such "center" or enduring, unchanging "self" within themselves, and that they find only a stream of thoughts and sensations, plus certain habits that provide continuity. If we are such a constantly changing stream of qualities, this would explain the fluctuations to which love is often subject.

me that he no longer loved his wife in any romantic sense at all. There were, to him, no lovable qualities left; she did not even show gratitude for what he did. What he did say was that he was in love with the *memory* of what she once was, the memory of the beautiful inner and outer qualities she once had that had appealed to him and given him pleasure. Cannot memory be a source of self-gratification, and thus was this man's motive for staying with his invalid?

Thus, in the case of this man, self-gratification was still at work in serving a kind of illusion. He was remaining with someone he remembered as beautiful *and with whom he still associated the rewards he once received in enjoying the qualities she once possessed.* Thus, those who think that cases of elderly and ill "lovers" serving each others' needs is a sign of altruism must ask themselves if such persons are really responding to each other's actual *present* personhood at all. (Another case that defenders of altruism might give is subject to the same analysis. If one's beloved is dead, he or she is surely no longer serving one's needs and interests. Yet one may continue to love the dead person deeply, even though she or he is gone. Once again, however, one is really in love with the memory of those charming qualities that once served one's needs and interests. Or one could say that one misses one's beloved because one misses the gratification of the needs he or she provided.)

How might a defender of erotic love respond to these arguments? One reply might be that the whole egoism-altruism controversy is irrelevant since if two lovers become one, whatever benefits one partner benefits the other as well and whenever one gives, one also receives in doing so. Thus the beloved's happiness becomes the lover's happiness as well, and the problem is apparently resolved. But this argument seems to involve a kind of enlarged egoism, where the beloved is but an extension of oneself; and the individuality of each partner is thus seriously threatened. And as long as each partner is also an individual, there could clearly be conflicting interests between the two; for one has obligations to oneself and not just to one's partner. If one partner desperately wants an abortion and her lover wants a child, then the old refrain of "If you really loved me, you wouldn't ask such a thing" will be heard from both sides. Nor can love always reach a compromise in such cases: one either has an abortion or one doesn't. Either way one partner is going to be deeply hurt because he or she feels that his or her own best interests have been sacrificed, and the relationship may be mortally wounded.

Another reply to the egoism theory is that there are other ways of being altruistic than the self-sacrificial variety. One might grant that each lover expects to "get" something out of the relationship, but doesn't each lover also know that he or she must *give* something in order to make the relationship work? Indeed, it might be argued that if one partner feels she isn't getting nearly as much as her beloved she will feel cheated and will look elsewhere for a more equitable relationship. It is not, however, clear how this equity theory of love, that love must be equal parts of give and take, can be viewed as being altruistic. Such a theory would seem to involve a kind of "you scratch my back and I'll scratch yours" business-like type of partnership, where each is constantly on the alert to get a fair return from what one has invested in the relationship. Indeed, on the equity theory, the lover who gives his beloved her fair share so she won't feel cheated actually seems to be operating out of enlightened self-interest. For if he doesn't give her what she wants, she will abandon him and no longer be available to serve his interests.

One might try to salvage altruism by claiming that one's primary motive is to give, while getting is only a side-benefit that is not directly intended or is, at most, only a secondary motive. A lover does, of course, want her lover to expect to get something out of the relationship, for she does not want charity or a self-sacrificing slave for a lover. But she wants to feel that her lover is not just giving in order to get something, and that his getting something is only a secondary consideration in his mind.

To be sure, it is true that one's initial impulse is to give to one's beloved without thinking of the benefits; in the initial stages of love, for example, one thinks only of laying sacrifices at the altar of the beloved. But what one thinks one's primary motive is and what one's real motive is are not necessarily the same thing. The way one selects one's lover for certain appealing qualities, the way one excludes others who may need one's love more, the way love relationships end when the rewards of love cease to be forthcoming are all commonly forgotten when one focuses simply on how charitable one feels at the moment of giving to one's beloved. Given the way love begins and ends, can giving have really been the primary motive for the relationship?

Thus the paradox of erotic love remains: One wants one's lover to be unselfish, yet one does not ordinarily want a self-sacrificing slave for a lover. (The latter would eventually come to be viewed with contempt rather than love and would probably be boring as well.) One might try to overcome this difficulty by finding someone who loves himself or herself in the sense of having a certain inner richness of being, thus making it possible for him or her to love others in an unselfish way without becoming a self-sacrificial slave. Many philosophers and psychologists have described such persons as being characterized by "being-love" rather than by self-centered "need-love." But if there are such persons who have this inner richness of being and unbounded generosity, they would surely be disturbed by the selectivity, possessiveness, and exclusiveness of erotic love. Uniting with one person in an intimate way would, to them, mean a withdrawal of their attention and resources from hundreds of others who need their help even more. Furthermore, such persons are quite secure and independent and they would seem to have no need for such a dependency relationship.[6]

6. The problem encountered by establishing a relationship with someone who is characterized by "being-love" is aptly illustrated by the relationship between Franklin and Eleanor Roosevelt. Mrs. Roosevelt's concern for mankind led her to undertake charitable activities throughout the world and constantly kept her away from her husband. President Roosevelt, in turn, had to turn to Lucy Rutherford for the affection and companionship he missed. Furthermore, Mrs. Roosevelt also illustrates how difficult it is to find someone who is characterized solely by "being-love." In her earlier years her feeling that she was physically unattractive apparently drove her into a state of "need-love." Nor did this possessive "need-love" ever vanish completely, for she was enraged when she was finally informed of her husband's relationship with Lucy Rutherford.

Another argument that an altruist might give is that even though love may begin for selfish reasons, the love will eventually develop into an essentially altruistic relationship. That is, what was once viewed as a means to an end may come to be loved for its own sake. Erich Fromm, for example, seems to think that love grows out of a self-interested need to overcome one's isolation; yet he holds that love can eventually become essentially a matter of giving rather than getting. And Theodore Reik holds that love arises from an attempt to overcome one's feelings of inferiority by identifying with someone who has those qualities one lacks in oneself. But he too thinks that love eventually outgrows its selfish motive and becomes something basically generous in nature. To borrow his words, a beautiful flower can grow out of manure.

It is not, however, clear that arguments such as these refute the claim that love is essentially self-interested. For example, someone who overcomes the sort of insecurity Fromm and Reik describe would probably have no further need for the beloved and would seek a more self-sufficient existence. And the claim that what was once used as a means to an end might come to be cherished for its own sake does not rule out self-interest. Someone may purchase a beautiful painting solely to cover a hole in the wall, but he may eventually come to love the painting itself. But he will love the painting not for its own sake, but because it provides him with an enjoyable aesthetic experience. And when the painting ceases to be interesting, he will discard it and find another. Thus self-interest was still the primary motive for his keeping the painting as long as he did, and the concept of loving something "for its own sake" may prove to be a myth.

Those who find themselves being asked for a divorce discover the same thing: they are no longer interesting to their partner. Indeed, however hurt they may be, they should not want the partner to stay with them out of sheer duty or charity. They want the beloved to be interested in them, which once again requires that the partner's self-interest be predominant. Thus the claim that love may arise out of self-interest and develop into an essentially generous phenomenon overlooks the way love also ends.

In summary, we have noted that even the most ardent defender of love's unselfishness does not want erotic love to arise out of mere charity or duty, however severe one's need for love may be. This demand is itself based on self-interest. For one's self-esteem is damaged if one feels one wasn't chosen for one's merits and appealing qualities and was only worthy of love that is given to just anyone in need of love. But if one wants to be chosen for one's appealing qualities, one is committed, willy-nilly, to the selectivity and exclusiveness that reveal the egoism of one's beloved. For he or she will be chosen on the basis of qualities that appeal to the beloved's needs and self-interests. Thus the contradiction of erotic love remains: one wants to be loved unselfishly for one's own sake, yet the one who seeks erotic love also presupposes that such love is essentially self-interested. (This issue will be developed further in the concluding chapter of this book.)

C. *Choice vs. Emotion.* A further contradiction to which erotic love is subject is the conflict between one's demands that one be chosen for what one is in some kind of rational way, and also that such love must include some degree of emotional involvement. But having an emotion does not seem to be a matter of choice at all. Let us explore these conflicting demands in further detail.

First, we commonly want to believe that our lover has chosen us for what we are, that his or her love was not the product of the blinding influence of drugs, alcohol, a love potion, some egocentric desire to prove one's own desirability in the marketplace of love, or something done to "get even" with his parents. When one has spent an evening in a nightclub with a stranger and he suddenly announces, "I can't help loving you," one might at first find this quite flattering, particularly if one is desperate to be loved. But a more thoughtful person to whom this declaration of love was directed might very well wonder how love could come about so suddenly. Is the love merely the product of viewing someone in especially glamorous surroundings after having had several cocktails? Is such a "love" being confused with infatuation or lust? And if someone says he "can't help" loving his partner, one wonders if he has any control over his emotions at all. *For an emotion that suddenly flares up out of the blue can die just as quickly.* Indeed, someone who says "I can't help loving you" may only be hooked on someone he knows he really doesn't like at all and who will only lead him to ruin. Or he may simply be a kind of "love addict," who is in love with falling in love, and who does not particularly care whom it happens to be he falls for.

Given these considerations, someone who hears the phrase "I can't help loving you" would surely not be impressed by such a declaration. For we want love to include some realistic view of what we really are, some degree of rational decision-making based on what we are as total persons. Otherwise it will possibly be just a brief infatuation with certain attractive qualities that we only seem to possess in the other person's eyes, blinded as they are by emotion.

Yet we also ordinarily want love to involve a deep emotional involvement and not just another "out of sight and out of mind" casual friendship. Not all lovers want an emotional involvement to the same degree, of course; perhaps only a few of the more conventional husbands and wives want to be like Romeo and Juliet. But all want some degree of emotional involvement unless it is just to be a marriage of convenience. And in the initial stages of even a conventional marriage it would not be uncommon for the partners to speak of having a deep, meaningful emotional involvement, even if the honeymoon soon wears off. The wedding anniversary is typically a tribute to this wish to return to that initial ecstatic state once again.

But if we want our lover to have chosen us, is this compatible with emotional involvement? It would seem that the more intense the emotion (which for many is synonymous with love), the less likely it is we can speak of choice. For example, *I can ask someone to do only those things he can freely choose or decide to do.* But I cannot ask someone to become emotionally involved with me. If they do not feel anything, they don't, and all the entreaties in the world are not going to produce an emotion. If love were a matter of choice, it would make sense to say "I have just decided to be in love with you"; but the oddity of such a declaration is quite obvious. Indeed, it seems that the part of love involving emotion is a discovery rather than a decision.

I can, of course, ask the one I love to be more open to feeling, to overcome possible mental blocks against me, to put herself in an environment where such feelings are more likely to occur, to try to get to know me better and to allow me to entertain her or otherwise impress her so that an emotion of love may arise. Such techniques may or may not work, but for a true romantic who insists on spontaneity of emotion, such methods would be an anathema. To have to subject oneself and one's beloved to such a grueling process of trying to wring an emotion of love out of the beloved would not only be a blow to the pride of the lover; an emotion that is produced under such contrived circumstances would also tend to be unstable, as well.

It seems clear, therefore, that to insist both on a rational choice and emotional involvement is a contradictory ideal. Let us examine a few further difficulties in trying to combine these alternatives into what some would want to call a rational love. A rational choice, for example, involves a degree of self-control over one's emotions. But would one really want to say to one's beloved: "I love you, but I would never allow myself to completely surrender my feelings to you"? Furthermore, choice often involves deliberation. But if one were to say to one's lover: "I don't want to say right now that I love you; I want to go away and deliberate about it," would she not be equally offended, if lovers expect the choice to be spontaneous rather than a cold, calculated decision? To deliberate about whether to love the person suggests that she is, as it were, on trial, and that one is weighing her good qualities against her bad qualities rather than accepting her for what she is. Indeed, insofar as choice involves self-control of one's emotions and careful deliberation, it is difficult to see how such calculating individuals are going to be capable of or even want the kind of spontaneous, profound emotional involvement the erotic lover ordinarily wants.

Despite all these considerations about the offensiveness of cold calculation, we still want to be chosen for what we are and not have our lover simply be driven into loving us by some blinding factor (including emotion) over which he or she has no control. In view of our criticism of the coldness of *deliberative* choice, it would seem that we want not just to be chosen, but to be chosen *spontaneously*. But to be chosen spontaneously includes strong emotional factors, which in turn make it difficult to say that there has been a genuine choice at all.

Thus, the lover who insists on a rational choice based on what one really is and also on a profound emotional involvement is faced with a dilemma. Not only are emotions not chosen, they can also interfere with being chosen *for what one really is*. For emotions are not necessarily lovers of realism, even though they are not utterly divorced from thought and may even have, as it were, a kind of wisdom or insight of their own. But emotions have a way of thriving on and creating mystery and illusion, and they can be unstable and unpredictable for that reason.

It seems, therefore, that for lovers to try to combine rational choice (as well as other factors such as commitment and responsibility) with emotion is like trying to combine cold water with a hot flame.[7] There are, of course, those who are not interested in any kind of profound emotional involvement and who want only a companionate form of love that is a kind of deep friendship. Here a rational choice may very well be possible because of the absence of deep emotions. But a romantic would insist that such a calm type of love is really only friendship. He would then argue that friends never taste the supreme ecstasy of a deep emotional involvement, and that a so-called rational love based on choice has been purchased at the price of sacrificing ecstasy.

D. *Security vs. Insecurity.* However strange it may sound from a psychological viewpoint, love seems to demand both a secure and an insecure beloved. How could such a contradiction ever arise? Or is it only more apparent than real?

One of the great joys of love is the knowledge that my beloved needs my love and that I am able to satisfy that need. But if the psychologist Lawrence Casler is right, those who need love suffer from such things as insecurity or sexual frustration or a desire to conform to society's demands that one must be loved to be of any value.[8] Casler's theory would then mean that those who need my love are not really loving me for my own sake. They would only be using me to overcome their own insecurities. Such persons certainly do not choose to love, and if one finds such a lover gratifying in certain ways one will have to keep him or her in a state of insecurity in order to be sure of maintaining the relationship. One who wishes to hold such a lover and who is also offended by the sadomasochistic overtones of such a relationship will surely find himself in a state of self-conflict.

Furthermore, such insecure lovers are quite jealous, possessive, and seem to have a kind of masochistic desire to enslave themselves to the beloved in order to be sure they will be loved and thus feel less empty and inadequate. But one does not ordinarily want a self-sacrificing slave for a lover.

Suppose, however, that one envisages having a secure lover. Implicit in Casler's paper is that this would be someone who could say: "I enjoy your love, I accept your love, and I'll return it in kind, but I don't really *need* your love." But this seems to make the relationship seem altogether too casual and superficial and too easily broken off. With such a self-sufficient person one may have the feeling of not really being important to or needed for his or her

---

7. There is one element of choice in love that cannot be overlooked, however. While it makes no sense to say (a) "I have decided to be in love with you," it does make sense to say (b) "I choose not to set up a *relationship* with you because it would be harmful to you or to me." Those who claim that they can choose to love or not to love are, I think, often confusing (b) with (a) and are assuming that what holds true of (b) also makes choice possible in (a).

8. Lawrence Casler, *op. cit.,* pp. 1–36.

happiness, a feeling that is incompatible with a deep erotic relationship. Indeed, it is not clear that such secure, self-sufficient persons would really want to become entangled in an erotic relationship at all. They would tend to prefer a more casual type of relationship such as friendship, where one can be more certain that the independence of each person is respected.

Thus, it seems that we are confronted with another paradox: The erotic lover wants to feel needed, yet this seems to require an insecure person with all of the faults such a person possesses that we mentioned above. On the other hand, the erotic lover wants a secure person, someone who can, as it were, stand on his own two feet and respect his own independence as well as that of the one he loves. But with such a self-sufficient person one is thwarted in his desire to feel needed. Furthermore, such an independent person would also thwart one's desire for a sense of total oneness with the beloved; for independent persons never allow themselves to become absorbed in some state of oneness with the beloved where their own identity might be threatened or where they might become dependent on the unpredictable emotions of their erotic lover.

Perhaps, however, the paradox can be resolved by the lover's searching for someone who is not utterly insecure and who is not also utterly secure. Such a person would not "need" me (something which suggests a compulsive neurotic attachment), but would "want" me (which need carry no such suggestion). Such a person would want my love, it would be important to her, but she would not need me in the sense that she would disintegrate as a person if I ceased loving her or were apart from her for other reasons. If this distinction between needing and wanting can be applied in this way, then I can feel wanted and the relationship is not a casual one in which we could separate without missing each other.

Will this reconciliation of the problem of security versus insecurity work? Could someone say to his beloved, "I want you but I don't really need you"? Right now, for example, I want a bottle of Coca-Cola, but I don't really need it; a soft drink would be a pleasant thing to have, but it is certainly not essential to my happiness. If it were, then I would not merely want a Coke; I would need it. But do lovers want to feel that each one is a pleasant thing to have around, but that they are not really essential to each other's happiness? One might reply that lovers do not want each other in the casual way I want a Coke; they want each other in some deeper sense. But where, then, does one draw the line between "wanting deeply" and "needing" one's beloved? It seems that one is somehow being drawn back into talking of one's needing one's beloved or of feeling that one is needed by one's beloved. But then it would seem that love once again seeks an insecure lover (which it does not really want for the reasons just mentioned); and if it then searches for a secure lover, it does not really want that either, again for the reasons mentioned.

If these considerations are valid, then our original paradox remains: love seeks the contradictory ideal of both an insecure and a secure beloved. And neither insecurity nor security is compatible with many of the other things I have previously mentioned that lovers consider esssential to a meaningful relationship.

E. *Oneness vs. Twoness.* Let us now turn to what might seem to be the most critical contradiction that erotic love faces. This sort of potential conflict crops up in the oft-repeated claim in books on love that lovers want to be "at one" with each other or "in each other" and at the same time to respect each other's individuality. Alan Lee describes this with the beautiful analogy of the sea and the seashore: They touch at every point and yet they are distinct entities.[9] The analogy would be apt if only it were not the case that seas have a way of eroding the seashore and that seashores bring the beautiful waves of the ocean to a dead halt. Do not the same difficulties arise when one tries to speak about two lovers becoming "one" and yet "two," a proposition which to a philosopher seems to be a blatant contradiction and an attempt to have one's cake and eat it too?

There does, to be sure, seem to be some sense in which lovers want to be a unity of heart, mind, body, and soul. Such a feeling of oneness gives one a sense of relief from the pangs of being a purely isolated being and provides a sense of security in being united with another. And at its most intense level such a sense of oneness with one's beloved approaches the ecstatic bliss that mystics feel when they claim to be, as it were, transported outside of themselves into a higher unity with what they believe is God Himself.

Yet, while many lovers insist on this oneness in which they are somehow mystically united in some kind of perfect psychic, emotional, and sexual harmony, they also commonly want to be two beings as well. That is, they do not want to totally sacrifice their freedom and independence and individual uniqueness to a state of mutual absorption. Indeed, if two lovers are not two strong individuals in their own right, what do they have to contribute to each other as a manifestation of their own unique inner resources? Furthermore, the quest for a kind of mystical unity of one partner with another will surely be sought primarily by those insecure individuals who have little love for themselves and who want to rescue themselves from their self-contempt and forlornness by being absorbed into a state of oneness with their beloved. In such a case any talk of such lovers being "one and yet two" is out of the question. To be one in the sense of a complete fusion of two beings and also to be two beings who retain their own individuality would require that such lovers be both insecure and secure. Then the very contradiction we explored in the preceding section would arise again.[10]

9. Lee, *Colors of Love,* p. 46.

10. The classic illustration of the insecurity of persons who seek total fusion with their beloved is found in a myth related by Aristophanes in Plato's *Symposium.* In this myth the world was once populated by round, two-sided creatures who had two eyes, arms, legs, and a sexual organ in both the front and the back of their bodies. The Greek gods, however, fearing that such creatures were becoming too defiant and powerful, decided to split them in half, so that each now had only two eyes, legs, and arms, and one sexual organ. They thus came to resemble what we are today. These half-men and half-women, however, felt forlorn and incomplete because the gods had severed the other half of themselves from them.

Thereafter, according to Aristophanes, such creatures roamed the earth seeking their other half so that they would feel complete once again rather than being only half a person. When one of these half-creatures met his other half, they immediately embraced, fell in love, and tried to stay as close together as possible so they would no longer feel incomplete.

However, even for those couples who do not seek a special form of total absorption in another and who try to be in some sense "one and yet two," there are plenty of difficulties.

For a couple to form, as it were, a harmony or unity of opposites presupposes that one's basic commitment is to the preservation of this unity. But doesn't one also have obligations to oneself as well as to this unity of opposites? If, for example, one partner wants to exercise his or her independence and, say commit adultery, then the other partner will insist that their oneness of mind, heart, and body is being torn asunder. Or, if adultery is considered an overly extreme way of being independent, then the abortion example would illustrate the difficulty just as well. The husband may very much want another child, while the wife may not want to endure the burden of bearing and raising more children. The woman has an obligation to her husband, but she also has an obligation to herself.

Which obligation will she fulfill? If she surrenders to her husband's wishes, then she has violated her obligation to herself. If she does not surrender to her husband's wishes, then the relationship may be mortally wounded. A feminist, of course, would argue that since it is the woman who must bear and raise the child, the husband should surrender his own interests and accede to his wife's wishes. But from the male's point of view, this argument assumes that his needs and interests are somehow less valid than those of his wife. One then has an irreconcilable conflict of interests, both of which are perhaps equally valid.

It seems clear, therefore, that any attempt to form a unity of heart, mind, body, and soul and also to retain one's own independence and respect one's obligations to oneself is doomed to fail unless one has a rare case where each partner thinks completely alike on all issues or where the partners can always find a way of compromising their differences without violating each other's legitimate interests.

There is, finally, one answer that is commonly found among defenders of "one but yet two" theory. It is that one somehow becomes more of an individual when he becomes at one with another person. Or the claim is made that we have a kind of "transpersonal" individuality that is very different from our isolated, self-sufficient individuality; and only through lovingly uniting with another can this transpersonal individual, defined in terms of its essential relatedness to others, be realized.

It is, of course, undeniably true that many of my potentialities will be called forth into actualization when I love another in the more ordinary nonabsorptive way; my love will inspire me to develop many traits that will enhance my uniqueness more than would otherwise be possible. But how this will be possible when love is interpreted as being "in" another or totally "one" with

---

From this myth, one might derive the notion that love is a search for wholeness and completeness, and that without love one feels like only half a person and about as useful as being only a half a pair of scissors. But when lovers who seek wholeness are described in these terms, it is clear that they are utterly insecure, helpless beings unless they are loved.

another is unclear. To absorb someone else's traits is not to develop one's own unique potentialities. Indeed, romantics focus on each other so much that it is hard to see how they have any time left to develop their own unique individuality. It is, of course, true that to combine two into one is to develop a kind of new, more complex individual that transcends what each one was alone; but then what becomes of their claim that they still respect each other's independence? Could not this new two-in-one "individual" develop a self-centered autonomy of its own that will look with scorn on whatever threatens its existence or refuses to gratify its needs, be it the rest of society or its own individual component numbers?

The claim that each of us is or must be a kind of "transpersonal" or "We-two" individual in addition to our own private selves is much more difficult to assess. The claim, as we noted above, is that love actualizes this important aspect of our individuality, and thus makes possible our claim to be a true individual in the full sense of the word. The isolated ego, proud of its independence of others, is said to be only an illusory or abstract or semi-individual.[11]

One difficulty with this "transpersonal" individual is that it is something that does not uniquely define the sort of relation one finds in love. Couldn't my transpersonal individuality be actualized by becoming at one with a crowd of persons with whom I feel united in response to a spell-binding orator? But there is clearly no intimacy between the members of the crowd (or even with the speaker) in a romantic sense. And the fact that such crowds are often swayed into believing things that their uniquely personal isolated selves would scorn in moments of private, sober reflection indicates that such a "transpersonal" individual is not an unalloyed good, however valuable such a concept may be as a form of recommending that we learn to be capable of relating to others.

If, therefore, we try to apply this concept of transpersonal individuality to the concept of love, we remain with the problem of reconciling the needs of my individual self with those of my "transpersonal" self. What if these two selves find themselves in some kind of quasi-schizophrenic disagreement about how I am to develop myself as an individual? Can the transpersonal individual

---

11. The concept of the "larger self of We" or "We-two" is defended in William Sadler's *Existence and Love* (New York: Scribner's, 1969). "The self," he writes, "is variously structured in terms of basic possible encounters which include the private, personal, and social modes of existence. From the viewpoint of love, the call of conscience is received as an address from a Thou beckoning me to an *authentic personal existence*. . . . The outlook of existential phenomenology suggests that the popular ethic of self-realization suffers from a gross myopia by exalting the individual over communal self-realization. . . . The realization of the *truly personal self* is not an individual accomplishment but a free gift of love." (p. 229; italics mine.) "The deepest and most essential voice within the phenomenon of conscience emerges from the dual reality of We. It is a call of an individual to become a truly personal self," where Sadler means that one must lovingly interpenetrate with another's existence in a larger "We-two" self (p. 231). "It seems clear that one of the most deadly enemies of love and hence of personal existence is man's own attempt to live autonomously. Because of the dual nature of man (by which Sadler means the "We" self as well as the personal self) it is sheer suicide to assert one's own autonomy (p. 238)." Despite Sadler's obvious disdain of personal autonomy, he takes great pains to insist that such a love "does not develop into a form of mutual absorption or immersion of one person into the other." His only explanation of this is that there remains a kind of "distance" between the two lovers (p. 233). But this is hardly a satisfactory reconciliation of what seem to be two contradictory claims: that personal autonomy is a sin against our social self, yet we must and can somehow retain such autonomy when we interprenetrate with another in the way he describes.

respect what my isolated self tells me to rationally do in my own best interests, which may include abandoning a destructive love relationship? Or will it overpower me in the way crowd psychology overpowers its members, often to their detriment?

It does not seem, therefore, that the "one-and-yet-two" theory is going to be rescued by talk of becoming a more unique, richer, or transpersonal individual thereby. The problem of respecting my own private individual needs remains to haunt such rescue efforts.

I conclude, therefore, that the "one but yet two" theory as traditionally expressed leads to an irreconcilable conflict with my needs to be at one with another and my further needs to be a unique individual who retains his or her own identity and independence. There are, of course, lovers who do not seek a quasi-mystical state of oneness or mutual absorption of each others' identity. For them there can be a milder form of love in which they can perhaps feel a kind of oneness with each other while simultaneously respecting each other's individuality. (However, as I have already noted, in any love relationship an irreconcilable conflict between one's obligations to oneself and one's obligations to the relationship is a permanent possibility.) But for those who think love must be a truly intense, deep relationship, this milder form of oneness is not going to be sufficient. This then leads one to the highly unwelcome conclusion that if one is going to enjoy love at its highest peak of ecstasy in a state of perfect oneness with one's partner, one's individuality is doomed.

F. *Opposites Attract vs. Like Attracts Like.* I would, finally, like to explore briefly two contradictory statements that have been made down through the ages by philosophers of love as to how love begins. On the one hand, there is the familiar claim that "opposites attract." On the other hand, it is just as frequently claimed that "like attracts like." We clearly seem to have a contradiction here, and each claim presents critical difficulties for a love that is derived from such theories.

What are the arguments for the claim that opposites attract? Heterosexuals often claim that even if homosexuality were to someday become socially acceptable, the vast majority of persons would still prefer a relationship with the opposite sex. They claim that being with someone different from themselves is a fascinating experience, as if one were exploring a foreign land for the first time and discovering something new and unfamiliar each day. A partner who is one's opposite is often said to thereby possess a certain mystique that is essential to produce the intoxicating emotions of love that transcend merely friendly feelings. Finally, someone who is looking for love is often thought to be searching for something that he or she lacks. Opposites could thus complement each other and provide each with what the other lacks in a kind of harmony of opposites. The man, it is often said, provides a strong shoulder on which the weak and helpless female can lean for security; and the woman provides the man with the tenderness and depth of emotion he is said to need.

One difficulty with the "opposites attract" theory insofar as it is used to defend heterosexuality is that it assumes that there are certain fundamental differences of temperament and outlook between males and females that are part of their very nature. Many feminists, however, would argue that the only natural difference between the two sexes is that women can become pregnant and men cannot. Other supposed differences are merely the products of sexist social conditioning in which men are conditioned into being rugged and aggressive and in which women are conditioned to feel that they are helpless, passive creatures.

Indeed, June Singer, in *Androgyny: Toward a New Theory of Sexuality,* has argued that we are all fundamentally androgynous, that is, we all possess both masculine and feminine temperaments. She argues, however, that males and females have been conditioned to repress the other side of their natures so that they can live up to traditional demands that men be masculine (by, for example, suppressing their emotions) and that women be feminine (by, for example, suppressing their assertiveness). But such forms of repression can produce many ills, such as sexism and neurosis. Ms. Singer argues that only when we can truly be open to both our masculine and feminine aspects and integrate them into a harmonious whole within ourselves will we be truly healthy beings and realize our full potentialities. But if such an androgynous society came into being, the traditional "opposites attract" argument for heterosexual love would no longer be valid. For if both males and females were equally masculine and feminine within themselves, there would no longer be any mystique that could arise merely from differences of gender. Nor would a masculine person need to seek out a feminine person to give himself a sense of completeness or provide a harmony of opposites; for both males and females would already have this harmony of opposites within themselves.

In such a society as Ms. Singer envisages individual differences would not, of course, disappear; only the traditional male-female dichotomy would vanish. One could then feel free to choose as a lover someone different from oneself in other ways: Thus a male might choose a male or female who has different interests from himself and this would provide the sense of mystique that love is said to require. On the sexual level, such androgynous beings could find equal satisfaction in taking either a passive or active role. And since each partner is equally masculine and feminine, the male could better understand and relate to feminine needs and the female could better understand the masculine point of view. Finally, such androgynous beings would no longer be confined to either a heterosexual or homosexual role. A man, for example, could be passive with a male partner and masculine with a female partner; bisexuality would then become a feasible option for all.

Let us now turn to the argument that love begins because "like attracts like." According to this theory, the claim that opposites attract is going to produce two beings who are fundamentally incompatible. Instead of talking about a harmony of opposites between males and females one should rather speak of the battle of the sexes. Furthermore, the so-called mystique that is said to arise from fascination with one's opposite is merely a kind of momentary infatuation with each other's differences that will evaporate once the two partners get to know each other better. Indeed, love can only survive if the lovers can also be friends, and friendship is based on a sharing of interests between two persons who are very much alike. And it would be argued that the claim of the "opposites attract" theory that each partner gives what the other lacks leads to a sense of mutual dependency that threatens the independence of each partner. Those who are alike, on the other hand, are attracted to each other because they share common interests. Such persons would respect each other's individuality and would not try to absorb each others' identity into some kind of perfect unity of opposites. Furthermore, on the sexual level two partners who have similar interests are far more likely to be compatible in the bedroom. If, for example, they were both of the same sex they would be more likely to understand and share each others' sexual needs and would be more at ease and familiar with someone whose body is like their own.

The defender of the "opposites attract" theory, however, would reply by claiming that "like attracts like" will produce only friendship or companionship, but not love. His claim would be that those who are alike know each other all too well, and that the magical ingredient of mystique that produces erotic love is missing. Nor will the element of mystique disappear if the two different partners are truly complex, inwardly rich beings; for them there will be a new discovery each day that will keep them eternally fascinated with each other. Their differences may, at times, cause conflicts, but will not love usually be able to prevail over these conflicts?

In surveying these two opposing arguments, one might argue that love actually seems to require that the lovers both be, as it were, opposite and alike, which seems to be a contradiction. If they are not in some sense alike, there is the strong possibility that they will be incompatible; love may at times triumph over such differences, but such a love is going to be a living hell if constant conflicts arise. On the other hand, one might argue that a relationship between two persons who are alike will most likely remain at the friendship level, although it is also true that a kind of love has often arisen between two persons who differ little from one another. (One thinks of the famous long-time relationship between Sartre and Simone de Beauvoir, two famous French writers who share many interests. Their love seems to be more than friendship, yet it falls short of being the ecstatic or erotic kind of love.)

Perhaps the solution to this supposed contradiction of love requiring both oppositeness and likeness is to make the simple observation that someone who wants both an enduring love (which requires compatibility) and an ecstatic love (which perhaps requires a certain mystique) should choose someone who is like oneself in certain ways and who is different from oneself in other ways. But then we are confronted with the problem we discussed at the beginning of this chapter: to have both ecstasy and endurance is a contradictory ideal that may be impossible to achieve.

Two

Can One Define "Love"?

1
Some Preliminary Difficulties

"If you truly love someone, you ought to do or be _____." Ought to do or be what? This problem has plagued philosophers of love down through ages. Many philosophers, for example, have been essentialists; that is, they believe there is some unique quality which love possesses which sets it apart from other human emotions such as hate. The difficulty with essentialism is that philosophers have traditionally been at odds about what uniquely defines love. For example, in attempting to define what it is to be a human being, some essentialists have argued that our distinctive trait is our rationality; others have claimed that it is our freedom. And so it is with love. Some would argue that its distinctive trait is a certain unique kind of emotion or degree of emotional depth; others would argue that the essence of love is benevolence; and still others would argue that love is a special kind of desire, that is, a desire to find completeness and wholeness by uniting with another human being such that each provides what the other lacks.

A further difficulty with traditional philosophies of love is that they radically disagree on what it is we should love. Some would claim that the truest or noblest form of love is love of God or love of all mankind or friends or love of country or love of ideals such as truth, goodness, justice and beauty. Those who argue this way tend to scorn erotic love between the sexes as essentially self-interested, and hold that erotic love is, in the final analysis, really only self-love. Whether the supposedly nobler forms of love are any less concerned with self-interest is, however, far from clear. Freud, for example, would argue that love of God is really only a love for a father-substitute who satisfies one's self-interested needs for security.

Indeed, it is clear that we can love many things, including persons of either sex, ourselves, a pet, a car, a fantasy, or even love itself. To define true love in terms what we ought to love is, I think, to make a moral claim that is designed to sustain a certain life-style. To say, for example, that the only true love is love of someone of the opposite sex is obviously designed to sustain a life-style based on family living and procreation. On the other hand, to condemn being in love with a fantasy as mere infatuation is perhaps like attempts to condemn masturbation as not being the "real thing." I conclude, therefore, that any attempt to define love should be divorced from considerations of what it is that is loved. Otherwise one's concept of love will involve a debatable moral claim about what it is that ought to be loved if love is to be true love.

When we turn to erotic love, which is the central topic of this section of the book, we find two basically opposing approaches. For some, erotic love should be an ecstatic experience based on a profound emotional involvement between two human beings who are united in a kind of mystical oneness of heart, mind, body, and soul. Their ideal would be Romeo and Juliet who fell in love at first sight and who were literally swept off their feet by intense emotions they could barely control.

For others, however, Romeo and Juliet's love would be condemned as mere infatuation because it would be, to them, an utterly irrational love. Those who defend a rational love insist that the two partners must be friends before they can be lovers. For if one falls in love at first sight, how does one know enough about the other person to make a rational assessment of whether he or she is really worthy of one's love or would make a compatible companion? For a rational lover, being swept off one's feet by intense emotions would prevent one from making a wise choice of someone to whom one could decide to commit oneself to an enduring relationship.

For an intensely romantic person, however, the so-called rational lover overlooks the possibility that emotions may, as it were, have a kind of intuitive wisdom of their own that provide an insight into the other's inner being that the rational intellect can never penetrate. The romantic might argue that his sense of total oneness with his partner makes it possible to know his beloved's inner being in a far more profound way than merely trying to assess the other person's traits on some kind of rational scale of desirable qualities.

Indeed, the romantic would argue that rational love is in the final analysis going to have to be devoid of emotion entirely if it is to be perfectly rational. Or if the rational lover does want some kind of emotional involvement, then he is going to have to realize that one cannot rationally choose to have emotions. For one may meet a partner whose qualities would make that person a perfectly rational choice, yet one may feel no erotic emotion whatever.

As for the rationalist's claim that unpredictable emotions provide a very shaky basis for an enduring relationship, the romantic would reply that one who is chosen in a calculating way on the basis of his or her desirable qualities will be abandoned in a similar way when his or her partner loses those desirable qualities. For what rational person would continue with a relationship when it would be irrational to do so? Thus the concept of rational choice does not necessarily entail an enduring commitment either.

This debate between the realistic and the romantic lover could doubtlessly go on forever. The realist would say that the fiery romantic lives in a fantasy world of perpetual infatuation, while the romantic would claim that the sober realist is a stick-in-the-mud who cautiously goes shopping for a mate in the way one goes shopping for a good steak. The romantic's ecstasy cannot last, of course, but he thinks the price he paid in terms of lack of endurance is outweighed by the sublime bliss of his relationship. The realist, on the other hand, carefully calculates his partner's good and bad qualities to see if the relationship will be an enduring one. For him, compatibility and companionship are the major goals rather than ecstasy. Neither the realist nor the romantic would claim that the other knows what true love is at all. The realist would label the romantic's love as mere infatuation, and the romantic would label the realist's love as being only a kind of deep friendship. Perhaps each should realize that labels like "infatuation" or "mere friendship" are often merely ways of expressing scorn for a kind of erotic love that does not suit one's own temperament and life-style.

Can love be defined? Or is love some kind of unique entity, act, or state of mind that cannot be reduced to anything else? Books about love are filled with claims that love is happiness, that love is trust, generosity, commitment, a unity of two beings in a harmony of opposites, and so forth. But a critic might argue that love is not these things themselves; he would hold that such things come about *because* one loves someone else. It is also commonly held that love is a desire for another person or that love is a certain kind of emotion. Yet a critic might argue that we desire the other person or feel certain emotions toward the beloved *because* we love the person. Thus love, on this view, would not itself be any of these things, but would be the cause of emotions, desires, and so forth. It is doubtlessly true that emotion and desire occur simultaneously with love, but this does not rule out a cause-effect relationship. For causes need not precede their effects, as in the case of drawing a line on a blackboard with a piece of chalk.

Does this sort of argument prove that love is some kind of mysterious entity that lies behind and causes the things in terms of which it has been traditionally defined? One might argue that such an argument overlooks the possible motives one might have for seeking these things, and that love could be characterized in terms of these motives. Thus one might argue that love is the desire to overcome one's loneliness or isolation or that love is a desire to overcome one's inferiority complex by uniting with and absorbing the identity of another person who has those qualities one lacks.

Yet a critic might argue that love is not itself a desire for these things. Rather these desires are themselves desires for love which in turn brings about a state of affairs which satisfies one's need to, say, escape loneliness and isolation. Thus the motive for seeking love and the state of affairs that love produces which would satisfy this motive would still be distinguishable from love itself. Once again, on this account, love would be some kind of mysterious entity that one seeks and which produces or leads to one's being happy, generous, filled with emotion and desire, and so forth.

Whether or not this argument I have invented proves that love is an indefinable and ultimately unknowable thing I will leave to the reader to decide. Philosophers are ill at ease with claims that there are mysterious and indefinable entities, acts, or states of mind. Yet it is clearly true that no particular set of traits in terms of which love of another person has traditionally been defined guarantee that there is any real love for that person. If one is generous towards another person, this may only be because one is trying to assuage one's feelings of guilt about having previously treated this person cruelly. If one unites with another person, this may be only a selfish need to escape one's isolation. If one is attracted to or emotionally involved with someone, this may only be because that person reminds one of a former lover.

Thus, no matter how many of the traditional criteria for love one may exemplify in one's behavior, it is always an open question as to whether they are really any indication of love for another person for that person's sake. The criteria for love become signs of true love only when they are motivated by or caused by a genuine love for the other person. Thus these traditional definitions of love for another person still presuppose rather than define the concept of love. If one still insists that love can be defined as a genuine concern for the beloved's welfare, one could reply that this concern is only the result of love or proof that love exists or is a way in which love manifests itself. But what love is in itself would still be a mystery.

It still might be argued, however, that if love invariably manifests itself in concern for the beloved's welfare, such concern would be a good clue as to what its inner nature is. But could there be cases in which love manifests itself in cruelty? If so, then the inner nature of love itself would be even more of a puzzle. In the play *Who's Afraid of Virginia Woolf?* the husband and wife constantly lacerate each other with vicious comments about each other's shortcomings. There was scarcely any evidence of tenderness or generosity or concern for each other's feelings. Did they merely hate each other or was their behavior a curious way in which love sometimes manifests itself? They obviously needed each other very much, for most people would separate rather than endure the torment they inflicted on each other. Furthermore, they were insanely jealous and possessive of each other, which indicates some kind of erotic love was present. In Camus's novel *The Stranger* an elderly man constantly beat and kicked his poorly fed, mangy dog; yet he wept bitterly when the dog disappeared. Did he in some sense love the dog all along? One could not say he cried merely because he no longer had anything to abuse; for he could easily have found another helpless animal to torture.

One might argue that these are instances of a sick or neurotic love rather than a healthy love. But once one admits that even a sick or neurotic love is a form of love, one cannot say that tenderness and concern for the beloved's welfare are necessary conditions for love as such; they would only be conditions for a healthy love relationship. Yet even here one must be cautious about labeling a love relationship that does not meet the idealist's criterion for true love as being neurotic or sick. I have been acquainted with a number of couples who seem to positively enjoy constantly quarreling with each other, and would resent an outsider's attempt to resolve their differences. Tenderness, trust, fidelity, and benevolence seem to be lacking in such relationships. Yet in an unguarded moment they would confess to me, although not to each other, that they truly loved each other. Indeed, they might argue that it is far healthier to openly express their own rather aggressive natures than to suppress their aggressions under a facade of tenderness and benevolence.

Furthermore, even in so-called healthy love relationships I have on numerous occasions been shocked by an occasional outburst of verbal or even physical violence that rivals anything one finds between bitter enemies. Perhaps the reason for this is that all erotic relationships, even those that are not possessive, are nevertheless to some extent dependency relationships. And perhaps the independent side of our nature which has obligations to itself which must often be sacrificed or at least compromised to make a relationship work, inevitably resents any form of dependency relationship, no matter how healthy such a relationship may be. Absolute independence and some degree of unity with another are contradictory ideals, no matter how much one tries to combine the two. Thus the couple in *Who's Afraid of Virginia Woolf?* whose quarrels reflect the terrible resentment they feel for knowing that each is so hopelessly dependent on the other simply represents to an extreme degree the resentment that is dormant in even the most supposedly healthy relationships and which is often suppressed behind a facade of tenderness and benevolence.

Are there any necessary conditions for being able to say that one is in love with someone else? Are there any traits that uniquely define erotic love and set it apart from other forms of human relationships? The traditional criteria of tenderness, trust, commitment, and benevolence do not, as I have noted above, seem to be found in all erotic relationships. These criteria represent the outlook of gentle, idealistic souls who overlook the possibility that love may have a demonic side. Even if such traits as trust and benevolence were held to be necessary conditions for a supposedly true love relationship, such traits are also found in friendship and in agapic love, that is, love for all mankind. Thus they would not uniquely define erotic love.

Is desire a necessary condition for erotic love? Some would argue that desire is not a necessary condition since one may love someone but not desire him or her because one knows that such a person would lead one to ruin. But although there may be no conscious desire for such a person, there are doubtlessly unconscious desires, needs, and interests that are operative in explaining why one was attracted to the harmful person in the first place. But even if desire is always present in one form or another in erotic love, desire does not uniquely define erotic love. For we also desire our friends, although perhaps not in an erotic way; but this still leaves "in an erotic way" undefined. Nor does desire uniquely define any form of love at all; for we often desire what we hate, as with those who are addicted to drugs or alcohol.

Could we define erotic love as a kind of total unity of heart, mind, body, and soul? But this is hardly a necessary condition for erotic lovers, since it would not apply to lovers who are very independent. Nor would it uniquely define erotic love, since extremely close friends could also be described in terms of this oneness of two beings.

In the following sections, I shall look at some other things that have been thought to uniquely define or be necessary conditions for erotic love. These include a distinctive type of emotion, a unique way of knowing another person's innermost being; I shall reexamine the claim that true love entails benevolence by examining the theories of Plato, Aristotle, and Erich Fromm. Finally, I shall devote a section to the problem of distinguishing erotic love from infatuation and friendship to see if we can discover any unique quality that distinguishes erotic love from these supposedly different types of human relationships.

2
Love as an Emotion

Is emotional involvement a necessary condition for saying that one is in love? Can erotic love be defined in terms of some kind of uniquely ecstatic emotion or degree of emotional depth that would distinguish love from friendship?

In examining the first question, could there be a type of love in which the lovers do not want any kind of emotional involvement? Love, for them, would be a search for a temporary intimate liaison in which there is some degree of affection, but no emotional involvement. The latter sort of involvement would, to them, trap them into settling down with one lover and prevent them from, as it were, playing the game of love and constantly wooing new partners. One is, of course, tempted to scorn this "playboy" concept of love as being much too vain, cold, calculating, and irresponsible. But given the criticisms we have already made of the idealist's concept of love in the preceding section, are we any longer in a position to say that the playboy concept of love is utterly invalid?

There is also another type of lover who is just as cool and calculating as the playboy mentioned, but who tries to fulfill the idealist's view that love should lead to a lasting marriage. This sort of lover is obsessed with compatibility, security, and permanence. He goes shopping for a lover with a strict set of criteria his partner must meet; and he does not allow emotional considerations to interfere with his making a perfectly rational choice. (To find a lover through computer-matching services would be his ideal.) Such ultrarational lovers are, to be sure, miles away from Romeo and Juliet's concept of love. Their love is a kind of business-like partnership in which they seek to satisfy only their minimal needs for affection, companionship, support, child-rearing, and so forth. Once such a person meets someone who fulfills his criteria, he immediately accepts her as his lover regardless of whether he feels any particular erotic emotion towards her.

Here the philosopher is faced with an important difficulty. Suppose that such calculating persons insist on calling themselves lovers, when a philosopher might insist that at least some degree of emotional involvement is necessary if the relation is to be worthy of the label of love? Does he have the right to tell such coolly controlled lovers that they do not know what love really is? Certainly they violate our traditional, conventional notion that love must involve the emotions in some way. But perhaps love is an "open concept"[1] that cannot be defined in terms of any traditional set of necessary and sufficient conditions, such that new forms of love are possible. (This has occurred in the world of art where paintings that do not represent or picture anything are now accepted by many as bona fide works of art.)

A defender of erotic love as necessarily involving intense emotions would, of course, claim that the cool forms of love mentioned above are just varieties of friendship and that such partners could not really claim to be in love with each other at all. Yet a critic might challenge this claim by asking how we are to specify just what that degree of affection is, where it stops being friendship and becomes the emotion of love, just as a critic of the art versus non-art distinction would challenge us to state that point where something must be labeled as art rather than non-art. Furthermore, even if one insisted erotic love must consist of some ecstatic emotion, this would still not distinguish love from either infatuation or friendship. For infatuated persons feel ecstatic emotions, and deep friends often have a degree of intense feeling for each other that is difficult to distinguish from the emotions of even Romeo and Juliet. Thus emotional involvement does not seem to be a necessary condition for erotic love or even a uniquely defining trait of such love.

Finally, let us consider some reasons why erotic emotions cannot be a sufficient condition for being able to say one loves another person.

The first reason is that if love were just an emotion it would be impossible to say that one was in love when one was not currently feeling such an emotion. No one, not even Romeo, feels such an emotion twenty-four hours a day.[2] For we have as many attitudes towards our lover as our moods vary: We may

---

1. Note that when I speak of love in this context, I am thinking of affiliative or erotic love *itself* being an open concept; I am not thinking of the traditional generic concept of love that is usually divided into erotic love, friendship, and charity or "gift" love: that is, *eros, philia,* and *agape.*

2. It might be argued that emotion is always present in the following sense: that if I do not currently actually "feel" the emotion, I could summon it up to my consciousness if I chose to do so. But if I am in the midst of a heated quarrel with my beloved, I might not be able to do this at all, although I would still remember that this is my lover toward whom I ordinarily feel this emotion.

be absorbed in our work, we may be bored with her at times, we may quarrel with her at times. When one is working at the level of sheer emotion, there is no guarantee of utterly predictable continuity. But despite these changes in our moods, it does not follow that one has ceased to love the person throughout these changes, so long as the changes are only temporary.

Secondly, when one places great emphasis on beautiful emotions to the exclusion of all else, then the beloved may be only an occasion for indulging oneself in such emotions rather than being the object of one's emotions. This is simply a way of saying that some people are in love with love, a common accusation directed against those who will settle for nothing less than the romantic ecstasy of the Romeo and Juliet type.

However, such an accusation is more appropriately directed against those who show a curious disregard for the one whom they profess to be utterly sacred in their eyes. For if the lover shows no serious concern for the beloved's welfare, then this would indicate that the accusation of being "in love with love" might be true. Of course, someone who shows regard for his beloved's welfare may also have selfish motives, such as the desire to be loved. But in the latter case the one who is loved is at least of some importance and could be the recipient of important benefits. Thus to love *someone*, for whatever motive, is very different from being in love with love feelings for their own sake. Indeed, if there were a love potion that caused one to have these "love emotions," then the person who is in love with emotions alone would simply take it and ignore other persons completely.

It should be noted that these two criticisms of emotions as a sufficient condition for love are equally applicable to the concept of love defined in terms of benevolence or concern for the welfare of the beloved. It is clearly not true, for example, that one's beloved is in need twenty-four hours a day. But if love were only a matter of giving to another, then I could not be said to love her at those times when there is no need to give her anything. One might argue that the beloved always needs at least one thing: love. But this need not be true if she becomes quite self-sufficent and doesn't even need my love. Yet one would ordinarily be said to love her, whether she is in need or not. The second criticism of emotion which raised the possibility that one may be in love with the emotions of love rather than the person who stimulated those emotions is also applicable to benevolence. For some persons may be in love with giving itself as a self-interested expression of their strength, wealth and power. Thus, while giving may result in benefits to another, it does not follow that benefiting another is always the motive for the giving.

In summary, it seems clear that emotion alone is not sufficient to define or guarantee love for another person. And, as we have already noted, emotional involvement is perhaps not a necessary condition for erotic love either.

3
Love as Knowledge of the Beloved

A further reason for thinking that love is not just an emotion arises from the oft-heard claim that emotions are blind, that they somehow prevent us from seeing the other person as she truly is. And if one wishes to love a *person* instead of a fantasy, would one not also need to have knowledge of precisely who it is one is loving? Furthermore, some would argue that knowledge of the beloved is a necessary condition for making a commitment to the beloved that can endure the fluctuations our emotions undergo. Emotions attach themselves to the beloved or are stirred by the beloved; but they do not by themselves commit themselves to the beloved, or make a decision to stay with the beloved through the temporary crises that love so often undergoes.

It might be argued, however, that emotions have a kind of wisdom of their own or create a unique non-intellectual capacity to intuit qualities in the beloved that ordinary cognition can never discern. For example, if there were really an ecstatic state of oneness with another person in which one were "in" that person in some psychic-emotional sense, then would one not be in a better position to know that person from the inside in a way that is unavailable to detached observers?

What can a philosopher add to this traditional debate about the "blindness" versus the "wisdom" of love? When I identify with my beloved in a way that transcends traditional cognitive or abstract ways of knowing, how do I know whether or not my oneness with the lover actually reveals more about me than my beloved? When mystics claim that they have a mysterious state of oneness with God, their reports of what God is like often conflict, despite the fact that there is only one God whose characteristics are unchanging. The claim that there is some pure mode of seeing of a mystical sort should reveal a likeness of vision, but does not seem to do so. The mystics' reports of what God is like seem only to reveal their own interests, needs, and preconceptions of what God is. And it is doubtful that two persons who have loved the same person give precisely similar accounts of what the unique qualities of the beloved are. For not precisely the same qualities may have aroused their emotions in the first place; and a defender of the claim that love is blind would argue that they saw in the beloved what they wanted to see, whether such qualities actually existed or not. Indeed, they would argue that for there to be an accurate knowledge of another person, there must be some kind of distance between knower and known that the oneness of ecstatic lovers does not permit. For if "I" am, as it were, "you," how do I distinguish knowledge of myself from knowledge of you, and know that it is really you whose unique self I am discovering?

However, the claim that there must be a certain distance between knower and the known itself introduces another problem of its own. For does this distance insure either objectivity or knowledge of the beloved's inwardness? Nietzsche, for example, argued that all knowledge is perspectival, that we all organize our perception of the world to fit our own needs and interests, and that the concept of any pure mode of seeing is a myth. This would mean that friends as well as lovers view other people from their own distinctive frame of reference. The claim that friends are more realistic than lovers and that lovers are more realistic than infatuated persons would then either collapse or would involve only distinctions of degree at best.

But there is an even graver difficulty in the claim that there must be a certain distance between two persons for them to see each other as they are. For if one puts oneself at a psychic distance, however small, from another, then can one claim to know the beloved in her true inwardness? The beloved may reveal to me only certain parts of herself for fear that if I knew her too thoroughly, I would be disillusioned or bored because her mysterious depths had been fully explored. Or if there are no conscious or unconscious needs for holding back one's reality and she does express her feelings as openly and honestly as friends are ordinarily said to do, then I could still be interpreting them in accordance with the way I wish to see her rather than what she really is. From my perspective I would see her as expressing the passion of Juliet, whereas she may only mean to demonstrate the affection of a housewife-type lover.

Thus, knowing the other person in his or her inmost inwardness runs into difficulties in whatever direction we turn. If I am ecstatically transported into a state of oneness with another, I am faced with the problem of whether I am really knowing her or just myself as transported into a new world of joy and beauty, the beloved's inner self, something which can create a unique state of mind that is hardly conducive to objectivity. And if I withdraw from her inner being, I see the outer person but not necessarily her inner self; and even this outer person from which I distanced myself may be distorted by my own emotionally colored perceptions.

Furthermore, one of the most famous traditional challenges to accurate knowledge of the beloved is that we somehow idealize the beloved, perhaps because our sexual frustrations make her seem more beautiful than she really is, or perhaps because we project the qualities we ourselves lack onto the beloved in order to vicariously possess these qualities. Another apparently less self-interested theory of idealization would simply be that we are so overwhelmed by the beloved that we bestow additional qualities on her as a kind of gift.

The classic statement of this theory comes from Stendhal's theory of idealization, which he labels as "crystallization."[3] He compares our response to the beloved to the dipping of a stripped bough into a salt mine; after a

3. Stendhal (Henri Beyle), *On Love*, trans. supervised by C. K. Scott-Moncrieff (New York: Grosset and Dunlap, 1967), pp. 5, 359-371. The problem with this theory, as will be developed in the text, is whether we first begin with some admiration of the beloved that had an objective basis and then, by being so highly impressed, go on to crystallize her further. Stendhal's example of the beloved as first being like a "stripped bough" before she is crystallized suggests she could not be admired just as she is. She becomes beautiful only after the imagination has done its work, and it is the imagined qualities that are loved and not the person she is. Elsewhere, however, he states that crystallization cannot proceed unless the man or woman is first objectively attractive in some way: "A woman woos the most well-bred man in the world; she soon learns that he has had certain ridiculous physical misfortunes; he immediately becomes unbearable to her. And yet she had never meant to resist him forever and these secret misfortunes do not affect his intelligence or charm in any way. *It is simply that crystallization has been made impossible*" (pp. 28-29; italics mine).

period it emerges covered with beautiful crystals. But if love is like this, then the security of the beloved clearly rests on her continuing to be seen as being "crystallized"; she would likely be abandoned if she returned to being seen as Stendhal's stripped bough.

The major difficulty with theories of idealization or overestimation of the beloved's qualities, however, is that we simply do not idealize just anyone. If the idealization theory held that we begin with someone who already fascinates us in an objective way and that we then idealize her further, there would be no problem. But some writers seem to suggest that it is the idealized qualities alone that we love. If this were true, it would seem as if we could idealize anyone, no matter how objectively unattractive he or she may be in a physical or spiritual sense. The individual would become just an excuse to indulge our imaginative powers, and he or she would merely be like a piece of ugly clay to mold into a beautiful shape of our own making.

The reply to this view, however, is that we do not ordinarily idealize just anyone: Romeo would not have idealized Juliet's grandmother, for example. This means that we already know what the beloved is like to some extent. If this is so, then the idealization theory could not itself be used as a proof that love is totally blind, for some knowledge of what the beloved is actually like is presupposed by the theory. Indeed, some might argue that the crystals on Stendhal's bough, rather than blinding us to the beloved's true qualities, actually serve as a kind of magnifying power that allows one to see the beloved's qualities more clearly.

In summary, what can we say of the conflicting claims that, on the one hand, erotic love is at least to some extent blind, and, on the other hand, that erotic love possesses some unique power of discovering the unique inner nature of the beloved or certain other qualities which a detached, objective observer would never notice? It is doubtlessly true that the beloved's response to her lover, blind or not, may very well cause him to see himself in a very different light and thus give him the confidence to actualize certain qualities which he only potentially possessed. As for the claim that love is utterly blind, this seems to be refuted by the fact that no twenty-year-old is going to blindly fall in love with someone who is ninety years old. Furthermore, despite the fact that in the initial stages of love even the beloved's bad qualities may be viewed

---

On the other hand, he writes: "Ah! I understand," said Ghita; "the moment you begin to be interested in a woman, you no longer see her *as she really is,* but as you want her to be . . ." (p. 368).

Yet he also notes that crystallization brings forth in the lover's eyes qualities which the woman possesses and which others cannot see: "Signora, this young man discovers qualities in you which we, your old friends, have never noticed. We could never, for instance, see in you an air of tender and sympathetic kindness" (p. 368).

Thus, Stendhal seems confused as to just what his theory of cystallization implies, although his overall view seems to be that the beloved must first be objectively admirable in some way before crystallization can begin. This seems to be confirmed by his famous list of steps by which love is born: admiration, one's saying to oneself, "How delightful to kiss her," hope, the birth of love, and finally crystallization (p. 5). Crystallization, Stendhal suggests, is simply a way in which we can increase our pleasure in being in the presence of someone who seems more beautiful than he or she actually is. But the concept of *increasing* one's pleasure means that one found the beloved in some way a pleasure to behold in the first place.

as lovable, the fact that love so often comes to an end when the beloved's bad qualities outweigh the good ones presupposes that one eventually comes to have some objective knowledge of what the beloved is like. (The exception would be when someone projects his own self-hate onto another and sees bad qualities in the beloved that are really his own.)

But if love is not utterly blind, can it claim to have some unique power of knowing the beloved's inner nature by uniting with the beloved in some quasi-mystical way? If this unique power of knowing means simply that one can empathize with another and, say, feel what the other is feeling, then such empathy is by no means the sole possession of lovers. And if one argues that one is somehow "in" the lover in some deeper sense such that lover and beloved somehow become one being, then it is far from clear that this peculiar state is going to reveal anything about one's beloved. For if the lover and beloved became, as it were, one being and all distinction between knower and who is known vanished, how would one know whether he has discovered anything about his beloved or only about himself? Or even worse, would one only have discovered something about some mysterious new composite of lover and beloved, such that knowledge of each in his or her own uniqueness would be obliterated?

Finally, it should be noted that knowledge is not a sufficient condition for love, since one can know someone quite well whom one hates. Nor do all persons think that knowledge, or at least complete knowledge, is a necessary condition for love. In contrast to the sober realist, the romantic prefers to veil his beloved under a cloak of illusion and mystery, things which he thinks create a mystique that heightens and prolongs love's ecstasy. The desire to have an accurate knowledge of one's beloved may be thought to be necessary if one is to love a person for his or her own sake, and not just an illusory being. But the desire to know one's beloved is not necessarily an expression of tender regard for the beloved's welfare; it may only be a way of checking to see if one's beloved is going to be, as it were, a "good deal" in the marketplace of love.

4
Is Love Benevolent? Fromm, Plato, and Aristotle

For most persons it would indeed be odd to say that one loved somebody or something if they didn't in some way care for it or show concern for its welfare. Indifference is marked by neglect, hatred by destruction, but love, it is said, must be essentially benevolent. In this section I will examine the theories of Fromm and Aristotle which make benevolence an essential ingredient of true love. However, neither Fromm nor Aristotle believe that true giving can come from a self-hating, self-sacrificial slave who has no concern for his or her own interests. Aristotle and Fromm both hold the view that we treat others in the way we view ourselves, and that only those who love and respect themselves can truly love others. Of course, self-love entails the fact that one also has certain obligations to one's own self-interests. It will, therefore, be interesting to see how Fromm and Aristotle can reconcile concern for one's obligations to oneself and one's obligations to others and prove that we are truly generous to others and not simply acting out of enlightened self-interest when we serve them. Finally, I will compare Aristotle's theory of love with that of his teacher, Plato; for Plato has often been criticized for holding a self-interested view of love that is diametrically opposed to that of his famous pupil.

Let us first examine Erich Fromm's philosophy of love found in his widely read *The Art of Loving* (New York: Harper & Row, 1956). For Fromm, love arises out of what is apparently a self-interested motive: the need to escape one's isolation and loneliness. He writes: "The awareness of human separation, without reunion by love, is the source of shame. It is at the same time the source of guilt and anxiety. The deepest need of man, then, is to overcome his separateness, to leave the prison of his aloneness" (p. 8). Many persons try to escape their anxiety at being alone by other routes than love; but Fromm claims none of these other methods will provide a real solution. "The unity achieved in productive work is not interpersonal, the unity achieved in orgiastic or sexual fusion is transitory; the unity achieved by social conformity is only a pseudo-unity" (p. 15). He claims that the only real answer lies in a love, which he characterizes as an "interpersonal fusion" with another human being.

Fromm goes on to argue, however, that this union with another commonly takes two forms: An immature symbiotic union and a mature union where each person retains his own individuality. The concept of symbiotic union derives from the biological relationship of the pregnant mother to the fetus where there is a physical relationship of complete dominance and dependence. In symbiotic forms of love, the dominance-dependence syndrome occurs on the psychological level. One form is the passive or quasi-masochistic person who tries to overcome his separateness by completely surrendering his individuality to another. Such a person "makes himself part and parcel of another person who directs him, guides him, protects him" (p. 16). The active or quasi-sadistic person, however, "wants to escape from his loneliness and his sense of imprisonment by making another person part and parcel of himself. He inflates and enhances himself by incorporating another person who worships him. The sadistic person is as dependent on the submissive person as the latter is on the former; neither can live without the other. The difference is only that the sadistic person commands, exploits, hurts, and humiliates, and the masochistic person is commanded, exploited, hurt, humiliated" (pp. 16–17).

In contrast with symbiotic union, true love for Fromm occurs when there is a fusion of two human beings who nevertheless preserve their own integrity and individuality. "In love the paradox occurs that two beings become one and yet remain two" (p. 17). Indeed, Fromm refuses to call the sado-masochistic form of love a kind of love at all. One might have thought that those who operate within a framework of dividing so-called sick or immature forms of love from what they think are healthy forms of love would have granted that love is love, even though it may take varying forms. (Similarly, there is good music and bad music, yet both are kinds of music.) But for Fromm love is union with integrity and benevolence, and nothing else counts as love. But if love is a desire to overcome one's separateness, then the symbiotic relationship he condemns does achieve this goal and should thus be considered a kind of love. Nor does he consider the possibility that union with another and benevolence may only be the result of love, and that love may manifest itself in many other ways that violate Fromm's moral ideals (Consider the example I mentioned earlier of the professor and his wife in *Who's Afraid of Virginia Woolf?*).

A further difficulty with his theory thus far is his picture of those who seek love: They seem to be forlorn beings who desperately fear being alone and who can only find relief in what Fromm calls "interpersonal fusion" with another. But this is precisely a description of persons who are very insecure and who naturally seek the symbiotic relationship Fromm condemns. Indeed, Fromm's phrase "interpersonal fusion" seems to describe a relationship where each surrenders his individuality rather than retain it as his theory requires.

Furthermore, Fromm constantly emphasizes the claim that one must first love oneself before one can love another. And at a later point in his book he writes: "Indeed, to be able to concentrate means to be able to be alone with oneself and this ability is precisely a condition for the ability to love. If I am attached to another person because I cannot stand on my own feet, he or she may be a lifesaver, but the relationship is not one of love. Paradoxically the ability to be alone is the condition for the ability to love."[4] But how does Fromm's original picture of the motivation for love fit with this requirement? Fromm originally stated that people come to love each other because they cannot bear the anxiety of separateness and can only find relief from their insecurity by interpersonal fusion with another person. But such persons clearly do not meet Fromm's requirement that one must first love oneself before one can truly love and not merely use another person to overcome one's anxiety-producing isolation.[5] Thus there is no possible way that the healthy loving relationship Fromm wants could ever begin if one accepts his original description of the motivation for interpersonal fusion with another.

Fromm might argue that those who love each other somehow eventually overcome their insecurity and are able to love themselves and stand on their own two feet as the result of being loved. But if one must be loved in order to have any sense of self-respect, this is hardly a description of a mature individual who can stand on his or her own two feet and who can love another without being a clinging vine. Indeed, it is far from clear that a self-loving, secure individual would want or need the kind of interpersonal fusion with another Fromm describes. Although Fromm insists that productive, creative activity cannot be a true substitute for loving a person, he overlooks the

---

4. Ibid., p. 94. Elsewhere he writes: "Love as mutual sexual satisfaction and love as 'teamwork' and as a *haven from aloneness* are the two normal forms of the distintegration of love in modern Western society" (p. 79; italics mine).

5. There is a further difficulty in deriving the concept of self-love Fromm's theory requires. If love is union or interpersonal fusion with another, how does one define love of oneself? (One obviously does not unite with oneself.)

many scientists, artists, and philosophers down through the ages who have lived quite fulfilling lives even though they often led a relatively isolated existence. Fromm spends pages glorifying family living and a mother's love for her children; yet he fails to realize that the creative loner may have left civilization with far more valuable "children," that is immortal scientific or artistic achievements.

Fromm's second criterion for mature love is benevolence. He writes:

> Love is an activity, not a passive effect; it is a "standing in," not a "falling for." In the most general way the active character can be described by stating that he is primarily giving, not receiving. . . . Giving is the highest expression of potency. In the very act of giving, I experience my strength, my wealth, my power. This experience of heightened vitality and potency fills me with joy. . . . In this giving of one's life, he enriches the other person, he enhances the other's sense of aliveness by enhancing his own sense of aliveness. He does not give in order to receive; giving is in itself an exquisite joy. But in giving he cannot help bringing something to life in the other person, and this which is brought to life reflects back to him; in truly giving, he cannot help receiving that which is given back to him . . . *Love is the active concern for the life and growth of that which we love.*[6]

Fromm mentions four characteristics which are essential to benevolence: *care, responsibility, respect,* and *knowledge.* Care is his key concept, for it is the "active concern for the life and growth of the beloved" (p. 22). The other characteristics are viewed as necessary conditions for caring; responsibility means being able and ready to respond to the needs of another. But responsibility without respect for the other person's own individuality could deteriorate into domination and possessiveness. Respect means that the other person should grow and unfold as he or she is. And knowledge is necessary if one is to know the beloved's needs and thus be able to respond to them.[7]

In developing his theory of benevolence, Fromm claims that giving is somehow an inevitable outgrowth of one's love for oneself and that one will

---

6. Ibid, pp. 20–22. Other benevolence theories include Otto Fenichel's claim that "one can speak of love only when consideration of the object goes so far that one's own satisfaction is impossible without satisfying the object." Fenichel's criterion makes one so dependent on making the beloved happy that it comes perilously close to having a self-enslaving quality. (*The Psychoanalytic Theory of Neurosis,* New York: W. W. Norton, 1945, p. 84). Rollo May defines love "as a delight in the presence of the other person and as affirming his value and development as much as one's own." (*Man's Search for Himself,* New York, 1953, p. 241).

7. Fromm also thinks that love provides a unique form of knowledge of the beloved. He writes: "The basic need to fuse with another person so as to transcend the prison of one's separateness is closely related to another specifically human desire, that to know the secret of man. . . . Love is active penetration of the other person, in which my desire to know you is stilled by union. In the act of fusion I know you, I know myself, I know everybody" (pp. 24–25). Fromm compares this unique form of knowledge to a mystic's union with God. Yet these quotations which reveal a desire for a quasi-mystical oneness with one's beloved are hardly compatible with his earlier claim that mature lovers must be one but yet two independent beings. The beloved's individuality seems to disappear completely when Fromm speaks of his act of fusing with another in order to acquire this unique knowledge of the beloved's inwardness.

necessarily treat others as one views oneself. He then argues that self-love is to be distinguished from selfishness. The selfish individual, he claims, does not really love himself at all and is obsessed with grabbing things for himself to try to fill his own inner emptiness and overcome his self-hate. He also argues that if one can love *only* others, but not oneself, then one cannot really love at all. Those who claim that they are purely unselfish and live only for others while caring nothing for themselves are only disguising their own self-hatred and their subconscious hatred for mankind, which is a projection of their own self-contempt. Their service to mankind is simply a means of trying to overcome their self-contempt and to assuage their guilt for secretly hating those they serve.

Finally, Fromm argues that one cannot really love an individual unless one has a brotherly love for all mankind. A lack of respect for mankind is a projection of one's own lack of self-respect onto others, and such a person will treat his beloved in the way he views himself and others. Similarly, a male who does not love (that is, respect) all womankind does not suddenly cease to be a sexist male when he is in love with a particular woman. He may, for a while, be overwhelmed by the emotions of love and treat his beloved as if she were a goddess; but this only means that his sexism has temporarily been pushed into his subconscious mind, and sooner or later it will manifest itself when the initial romantic glow has evaporated. Brotherly love for all mankind or "love thy neighbor as thyself," is thus the most basic form of love for Fromm, and must underlie all other forms of love if the latter are to be worthy of being called love.

Although I would not myself wish to deny that some persons are benevolent, it is not clear that Fromm's way of defending benevolence will work. The concept that regard for others rests on love for oneself is, for example, fraught with many dangers. This becomes evident when Fromm writes that "giving is the highest expression of potency. In the very act of giving I experience *my* strength, *my* wealth, *my* power. The expression of heightened vitality fills *me* with joy. . . . In truly giving *he* cannot help receiving that which is given back to *him*" (p. 20-21; italics mine). Nietzsche, however, would argue that my experiencing my strength, wealth, and power is merely a sign of the fundamental will to power in all of us, and that the giver secretly wills to be exalted when he serves others.[8] And an egoist would note with interest how Fromm constantly appeals to our own self-interest in urging us to be benevolent. (One thinks of the familiar warning: "Drive safely; for the life you save may be your own.")

Fromm does, of course, require some degree of self-interest to be present in the giver; for he has already argued that the purely self-sacrificial person is a self-hating masochist who secretly despises others. But once one has

---

8. Such motives, of course, often exist largely on the subconscious level, a terrain Fromm does not explore adequately. Although he praises mother-love, for example, as one of the purest forms of benevolence, he never answers the claim made by Plato and countless others that having children is primarily motivated by the parents' desire for immortality. Fromm, a psychoanalyst, of all people should be aware that what we consciously feel our motives are and what our real motives might be need not coincide.

admitted that self-love involves self-interest, how does one know that one is not actually giving in order to get? Fromm, of course, would argue that one's increased joy, potency, and vitality are merely the rewards, but not the motives for giving. But what if one found that one's joy, potency, and vitality were being drained instead of enhanced by giving? Would such a person still continue to give? If one has to sacrifice his life for his lover or for mankind, how does this enhance one's joy, potency, and vitality or fulfill Fromm's claim that "in truly giving he cannot help receiving that which is given back to him?" (A Christian would argue that the one who sacrifices his life is rewarded in heaven; but Fromm works within a strictly secular framework.)

Finally, Fromm's claim that our love for others presupposes and is an extension of our love for ourselves makes one wonder if our giving to others is not really an attempt to make others into mirror images of ourselves. Fromm constantly praises the Christian ideal "Love thy neighbor as thyself," but Christians down through the ages have been notoriously prone to want, as it were, to *make* their neighbor like themselves. Either one must worship God or be sentenced to eternal damnation. The notion that giving to others makes them mirrors of ourselves is suggested when Fromm writes: "But in giving he cannot help bringing something to life in the other person, and this which is brought to life *reflects* back to him. . . . If I can say to somebody else, 'I love you,' I must be able to say, 'I love in you everybody, I love through you the world, *I love in you also myself*'" (pp. 20–21, 39; italics mine).

Fromm repeatedly denies that love is only an enlarged egoism, but it is not clear how his theory can avoid it. Indeed, although he insists that each partner should respect the other's individuality, his talk of love as being "interpersonal fusion" does seem to be just such an enlarged egoism, that is, where each partner tries to absorb the other's identity into his own. And his criterion of respect for the other person to develop in his or her own way might require that the beloved leave her mate and develop her potential elsewhere. But Fromm's lovers are motivated by a desperate desire to overcome their separateness; how is the partner who is left behind while his mate goes to New York to become a ballerina going to endure the isolation this will bring him? Won't he insist that she stay with him to overcome what Fromm calls the anxiety of separateness?

Finally, we must see how Fromm is going to reconcile his agapic "love all mankind equally" with erotic love, which he admits to be by its very nature selective and exclusive. Fromm firmly rejects concepts like "falling in love" as being mere infatuation. Since love for Fromm is motivated by a desire to escape one's isolation, he wants to make sure that such a love is going to endure. He writes:

> [Erotic] love is supposed to be the outcome of a spontaneous, emotional reaction, of suddenly being gripped by an irresistible feeling. In this view, one sees only the peculiarities of the two people involved—and not the fact that all men are part of Adam and all women part of Eve. One

neglects to see an important factor in erotic love, that of *will*. To love somebody is not just a strong feeling—it is a decision, it is a judgment, it is a promise. If love were only a feeling, there would be no basis for the promise to love each other forever. A feeling comes and it may go. How can I judge that it will stay forever, when my act does not involve judgment and decision? (p. 47)

Here Fromm runs into the obvious difficulty of trying to combine emotion with commitment and decision. For emotions are not matters of decision, and since Fromm has admitted that feelings can always come and go, no one can make a promise that one's emotions will never change. Thus it seems clear that if Fromm's lovers are looking for the security that permanent commitment provides (a fact that further reveals their insecurity rather than their self-respect), then Fromm is going to have to dispense with emotion altogether. For many this would mean that Fromm would have to push his quest for a so-called sane, enduring relationship to almost insane limits.

The central difficulty with Fromm's concept of erotic love, however, is how he is to reconcile the exclusiveness and selectivity of erotic love with the basic brotherly love that he thinks must underlie all other forms of love. Of brotherly love, he writes:

Brotherly love is love for all human beings; it is characterized by its very lack of exclusiveness. . . . Brotherly love is based on the experience that we are all one. The differences in talents, intelligence, and knowledge are negligible in comparison to the identity of all men (pp. 39-40).

Yet in describing erotic love he writes that one must make a decision, a *judgment*. But when one makes a judgment, isn't one trying to see if this particular person has the qualities that satisfy one's needs? But in brotherly love individual qualities are, he claims, negligible in worth as compared to the identity of all humankind. Indeed, making a judgment also seems to contradict his criterion for respect: "I feel one with him or her but with him *as he is,* not as I need him to be or as an object for my use."[9]

In describing erotic love, Fromm writes:

Erotic love is exclusive, but it loves in the other person all of mankind, all that is alive. It is exclusive only in the sense that I can fuse myself intensely with one person only. Erotic love excludes love of others only in the sense of erotic fusion, full commitment in all aspects of life—but not in the sense of brotherly love. . . . Inasmuch as we all are one, we can love

9. Ibid., p. 24. At the conclusion of his section on erotic love he writes: "The idea of a relationship which can be easily dissolved if one is not successful with it is as erroneous as the idea that under no circumstances must the relationship be dissolved" (p. 48). But if, as Fromm insists, true love is basically love of persons for their own sakes, and not primarily for their pleasing superficial qualities, then love should never cease since persons are always persons until they die.

everybody in the same way in the sense of brotherly love. But inasmuch as we are all also different, erotic love requires certain specific highly individual elements which exist between some people but not between all (pp. 46–47).

It is now clear that selectivity, preferring one person over another because he or she has more erotic qualities than others, has arisen within the framework of treating all humankind as one, with none to be preferred to another except perhaps on the basis of who needs one's help the most. There is, to be sure, nothing wrong with two people working as loving partners in serving mankind, yet Fromm speaks of erotic love as "fusion, commitment in all aspects of life." But if I am this tightly linked to one person, how could I simultaneously serve mankind as well if I had to do so at the expense of my total erotic fusion with and commitment to one person? I may very well, as Fromm says, show my love for mankind in loving my partner, but it would seem to be only in a symbolic way. It is clear, therefore, that Fromm's attempt to reconcile erotic love with benevolent brotherly love is a failure.

In summary, Fromm's method of developing his twin concepts of union and benevolence as definitions of love have led him into a fundamental contradiction. On the one hand, the desire for interpersonal fusion presupposes self-interested "need-love," while his concept of benevolence presupposes persons who are overflowing with brotherly love or "being-love." And the two concepts of need-love and being-love are never adequately reconciled in his book. Indeed, his elaborate, impassioned defense of benevolence certainly indicates that egoism is a very widespread phenomenon if it requires an entire book to defend its opposite. And the fact that his book has had such wide appeal indicates that millions of persons are searching for what they have not found in their own love relationships. Does this indicate that at least erotic love is by its very nature essentially self-interested?

Now that we have examined Fromm's defense of love as benevolence, let us turn to two philosophers of ancient Greece, Plato and his most famous pupil, Aristotle. Plato has often been accused of holding an essentially self-interested theory of love that somehow uses individual persons as mere stepping stones to his desire for a quasi-mystical vision of absolute Beauty and Goodness and the consequent self-fulfillment, happiness and immortality (of a sort) that he claims result from this vision. Aristotle, on the other hand, has been praised because he claims that friends respect each other for their own sakes. Plato's critics charge that he could only love, as it were, mere abstractions and not persons in the full sense of the word at all. Let us first examine Plato's theory as it is found in the *Symposium* and the *Phaedrus* to see if these charges are true. (It should be noted that Plato was not himself particularly concerned with the age-old egoism-benevolence controversy; his main concern was with *what* it is that must be loved if we are to be lovers in the noblest and truest sense of the word.)

In the *Symposium,* Socrates first makes the startling announcement that love is not a god or goddess of some sort, and that love is not itself good and beautiful. Love, he claims, seeks beauty and goodness and thus cannot itself be beautiful or good; for if it were itself already beautiful and good, there would be no reason for it to seek these things. Thus, Socrates' argument shows that he thinks that love seeks beauty because it lacks beauty. And if love is a kind of lack or deficiency in the lover, then the desire to overcome one's deficiency will entail that such love will be essentially self-interested and possibly exploitative of others in some way.

However, if love is neither divine nor beautiful nor good, does it follow that love is therefore mortal, ugly, and evil? Socrates then recalls what a priestess named Diotima (the spokeswoman for Plato's theory) once taught him about love: Because love is not divine or beautiful or good, it does not follow that it is mortal or bad or ugly either. Love is rather a kind of intermediate state between these things in the way that a correct personal opinion not backed by proof is an intermediate state between ignorance and true knowledge. More importantly, although love is not divine and immortal, it is not a merely mortal thing either. Rather it is a kind of intermediary between the mortal and the immortal; that is, *eros* is a drive that prompts man to leave behind for a while the world of mortal, changing, temporal things and is a desire for a vision of that which is immortal, changeless, and outside of space and time. (The vision of the immortal that Diotima had in mind was not that of an immortal person or deity.)

Love, then, is a desire for a vision of absolute Beauty. But why should one desire this vision? Diotima answers that beauty is but one striking instance of what all love is searching for, that is, the possession of what is good and the personal happiness this brings. She says:

> May we then say without qualification that men are in love with what is good? But we must add, mustn't we, that the aim of love is the possession of the good *for themselves?* (Italics mine) . . . And not only its possession, but its perpetual possession? . . . To sum up, then, love is the desire for the perpetual possession of the good. . . . If as we agreed, the aim of love is the perpetual possession of the good, it necessarily follows that we must desire immortality together with the good, . . . and that love is love of immortality as well as of the good.[10]

Thus far, it seems clear that Diotima's theory of love is essentially self-interested. Love primarily seeks one's own good, happiness, and immortality. The way in which love might benefit others will be discussed later when we explore Diotima's further claim that beholding absolute Beauty leaves the philosopher with a desire to procreate, as it were, "spiritual children" and to bring forth immortal beauty of his own into the world.

How does one attain this vision of absolute Beauty to which the noblest kind of love aspires? One first ascends Diotima's "ladder of love" by beginning with the admiration of physical beauty as it exists in one individual.

10. Plato, *The Symposium*, trans. W. Hamilton (Baltimore: Penguin Books, 1951), pp. 86–87.

The common man, overwhelmed by lustful desire for such a beautiful body, never progresses farther than this. The philosopher, however, is inspired by love of this one beautiful body to see that the beauty exhibited in all bodies is one and the same, and will go on to become a lover of all physical beauty. His love of physical beauty will, however, eventually become further sublimated into love of the soul. He will recognize that beauty of soul or moral beauty is far worthier of one's attention than mere physical beauty. But then, Diotima argues, one must leave behind love of persons, be they physically or spiritually beautiful, and ascend to ever more spiritualized and universal concepts of beauty. One must attend to the moral beauty of the laws and institutions of a just and well-ordered society. (Order and harmony were central to the concept of beauty in the Greek world.) One must then engage in a lengthy study of the order and harmony found in various fields of knowledge, such as the sciences. Finally one will reach a point where one can have an intuitive vision not merely of this or that kind of beauty, but of Beauty itself.

Diotima describes ideal Beauty in the following way:

This beauty is first of all eternal; it neither comes into being nor passes away, neither waxes nor wanes; next it is not beautiful in part and ugly in part, nor beautiful at one time and ugly at another, nor beautiful in this relation and ugly in that, nor beautiful here and ugly there, as varying according to its beholders; nor again will this beauty appear to him like the beauty of a face or hands or anything else corporeal, or like the beauty of a thought or a science, or like beauty which has its seat in something other than itself, be it a living thing or the earth or sky or anything else whatever; he will see it as absolute, existing alone with itself, unique, eternal, and all other beautiful things as partaking of it, yet in such a manner that, while they come into being and pass away, it (Beauty) neither undergoes any increase or diminution nor suffers any change.[11]

Furthermore, for Plato beauty and goodness were closely connected. A beautiful thing is one, all of whose parts form an integral, harmonious whole. In *The Republic* Plato states that the good man is one whose nature is a harmonious blend of reason, emotion, and bodily appetites (one of which is sex), with reason being the prevailing force to see that none of the other

11. For Plato, ideal Beauty was only one of his otherworldly absolutes or Forms. A thing is good or just, for example, only to the extent that it approximates ideal Goodness or Justice. Whereas Socrates had sought only for a definition stating that unique quality which enables us, for example, to say what it is that makes all just acts instances of justice, Plato elevated the Socratic definitions into non-corporeal, unchanging entities of some kind. Most persons would consider such concepts as truth, beauty, goodness, manhood, and so forth as mere abstractions or concepts. But for Plato these things were the ultimate realities or archetypes in which a thing is what it is to the extent that it approximates its ideal Form. How, a Platonist might ask, could we claim that the Parthenon is more beautiful than a shack unless we already have some idea of what ideal Beauty is? (In the *Phaedrus* Plato claims that before our souls entered our bodies, they had a vision of these archetypes which we now only dimly recollect in our mortal existence. And a Platonist would argue that it is the memory of what absolute Beauty is like that enables us to know that one thing is more beautiful than another or that two things are equally beautiful.)

aspects of his being control him. A bad man is one who, instead of leading a balanced life of moderation and rational self-control, allows the baser portions of his nature to take control. Thus a Platonist might argue that the vision of ideal Beauty Plato describes would, insofar as one incorporates it into his or her being, lead to what Plato considers moral self-development as well.

At this point a critic might still argue that Plato has merely been interested in persons (and only beautiful persons, at that) as a means of inspiring him to his own self-perfection. A critic would claim that he is interested in persons not as persons, but simply in terms of the beauty they have which inspire him to seek absolute Beauty and leave the world behind. In *The Phaedrus,* for example, Plato remarks that when we see a beautiful person for the first time, that person's beauty inspires us with a kind of divine madness. But this love that is a divine madness is not really for that person himself or herself, but rather occurs because his or her beauty reminds us of the ideal Beauty our souls perceived in the Platonic heaven before we were born as flesh-and-blood mortals. This divine madness or love is, then, not for the person himself, but is a desire to see once again that ideal Beauty our souls once perceived in its pure form in the Platonic heaven. The Platonic lover seems to see not persons but, as it were, to see through them with a desire for a vision of the ideal Beauty of which their own imperfect, mortal beauty is only a reminder and a source of inspiration.

Indeed, when Diotima says at one point: "This above all others, my dear Socrates, is the region where a man's life should be spent, in the contemplation of absolute Beauty," it would seem as if she were advocating an otherworldly existence (p. 94). For certainly one cannot spend one's mortal existence eternally contemplating the Platonic absolute, what with need to eat, sleep, and the like.

Diotima's contempt for the world in which we ordinary mortals live is further revealed when she asks:

> What may we suppose to be the felicity of the man who sees absolute beauty in its essence, pure and unalloyed, who, instead of a beauty tainted by human flesh and color and a mass of perishable rubbish, is able to apprehend divine beauty where it exists apart and alone? (p. 95)

Thus, a critic might argue that the Platonic lover in a way secretly yearns for death so that his soul may return to the Platonic heavens and blissfully spend eternity contemplating Beauty.[12] This otherworldly side of Plato would certainly rule out any possibility of the Platonic lover's being able to be benevolent to others. And one could not be benevolent towards absolute

12. Irving Singer in his *The Nature of Love: Plato to Luther* (New York: Random House, 1966) also argues that the Platonist is seeking a kind of death. He writes: "Indeed, the union (with absolute Beauty) for which Platonic love aspires sounds more like an act of surrender, a yielding up of desire at the moment one is possessed *by* perfection. If *eros* is just a striving to satisfy organic needs, it must die and all desires end once absolute fulfillment has been achieved. This would be the dark side of Plato, true love culminating in self-destruction, the philosophic quest being as suicidal as Socrates' later life often seemed to be. The view presupposes that only in extinction are desires fulfilled, which is a poetic way of expressing love of death (p. 90).

Beauty or the other Platonic Forms since they are already perfect and complete in themselves.

Furthermore, this otherworldly strain in Plato's philosophy where the eternal contemplation of absolute Beauty would seem to be the ideal love violates Plato's insistence in his other works (especially in *The Republic*) that the good or just man is one who does justice to all aspects of his being, including one's reason, emotions, and bodily appetites. But one of these bodily appetites is sex. In the love of Plato's non-corporeal, absolute Beauty, however, one seems to have ascended to a realm where sexuality is left behind completely. And Diotima seems to suggest that even during our mortal existence the perpetual contemplation of Beauty would be the theoretical ideal. "Do you (she asks) think that it would be a poor life that a man leads who has his gaze fixed in that direction, who contemplates absolute Beauty with the appropriate faculty and is in constant union with it?" (p. 95) Thus the desire for the perpetual (and sexless) contemplation of the Platonic forms would contradict Plato's other conception of what a truly just or good man must be like.

Indeed, even if one didn't contemplate Beauty eternally but had only one vision of this otherworldly transcendental glory, would one ever again feel at home with or satisfied by the merely worldly pleasure of sex? Furthermore, if the Platonist were to argue that one should model the more worldly forms of love in terms of Plato's ideal love, then it would seem that we would be left with the view that all love should be devoid of sex. But this would, for example, contradict Plato's apparent defense of homosexual love elsewhere in his dialogues.

Could Plato's theory of love still be benevolent in some way? Irving Singer answers this question with a resounding no. He writes:

> [For Plato] in loving something, man is really seeking to possess the goodness in it. For Plato, as for all the Greeks—as well as Freud and many others—man is basically acquisitive. His life is a continuous search for things that will satisfy, things that fulfill his needs and provide happiness. Man striving, man in motion, man desiring and struggling to achieve the culminating objects of his desire—this is the prime category of Plato's psychology (p. 55).

In the *Symposium,* however, Diotima speaks of two kinds of pregnancy. One kind occurs between those lovers who never pass beyond the first step of the ladder of love. Such persons, attracted only by physical beauty, are thereby inspired in a purely sexual way to procreate mortal children. She makes it clear that their motive for doing so is essentially self-interested: They want to achieve a kind of immortality for themselves through the children they bear.

However, Diotima then adds that there is a higher kind of pregnancy of a spiritual nature. For example, one remembers the immortal plays of Shakespeare, his "spiritual children," as it were, but who remembers the children borne him by his wife? In the Platonic system this nobler kind of pregnancy is typically found in an older, wiser man who has ascended

Diotima's ladder of love and has attained a vision of absolute Beauty and Goodness. A Platonist might argue that one who has achieved this philosophic wisdom no longer loves because of some lack or need as Socrates described earlier. For he has attained the self-interested goal of his earlier *eros* in beholding absolute Beauty and is now, as it were, full and content. Indeed, this fullness is a kind of spiritual pregnancy in which he now desires to procreate beautiful things of his own: immortal children of the spirit, as it were, that are far more lasting in value than mere mortal children. His love, the Platonist might argue, is no longer a kind of deficiency or lack, but a fullness of being in which he desires to share his wisdom with others and to create beautiful things that are reflections of and inspired by his vision of absolute Beauty. (Whether a Platonist could ever be fully content during his mortal existence and thus be totally free of self-interested desire is, however, doubtful. The Platonist, as Diotima's earlier remarks indicated, seems to be content only when he is eternally contemplating Beauty, something which is obviously impossible to do while he lives in this world. This will become evident later when we discuss the philosopher's self-interested desire for immortality.)

For a philosopher, this apparently benevolent desire to share one's bounty might involve developing new philosophical theories of his own. More typically, however, it would take the form of teaching a beloved youth how to attain the same philosophic wisdom he possesses. The Platonic philosopher is, however, quite selective about whom he teaches. The youth must be spiritually beautiful and wise and (hopefully) physically beautiful as well. Like ordinary lovers who are inspired by beauty to procreate mortal children, the Platonic lover who desires to procreate spiritual children is also repelled by ugliness. In *The Phaedrus* Socrates says:

> Every lover (desires) that his beloved should be of a nature like his own god, and when he has won him, he leads him on to walk in the ways of their god (absolute Beauty) and after his likeness, patterning himself thereupon and giving counsel and discipline to the boy. There is no jealousy nor petty spitefulness in his dealings, but his every act is aimed at bringing the beloved to be every whit like unto himself and unto the god of their worship.[13]

Is it true, however, that benevolence is really the motive for the desire to procreate immortal things or to lead others up the ladder of love to behold absolute Beauty so that they may become like oneself? At one point Diotima says: "The object of love, Socrates, is not, as you think, beauty. . . . Now why is procreation the object of love? Because procreation is the nearest thing to perpetuity and immortality that a mortal being can attain. . . . So do not feel surprised that every creature naturally cherishes its own progeny; it is in

13. Plato, *Phaedrus,* trans. R. Hackforth (Cambridge, Cambridge University Press, 1952), p. 100.

order to secure immortality that each individual is haunted by this eager desire and love."[14]

Since Diotima's reference to progency includes both physical children and immortal children of the spirit, it would seem clear that the Platonic philosopher's sharing his bounty with others is still motivated by a self-interested desire for a kind of worldly immortality. Isn't such a philosopher trying to assure his own immortality by educating youth to be like himself? This self-interested motive would, of course, be quite noble if teaching the Platonic view of the world were really a route to the self-perfection of those whom he teaches. But is it really benevolent to teach others that they must use human beings as mere stepping stones to their own self-perfection? (Diotima says that one must "begin with examples of beauty in this world—including the beauty of persons—and *using them as steps* to ascend continually with that absolute Beauty as one's aim" (p. 94; italics mine).

Furthermore, is it benevolent to teach a philosophy to a gifted elite who then claim that only they know what is absolutely beautiful, good, and perfect for everyone? (Plato's *Republic* claims that the ideal society should be ruled by such philosopher-kings and that no dissent is to be tolerated. In this dialogue, as in his other writings, Plato's contempt for the masses of ordinary mortals is obvious.) Finally, despite Diotima's insistence that the beholder of absolute Beauty must bring forth beauty and wisdom into this world, there is the distinctly otherworldly strain in Plato's philosophy which implies that the things of this world, including human beings, are virtually without value as contrasted with the Platonic Forms. It is not human beings, but abstractions such as Beauty, Goodness, and the like that are, in the final analysis, the only things that are worthy of the truest and noblest love for a Platonist. One does not, of course, have to love human beings in order to be benevolent; one can be benevolent towards one's cat. But the Platonic Forms need nothing at all, and one could therefore hardly be benevolent to them.

In summary, Plato's lovers of wisdom are still self-interested in trying to ensure the immortality of their own ideas (that is, their dubious Platonic vision of the world) by teaching them to succeeding generations.

Let us now examine the theory of benevolence found in the philosophy of Plato's most famous pupil, Aristotle. Unlike Plato, Aristotle was very much concerned with the self-interest versus benevolence controversy, and he was eager to show that the truest love must be benevolent. Aristotle was, however, realistic enough to recognize that some self-interest is involved even in the most seemingly pure benevolent relationships. As we shall see, however, his desperate desire to reconcile self-love with benevolence seems to lead to a theory in which self-interest is predominant, his own intentions notwithstanding.

---

14. Plato, *The Symposium*, pp. 87–89. At another point Diotima says: "Do you not see that in that region alone where he sees beauty with the faculty capable of seeing it, he will be able to bring forth not mere reflected images of goodness but true goodness because he will be in contact not with a reflection but with the truth? And having brought forth and nurtured true goodness he will have the privilege of being beloved of God, and becoming, if ever a man can, immortal himself?" (p. 95).

Unlike Plato, Aristotle discusses benevolent love not in terms of eros, but in terms of friendship. He scorned erotic love as a kind of "excess of emotion" which he perhaps thought was too unstable a basis for a lasting commitment to another person. Such a commitment can only occur when a relationship arises as the result of rational choice based on affection rather than erotic desire. And it is a hallmark of friendship, Aristotle argued, that it is based on just such a rational choice of one's partner. In contrasting erotic love with friendship, Aristotle writes:

> Love has the character of an emotion, friendship of a confirmed disposition (a state of character). Thus love can be felt even for lifeless objects; but that reciprocal liking which we call friendship involves deliberate choice, and such choice involves the action of a disposition (that is, it springs from a state of character). Now in wishing the good of their friends for the sake of those friends, men are influenced not by an emotion but by a disposition—a settled state of mind.[15]

In an early work of Plato, however, friendship is subjected to a harsh attack. Aristotle argued that friendship is based on the principle of sharing similar interests and on the partners being fundamentally alike. But Plato attacked this like-attracts-like principle in the following way:

> Can like do any harm or good to like which he could not do to himself, or suffer anything from his like which he would not suffer from himself? And if neither can be of any use to the other how can they feel affection for one another?[16]

Plato is arguing that those who are alike have nothing to contribute to each other since each one already has what the other has. Plato further tries to undermine the possibility of friendship by arguing that the bad cannot love the bad since they would only exploit each other. Nor is a friendship possible between a good man and a bad man since the bad man would still exploit the good man. Thus a true, non-exploitative friendship could arise only between two good persons. But then Plato tries to destroy this remaining definition of friendship by saying:

> But then, again, will not the good, insofar as he is good, be sufficient for himself? Certainly he will. And he who is sufficient wants nothing (including friends) for himself—that is implied in the word sufficient.

---

15. *The Ethics of Aristotle (The Nichomachean Ethics),* trans. J. A. K. Thompson (Baltimore, Md., Penguin Books, 1953), p. 237. Aristotle's philosophy of friendship is found primarily in Books VII and VIII of *The Nichomachean Ethics.*

16. *The Lysis* from *The Dialogues of Plato,* trans. Benjamin Jowett (London, Sphere Books, 1970), pp. 86–87. It should be noted that *The Lysis* is an early, exploratory dialogue that perhaps does not represent Plato's final views on the subject.

And he who wants nothing will feel affection for nothing. Neither can he love that for which he has no affection. And he who loves not is not a lover or friend. What place is there for any friendship at all between good men if, even when absent, they do not feel the loss of one another (for even when alone they are sufficient unto themselves) and when present have no use of one another? How can such persons ever value another?[17]

Thus, Plato concludes that since persons who are alike have nothing to contribute to each other (for each one already has what the other has), and since good persons do not need each other (for both are self-sufficient), friendship is impossible. (It should be noted that Plato's arguments against the possibility of friendship again reveal a self-interested concept of love. For in discussing friendship between like persons and two persons who are equally good, he makes it clear that he thinks no affection can arise unless each partner can first see that there is some way in which the other partner could benefit him.)

Aristotle would agree with Plato's reasons for holding that a true, non-exploitative friendship would have to occur between two good or just persons. The Christian idea that one should love all human beings, be they good or evil, or that one should befriend a sinner and try to make him better is completely foreign to both Plato and Aristotle. For them, true love or friendship is highly selective and is given only to those who merit it in terms of the nobility of their character, their wisdom, and the like. Aristotle, however, would utterly reject Plato's dour conclusion in *The Lysis* that there is no philosophical basis on which to justify any form of friendship. For he thought that man was essentially a social creature, and that a life devoid of friendship would be worthless. Nor did he think that those who were alike had nothing to contribute to each other: The delight in sharing common interests is one obvious benefit. Nor would Aristotle agree with Plato's claim that a good man (or even a perfectly good man) is somehow self-sufficient and never needs the aid and comfort of a friend. The only beings that are totally self-sufficient, he would argue, are the gods.

Aristotle divides friendships into three kinds: friendships of pleasure, utility, and virtue. The only true friendship is that of virtue where the two friends love each other for their own sakes and not primarily for what each can get from the other. Such friendships, he argued, are quite rare, while the vast majority of friendships are of the inferior kind based on pleasure and utility. Friendships of pleasure occur between those who find each other witty or fun to be with, and such friendships dissolve as soon as one no longer finds the friend entertaining. The focus of such a so-called friendship is not on the friend as a person, but strictly in terms of how much pleasure he or she can

---

17. Ibid., p. 87. Plato's theory that the good man is somehow self-sufficient is perhaps based on his definition of a good or just man as being one, all of whose aspects of his inner being are in harmony with each other. A man of moderation and rational self-control has a kind of inner balance or, as it were, an inner gyroscope that allows him to be autonomous and secure within himself. Or perhaps he feels that the good man is one who has ascended the ladder of love and has modeled himself after the self-sufficient archetypes of absolute Goodness and Beauty.

provide. Friendships of utility are formed on the expectation of some material gain one can expect from the relationship. A typical example would be that of an ambitious businessman who befriends influential persons who will be able to help him up the ladder to financial success. Both friendships of pleasure and utility operate on a strict quid pro quo basis, and they are highly unstable since such friends will be dropped as soon as the relationship ceases to fulfill one's own self-interest. In describing these two inferior forms of friendship, Aristotle writes:

> Thus friends who have been brought together by a feeling that they will profit by their association do not love one another for their personal qualities, but only so far as they are useful to one another. It is much the same with those whose friendship is inspired by pleasure they have in each others' society. Thus the company of witty persons is agreeable, not because of what they are in themselves, but because they are agreeable to us. This means that when a friendship is founded on the expectation of some advantage to be received, what the friends are thinking of is their own good; when it is based on the expectation of pleasure, they are thinking of what is good for themselves. Their affection is not for the object of their affection as such. These two forms of friendship are then grounded on an inessential factor—an "accident"—because in them the friend is not loved for being what he is in himself, but as the source, perhaps of some pleasure, perhaps of some advantage.[18]

The only true friendship, however, is what Aristotle calls the friendship of virtue. He describes it in the following way:

> But it is only between those who are good, and resemble one another in their goodness, that friendship is perfect. Such friends are both good in themselves and, so far as they are good, desire the good of one another. But is it those who desire the good of their friends for their friends' sake who are most completely friends, since each loves the other for what the other is in himself and not for something he has about which he need not love (p. 233).

Aristotle, however, immediately adds the following disturbing comment: "Accordingly the friendship of such men lasts as long as they keep their goodness—and goodness is a lasting quality."[19] But what if one's friend loses his goodness? That good men can turn bad is certainly not unheard of. Aristotle's good man would, of course, try to rescue his friend from evil. But what if he failed to do so? Aristotle then holds that the friendship must end. But wouldn't someone who loves another as a person and not just for

18. *The Ethics of Aristotle,* pp. 231-32.

19. Ibid. Aristotle's reason for insisting that one's friend must remain good is that no good man can love that which is evil.

his or her virtuous qualities continue to be friends with someone who has gone astray?

An Aristotelian would criticize Plato for viewing persons only in terms of their beauty and using their beauty as an inspiration to leave persons behind altogether and contemplate absolute Beauty. But while Aristotle has no concern for absolute Beauty, it would seem as if he, too, were in love not with total persons for their own sake, but were in love primarily with their goodness. Aristotelian friendship thus resembles a kind of miniature National Honor Society to which one is admitted if one has the proper character references, and from which one is expelled if one violates its norms for virtue. Loving a person on the basis of his goodness or merits rather than for what he is as a human being is also suggested when Aristotle writes: "So the kind of friends who stay friends, and whose friendship is lasting, are those who give to each other that amount of affection *which is proportionate to their deserts*" (p. 243; italics mine). The link between one's goodness and the amount of affection one merits is further revealed when he argues that one who is more virtuous or noble than his friend should receive a greater amount of affection from the latter:

> But in all those relationships where the parties are not on the same footing it is necessary that the feeling between them should be equalized according to a ratio or proportion. That is to say, the more virtuous friend should receive more affection than he bestows, and so should the more useful, and in every case that which has superiority. It is when the superior is balanced by an equivalent amount of affection that we get in a manner that equality which, as agreed, is the essence of friendship (p. 242).

It is clear, therefore, that those who define benevolence in terms of loving a person for his or her own sake, regardless of whether or not he or she merits love, will reject Aristotle's concept of a perfect friendship as being truly benevolent. To be sure, most persons want to be loved at least in part because they feel they merit affection; they do not want a merely charitable love. But this desire is, of course, self-interested. As Aristotle writes in another context: "But those who desire to be honoured by the good and the wise are really seeking to be confirmed in the favourable opinion they have of themselves."[20] However, he then adds: "It is different with affection, which men like to receive for its own sake." But is it really the case that those who seek affection do so for its own sake? Aristotle, while often vehemently claiming that his virtuous form of

---

20. Ibid., p. 240. Freud also links love with merit, and argues that the claim of universal benevolence implied in the commandment "Thou shalt love thy neighbor as thyself" is unsound. He writes: "My love is something valuable to me which I ought not to throw away without reflection. It imposes duties on me for which I must be ready to make sacrifice. *If I love someone he must deserve it in some way.* . . . He deserves it if he is so like me in important ways that I can love myself in him, and he deserves it if he is so much more perfect than myself that I can love my ideal of my own self in him. Indeed it would be wrong to (love a stranger who does not merit love) for my love is valued by all my own people as a sign of preferring them, and it is an injustice to them if I put a stranger on a par with them. (*Civilization and Its Discontents,* New York: W. W. Norton, 1961, pp. 56-57; italics mine.)

friendship is benevolent, nevertheless makes repeated reference to the self-interest of the partners who seek this noblest form of affection. At one point Aristotle notes that when two friends start to become dissimilar, as when one remains a manual laborer and the other becomes a doctor, it is only natural that they will cease to be friends. For friendship, Aristotle argues, is based on the principle that "like attracts like." Should one person therefore exercise his benevolence and try to help his friend become better than he is? Aristotle seems to think that one should not do so, for one then risks losing the friend. He writes:

> But when a great gulf is fixed, as between God and man, there can be no friendship. This has given rise to the question whether it is a mistake to say that friends wish the greatest of goods for each other. . . . If they do cherish such wishes for them, they will no longer have them for friends, and so shall not have certain goods, for friends are goods. They will thus be defeating the very object of their wishes. If then we were right in saying that a friend, truly so-called, wishes his friend well for that friend's sake, we are bound to conclude that the *latter must continue to be exactly the sort of person that he is.* Therefore he will content himself with wishing for his friends the greatest goods available to a human being. *And perhaps not all of these. For everybody who forms a wish thinks first of himself* (p. 241; italics mine).

Here, the self-interested need to hold on to a friend reveals itself most strikingly. For apparently Aristotle will benefit his friend only up to a certain point; beyond that he will not wish for him all the greatest goods available to a human being lest his friend become so much loftier in station that they will no longer have anything in common. In trying to keep the friend just as he is, Aristotle (as the last sentence grants) is admitting that a friend thinks of himself first in trying to hold on to his friend even at the expense of the development of one's friend into a higher status than he possesses.

Furthermore, although Aristotle has relegated friendships of pleasure to an inferior status, he makes it clear that any form of friendship (including friendships of virtue) must yield *mutual* satisfaction. He writes:

> The ability of grim and elderly persons to make friends is limited by the fact that they tend to be cross-grained and take small pleasure in society; for it is qualities just the opposite of these that are most amiable and most apt to win friendship. Hence the young strike up friendships quickly but not the old, *for one does not make friends with people whose company gives us no satisfaction.* And much the same may be said of morose persons (p. 238; italics mine).

And although he had condemned the "you scratch my back and I'll scratch yours" aspect of the inferior friendships of utility and pleasure, Aristotle comes perilously close to asserting a quid pro quo aspect to friendships of virtue, as well. He writes: "This, then, is the perfect form of friendship both on account of the time it lasts and because it has all the other good points of a friendship. In every way each friend—*as between friends is only proper*—receives from the other the same or like advantages."[21]

An Aristotelian might, however, argue that the satisfaction and advantages demanded of the friendship virtue are perfectly innocent since the satisfaction in such a relationship is found primarily in giving rather than receiving benefits. Aristotle writes:

> Now friendship surely consists in giving rather than accepting affection. Think, for example, of the joy that mothers have in loving their children. Sometimes they give them out to nurse, still knowing and loving them, but not asking to be loved in return if they cannot have that too (p. 242).

Yet it is not clear just how benevolent this or the other forms of giving are for Aristotle. Of parents he writes: "It is certain that parents love their offspring as themselves in the sense that one's offspring is *a kind of second self*" (p. 250; italics mine). Elsewhere, he describes every friend as a kind of alter ego. Since Aristotle's entire concept of friendship rests on the idea that "like attracts like," he is now faced with a familiar criticism of this principle: that each partner is narcissistically viewing the other as a mirror image of himself or herself. That is, when one speaks of one's friend as a second self, one is immediately open to the charge that he gives to his friend only because he loves the image of himself in the other. Loving others then becomes merely a circuitous route to loving oneself, and giving to others is really giving to what is only an extension of oneself.

Aristotle himself repeatedly points out that when two friends become too dissimilar, the relationship will end. And the egoist would argue that this is not merely because that they no longer have any shared interests; it is rather that dissimilar persons end their friendship because each can no longer see the other as a reflection of or an enlargement of his or her own self. (If the like attracts like principle is open to the charge of narcissism, it does not follow that the claim that opposites attract avoids egoism either. For with opposites, each partner may only be trying to get from the other in some vicarious way what he or she lacks. A familiar example is the attraction between an ugly, but powerful male and a beautiful, but insecure female.)

In developing his theme that a friend is a kind of alter ego, Aristotle opens with a claim that Fromm developed as well: that the love for others is derived from self-love. He writes:

> The characteristic elements in our friendship for our neighbours . . . seem to have their origin in the sympathetic feelings we have for ourselves. . . .

---

21. Ibid., p. 234; italics mine. In *The Topics,* however, Aristotle writes that we "prize friendship for itself, even though nothing else is likely to come to us from it."

The good man wishes whatever things are good for himself . . . and seeks to realize them in his actions, the good man showing his character in this, that he labors to establish the good. And this he does for his own sake, that is, for the intellectual part of his being, which is, we believe, the essential man. Again he desires his own life and safety, more especially that of the rational part of his soul. For existence is good in the eyes of the good man, and everyone desires his own good. No man would choose to have all the blessings in the world as his own at the price of becoming somebody else. . . . It is then because the good man has these (benevolent) feelings towards himself, and because he feels towards his friend as he feels towards himself—for a friend is a second self—that friendship can be regarded as an expression of one of these feelings, and friends as those who experience them. . . . To which we may add that devoted attachment to someone else comes to resemble love for oneself (pp. 266–67).

Here the threat to the concept of serving others for their own sake is clearly revealed in the claim that one must first love oneself before one can become a lover or that love for others is but an extension of love for oneself. Aristotle seems to imply that the concept of self-love entails the claim that one has obligations primarily to oneself. For example, Aristotle mentions the obligation to preserve one's own existence. ("For existence is good in the eyes of the good man, and *everyone desires his own good*"; italics mine). But this would seem to conflict with the claim that benevolence may have to involve sacrificing one's life to save another's life.

Furthermore, Aristotle's remarks indicate that he feels one is benevolent primarily because he regards his friend as an alter ego, and that loving one's alter ego is merely a way of loving oneself or an enlarged self. ("Devoted attachment to someone else comes to resemble love for oneself.") But benevolence surely means that one should aid another because he or she is a human being and not merely because he or she resembles oneself and thus qualifies to be a "second self."

Thus, linking self-love to benevolence faces an apparent dilemma: On the one hand, one who has no love for himself will treat others as he treats himself, that is, with indifference or contempt. On the other hand, if it is claimed that one must first love oneself before one can love others, those who love themselves seem to have obligations primarily to themselves. Their love for others is an extension of their love for themselves, but this seems to imply that in loving others they are really only loving themselves. And this means that they could not love others (or at least love others as friends) unless they could see in them their own self-image. (As we noted earlier, Aristotle repeatedly insists that in friendship, one can only like one who is like oneself.)

Let us conclude our discussion of Aristotle by noting his classic attempt to try to overcome the difficulties mentioned above and to somehow reconcile self-love with benevolence to one's own friend for his or her own sake. He begins, once again, by defending self-love:

The good man is supposed to never act except on some lofty principle . . . and to neglect his own interests to promote that of his friend. It is a view which is not borne out by the facts. Nor need this surprise us. It is common ground that a man should love his best friend most. But my best friend is the man who in wishing me well wishes it for my sake, whether this shall come to be known or not. Well, there is no one who fulfills this definition so well as I do in my behaviour towards myself. . . . For a man is his own best friend. From this it follows that he ought to love himself best (p. 274).

But Aristotle then tries to link self-love with benevolence to others by distinguishing between two types of self-love. One is the vulgar self-lover who greedily seeks money, sexual pleasure, and fame; the vulgar self-lover seeks only to gratify his baser instincts. The noble self-lover, however, seeks only his own moral self-perfection by performing acts which benefit and ennoble others. The noble self-lover is, of course, self-interested in that he seeks to become a man of honor, a man of virtuous nobility. Aristotle writes:

But there is something else which we can say about the truly good man. Many of his actions are performed to serve his friends or his country, even if this should involve dying for them. For he is eager to sacrifice wealth, honours, all the prizes of life in his eagerness to play a noble part. He would prefer one crowded hour of glorious life to a protracted existence and mild enjoyment spent as an ordinary man would spend it—one great and dazzling achievement to many small successes. And surely this may be said of those who lay down their life for others; *they choose for themselves a crown of glory.* It is also a characteristic of the good man that he is prepared to lose money on condition that his friends get more. The friend gets the cash and he gets the credit (for being virtuous), *so that he is assigning the greater good to himself.* . . . It is natural then that people should think him virtuous, when he prefers honor to everything else. He may even create opportunities for his friend to do a fine action which he might have done for himself, and this may be the noble course for him to take. Thus in the whole field of admirable conduct we see the good man *taking the larger share of moral dignity.* In this sense, as I said before, it is right that he should be self-loving. But in the vulgar sense no one should be so (p. 276; italics mine).

Has Aristotle succeeded in reconciling self-interest with benevolence? Is seeking "a crown of glory" any less self-interested than is seeking money or sex? Is Aristotle's noble self-lover any different from a student who performs virtuous actions so that he may be elected to the National Honor Society? If one's actions are to be truly noble, they must surely be done for their own sake or at least be done primarily to benefit others and only secondarily to ennoble oneself or to enhance one's feeling of self-esteem. But one gets the impression from the preceding quotation that one benefits others primarily because one's own "honor" is at stake. At one point he writes: "Therefore it is right for the *good* man to be self-loving, because he will thereby himself be benefited by performing fine actions." Then, almost as an afterthought, he adds: "And by the same process he will be helpful to others" (p. 276).

However, if one's actions were not meant primarily to benefit others for their own sake, then they would be a self-interested form of self-aggrandizement, and one could not claim to be a man of honor or virtuous nobility. To be sure, Aristotle elsewhere repeatedly insists that one wishes one's friends well for their own sake. A defender of Aristotle might then argue that his man of honor is seeking honor only as a byproduct of his benefiting others. But then one is still faced with the fact that what we think our motives are and what our motives really are need not coincide. And Aristotle's description of the man of honor in the preceding quotation certainly gives one reason to think that his motives are essentially self-interested, whether he may himself realize it or not.

5

Can We Distinguish Love from Infatuation and Friendship?

In this section I will try the device of trying to become clearer about the nature of erotic love by attempting, if possible, to distinguish love from infatuation and friendship. Many people agree that it is, indeed, often impossible to say where friendship ends and love begins; on the other hand, most people are quite confident that there are important differences between love and infatuation. Could it be possible, however, that those who accuse others of being merely infatuated or those who later say they were just infatuated "all along" are mistakenly presupposing that there is some one thing called "true love" and that whatever deviates from this is infatuation?

Let us first see if we can distinguish love from infatuation. Suppose, for example, that lucious Lolita, aged sixteen, "falls for" a middle-aged teacher. Her mother would insist that this is only an immature, irrational "crush" that she soon will outgrow, as soon as she becomes more "realistic and mature." And while her mother would insist that Lolita's apparent infatuation is not love at all, there still remains the possibility that it is a *kind of love,* albeit perhaps an immature or blind or irrational one. Of course, if there is an element of blindness and irrationality in most forms of erotic love, then the distinction between love and infatuation would be a matter of degree, at best.

There is the further possibility that when someone says, "You're not in love; you're just infatuated," they may be trying to "put down" a love affair of which they are subconsciously jealous. Or when those who think that love, like God, is perfect come across an unhappy love or some imperfection love has, there may be a tendency to defend love by saying that such flaws belong to infatuation and not to true love at all. But this would be an attempt to hide love's flaws by simply transferring them to a different concept.

Let us quote a letter to "Dear Abby" that professed to know the precise difference between the two concepts:

1. Infatuation leaps into bloom. Love usually takes root slowly and grows with time.
2. Infatuation is accompanied by a sense of uncertainty. You are stimulated and thrilled, but not really happy. You are miserable when he is absent, and you can't wait to see him again.
3. Love begins with a feeling of security. You are warm with a sense of his nearness, even when he is away. . . . You want him near, but near or far, you know he's yours and you can wait.
4. Infatuation says: "We must get married right away. I can't risk losing him." Love says: "Don't rush into anything. You are sure of one another. You can plan your future with confidence."
5. Infatuation is mostly physical, sexual. You find it difficult to enjoy one another unless you know the evening will end in bed.
6. Love is the maturation of friendship. You must be friends before you can become lovers.
7. Infatuation is linked with jealousy, lack of confidence. When he's away you wonder if he's with another girl. Sometimes you even check to make sure.
8. Love means trust. You may fall into infatuation, but you never fall in love. . . .

> (signed)
> I Know The Difference

Abby was highly impressed with this letter, and said she agreed with it wholeheartedly. But Romeo or Errol Flynn would find such a love an utter bore; for between the lines of this letter is a clear preference for a certain kind of love, a certain life-style involving primarily security and companionship between two people who perhaps grew up together. There is a curious lack of deep emotional involvement, of romantic ecstasy, of the mystery and charm of a less predictable companion. It is more the outlook of an older couple or a pair of friends who have little concern for sex and who feel utterly secure in their relationship because they view love more as a commitment than as emotion. From a sociological point of view, it might be found in rural areas where everyone knows each other well and where novelty, mystery, and illusion are scorned; or it would be found in ethnic groups in large cities where one is expected to marry within one's own clan those whom one has known from childhood and who share similar religious and moral outlooks.

Let us look more carefully at the first criteria mentioned in the letter—that love which slowly "grows with time" is a truer love than one which happens at first sight. Those who do fall in love at first sight feel "captivated" as if they had been semi-hypnotized, but those who describe this experience also report a curious feeling of being liberated, as well. Such a love may not be so long-lasting once the spell has worn off, or it may be the beginning of long-lasting love. If the latter is the case, why call the initial stage of a solid love relationship infatuation with all the negative connotations such a term has?

On the other hand, what if the relation does not last very long and one "comes to his senses" in a few days and realizes he was in love with an illusion? Two questions face us here: How long does love have to endure to be "true love"? Who must one be in love with for it to be true love? If love is defined as being in love with the unchanging inner person whose personal qualities are of no concern to love, then (as I noted in an earlier section) the love would have to be eternal since the inner self is said to be unchanging. If love did die, then in such a view one was only in love with those qualities which met one's needs, and not unselfishly in love with the true "inner person" at all. And in such a view love that perishes was never love to begin with because it did not love the right part of the person—the inner self cherished for its own sake and which is said never to change.

Such a view, however, is hardly in accord with how we ordinarily view the length of love; scarcely anyone thinks that a couple who breaks up after five years of marriage were necessarily never in love at all. But then how long must love last to be true love? (My students often ask me if one night would be enough!) Are there not true lovers who so prize variety instead of constancy that they want no lasting commitment? Nor would they necessarily be immoral if the beloved had similar beliefs. Perhaps security and predictability are necessary for marriage, but love is not the same as marriage. The question of how long love must last is certainly too controversial to offer the clear distinction that infatuation is brief and love is long lasting. (My students tend to take the view that it is up to the lovers to decide how long they want their love to last and that there is no minimum time that they must remain together to merit the label "true love.")

Another problem with love at first sight is that I may be loving only an illusion; I may be so desperate for love that I read into the other person all sorts of qualities that are not really there. Am I then just infatuated in the sense that I am not in love with the person as he or she objectively is? Here I deceive myself with a fantasy typical of the "mad crush" to which our Lolitas are sometimes prone. Note that the fantasy may or may not wear off in time, for the need to project traits onto the beloved and cherish what I cannot find in reality may be so great that the fantasy may become an enduring one. Do we invent a word like *infatuation* to convince others to "return to reality," as viewed from the perspective of the majority of mankind? This "reality" could obviously not function if too many people escaped into such fantasy worlds; the solution would obviously be to make reality itself more appealing or else to deemphasize the idea that love can only be love of the enchantingly beautiful.

The question still remains, however, whether we can distinguish love from infatuation in terms of *what* is loved. If I love a fantasy, or if I love "love" and not a person as she actually is, can I not still be truly in *love* with a fantasy or with love? Loving a person as she actually is is obviously a prerequisite for enduring the realities that marriage forces upon us in living together day in and day out; and perhaps there is something immoral in refusing to look at a person as she truly is. But these introduce sociological and moral considerations into our attempt to make a distinction (which should be worked out in terms of the language of love itself). The sociologists' and moralists' distinction between love and infatuation is a prescriptive one, used to advocate certain social and moral views, and is not a description of the actual difference between two concepts. (My own suspicion thus far is that so-called "true" love, when it is contrasted with infatuation, is actually a prescriptive term used to promote a certain type of love and its associated life-style of security and predictability, that is, a "companionate" form of loving that knows few of the highs and lows of romantic passion and which ensures the institution of marriage.)

Another point made in the letter to Dear Abby is that infatuation is mostly sexual, that one confuses an attraction that is primarily physical with love, which is of the entire person. The key word here is *primarily,* for if it were *purely* physical, it would be difficult to see how the partners could confuse it with love. But if it is only primarily physical, this means that there are other things one finds appealing in one's partner. For if one thinks that such a relation is love (even if others call it infatuation), then one must find one's partner to be warm, sensuous, handsome, charming, and so forth. Perhaps the physical aspect—concluding the evening in bed—*is* what they look forward to most; but it is not unusual for lovers to find some particular aspect of the relationship as its central focus. Ordinary married lovers focus on home and children, for example, and this is often what makes all the other aspects of the association lovable—by association with this central focus of interest.

The preceding theory of infatuation might be called the one-facet-of-the-diamond theory: that one is enchanted primarily with only one facet of the other person and that one thinks one loves the whole person because the rest of him or her is bathed in the glow of that one particular facet. But surely this is the way love itself often begins. It need not begin by one's loving every aspect of the other person; one may not come to know these until years later. Certainly it would be a rare thing to find someone whose every quality is instantly enchanting or lovable. One may begin by being struck by the other person's power or intellect or personality, or maybe her fascinating rump or his blue eyes. The other traits—including the faults—may then become lovable by association with this central fascinating aspect. And this need not be only the beginning of love; it may be the source of its continuing appeal. If this account of the origins and continuance of love are correct, then the one-facet-of-the-diamond theory of infatuation fails to separate infatuation from love with clear distinctness.

There is one other significant comment in the letter to Dear Abby: the claim that jealousy and insecurity are linked to infatuation. However, some degree of jealousy and insecurity are not unknown to even the most seemingly stable of relationships. One need only test this by asking a secure married couple if the husband would mind sharing the wife for the evening or by noticing what happens if the husband suspects his wife of "cheating" on him. (On the other hand, romantics have long known that fear of the loss of a loved one can also be a way of enhancing the passion and ardor one feels for the beloved.)

There may well be, of course, a considerable degree of possessiveness between many infatuated couples, especially those who are undergoing such experiences for the first time. It is tempting to cite all sorts of psychological theories to the effect that they have very low self-esteem, which they are trying to overcome by possessing another's love at all costs. They are in love with being loved, as the saying goes, and they blindly enslave themselves to the beloved to receive the affection they need so badly. But so long as the relation lasts it may be a very ecstatic one in which the person is transformed in ways that may be analogous to a religious conversion. There is the danger of the loss of one's individuality, but there is also the possibility that a new self will emerge if only the so-called infatuation can cool down to the point where each can feel more secure as an individual.

Nor is it the case that every supposedly infatuated individual is somehow a person who hates himself; one can, for example, imagine a perfectly secure person transported into heights of ecstasy over a painting others would scorn as trash, and he may sacrifice greatly to secure the painting. But it does not follow that an act that seems irrational to most people is an indication that this individual hates himself and needs to possess this painting to secure his self-esteem. His aesthetic appreciation is simply attuned to this work to the highest degree, and that's it.

Finally, infatuation has been called "irrational love." But how many perfectly secure couples with a mature love have actually chosen the beloved on the basis of purely rational considerations? Except for those who follow the compatibility fetish to its extreme by computer matching, it is perfectly common for even the most mature lover to withhold his or her love from the one who would be best from a strictly rational point of view. For both love and infatuation (if there be such distinct concepts) are personal matters that involve feelings about another person. Can one then say that the value judgments I make in either love or infatuation are going to be objective or sensible, in the sense that anyone else need agree with me in my judgment of my beloved's worth? (Or if they did agree with my judgment, there is no guarantee that anyone else in the world would *love* my beloved.) A value judgment about another human being that may seem utterly silly and immature to someone who is indifferent to my beloved might seem quite valid *for me.* (I recall the comment of the singer in the film *Cabaret* who danced with an ape dressed as a woman: "If you could see her through my eyes, she wouldn't look ugly at all!")

Furthermore, someone may have everything to offer me and yet I may not choose her, if there is such a thing as choosing love. For as long as mind and heart are both involved in love, there will be a degree of irrationality in all our selections; thus those who accuse the infatuated of irrationality can draw, at best, only a distinction of degree between love and infatuation. And even if we grant that infatuation is immature or irrational love, it does not follow that it is not a form of love, any more than one can say that Eva Braun's feeling for Hitler was not also a form of love. Many loves that are invidiously compared with secure, bourgeois love often have a degree of depth, dedication, sincerity, and ecstasy that saner forms of love could well envy, however tragic and short-lived the less "solid" forms of love may often be.

Finally, it might be argued that love and infatuation involve very different kinds of feeling: infatuation is a state of feeling a violent emotion that sweeps one off one's feet and makes one possessive, irrational, and a slave to the beloved. Love, it might be claimed, is a calmer, saner emotion that one can control and that deepens as the years go by, instead of fading in a few weeks or months. But is one really to say that the violent emotions between the historical Antony and Cleopatra, the legendary Tristan and Iseult, or the imaginary Romeo and Juliet were not love? Why is it that thousands of readers of these great plays or tales do not doubt for a moment that they are great love stories, even though someone may insist that his or her son or daughter who exhibits Romeo's or Juliet's passions is "just infatuated"?

It seems evident, therefore, that attempts to delineate sharp differences between love and infatuation are doomed to failure. If we had hopes of defining true love by distinguishing it from infatuation, then it would seem that our effort will be unavailing.

I now wish to turn to the question of whether we can draw any sharp distinctions between love and friendship. A father once asked his daughter's suitor, "I know you love my daughter, but do you really like her?" What does the strange question mean? Apparently he was asking if in addition to being lovers they were also good friends. It is clearly possible that one might be a lover but not a friend. One may become emotionally "hooked" on someone (perhaps because of outstanding beauty or sexual prowess) whom one does not really "like" at all (perhaps because of that person's nasty disposition or because they share few or no common interests). For a love to last, or at least be a joyful love, the lovers must clearly also be good friends.

But can we distinguish sharply between love and friendship? One common answer is that one has sex with lovers but not with friends, and that if one does become sexually intimate with a friend, that friend is now actually one's lover. But this is certainly not necessarily true: friends often kiss or hug each other or even have sexual relations, but they would not claim that they are thereby in love with each other.

Does deep devotion constitute the difference? Clearly not, since both friends and lovers can be deeply devoted to one another. A close friend is just as likely to sacrifice his life for his companion as a lover would sacrifice his life for his beloved. Is the difference the fact that lovers are emotionally attached to each other but friends are not? Friends are said only to "like" each other. But this is not absolute either: if one's best friend dies, one may suffer as much emotional loss as if one's lover had died.

Is the difference that one feels a certain unique kind of emotion only for a lover (the wings-on-the-feet, supreme state of ecstasy sort of feeling)? This may be a difference, but it is by no means absolute. One can be in love without feeling ecstatic, and any uniquely ecstatic emotions can wear off quickly without the partners ceasing to be lovers. On the other hand, I may very well also feel ecstatic when I have been able to make friends with someone I have deeply admired for a long time.

Let us try yet another argument to distinguish the two. Suppose that we claim that in friendship the primary focus of the relationship is on common pursuits and common interests. This is not, of course, a sufficient condition for friendship since enemies can have common interests also. So they must also be devoted to each other. Still they are devoted primarily as companions having common interests. Thus, being focused on companionship and common interests, friendship is always mutual. "I am a friend of his" entails "he is a friend of mine."[22] But to say "I am in love with her" does not entail "she is in love with me," for love may be unrequited.

One might then argue that while the primary focus of friendship is on mutual interests, the primary focus of lovers is on each other, even though they also may (or may not) have common interests. Thus lovers might spend an evening holding hands, strolling through the park, looking into each other's eyes, and perhaps saying nothing. On the other hand, friends ordinarily want to do something that reflects their common interests, such as go bowling or at least talk about topics of shared interest. For friends merely to sit together in silence and hold hands would, unlike the case of lovers, commonly lead to boredom. One can illustrate this further: If one invites a friend to one's apartment to listen to music, the focus would be on their shared interest: the music itself. But for lovers the music would ordinarily be only a background for their being together. This distinction is not, however, absolute. Love often grows out of shared interests, and friends sometimes go for a silent stroll in the moonlight too.

Another possible distinction is that since friendship is a matter of shared common experiences and interests and since one may have several different interests, one may have several friends also. And one may assume that one's friends have several other friends as well. Unlike lovers, we are inclined to share friends, to respect their freedom to be friends with others, and to respect their freedom to develop themselves in ways that may require the departure of the friend from one's life.

On the other hand, we ordinarily have only one lover. Furthermore, lovers are often much more selective, exclusive, and even possessive in many cases. And, unlike friends, one is ordinarily quite disturbed to discover that one's lover has another lover as well. But this distinction is not absolute either. For although one may have many friends, one has only one "best" friend, and one may be quite selective and possessive about that best friend as well.

---

22. This means that friendship is something more than merely "liking" someone; for I can like someone who does not like me. One can, of course, be friendly toward someone who does not want to be one's friend. But one cannot be someone's friend unless the friendship is mutual.

A further possible distinction is that we believe that our lover is the most important person in our life and that the lover's needs take precedence over a friend's needs should a conflict arise. If one had to make a choice between taking one's lover or a penniless friend on a Caribbean vacation, wouldn't one ordinarily take the lover rather than the friend? Of course, if the friend had a suicidal fear of rejection, one might very well take the friend. But while one might argue that the lover's needs ought to take precedence over others', this frequently does not happen. We only need to remember the thousands of husbands who prefer to spend an evening with their friends at the bar and leave their wives sitting home alone. And there are cases where the friend's needs should take precedence over the lover's needs. If a friend is in a suicidal state of depression, one should want to spend much time trying to console him or her, even if this means the lover's need for companionship will have to be sacrificed temporarily.

Another possible distinction is that, while both love and friendship can be irrational, they differ in the following way. An irrational friendship is when the partners share common interests, such as drugs or stealing, that are destructive to one or both partners. But love can be irrational in quite a different way. I can be insanely jealous of my lover, or I may find myself falling in love with someone whom I thought I despised or with whom I have nothing in common or who could lead me to ruin. But this distinction is also far from absolute. Lovers can share irrational interests that harm them; and you might find yourself unable to resist trying to make a friend of someone you admire but who you know may lead you to ruin, particularly when this involves having to take up some harmful pursuit in order to win the friendship.

A final possible distinction is that, with the exception just mentioned, one is ordinarily said to choose one's friends either wisely or foolishly. One ordinarily does not find oneself "falling" into a friendship as lovers sometimes do against their better judgment. On the other hand, one does not speak so easily about choosing to love someone or choosing to fall out of love. Insofar as love may involve deep emotions, the arrival or disappearance of such emotions is not a matter of choice. One does not say, "I have just decided to be in love with you." One might say: "I found myself falling in love with him. I fought it all the way, but I couldn't help myself." Or one might say: "I'd like to love you, for you'd certainly make the ideal partner and you've done a great deal to merit my giving my love to you. But still I find that I feel no emotion of love for you at all, though I like you very much." (One can, of course, often choose not to establish a *relationship* with the beloved, but that is another matter.)

But this distinction between friendship as choice and love as an emotion that is not open to choice is not absolute either. We have already noted that in some cases one might say: "I can't help wanting to be your friend, even though I know you're going to lead me to ruin." And there are forms of love that border on friendship and that therefore involve relatively mild emotions that do not sweep one off one's feet; here choosing to love would clearly be possible.

None of these distinctions between love and friendship are absolute but are only matters of degree. To draw a clear line between love and friendship so that one knows precisely where one ends and the other begins is obviously impossible to do.

6
On Defining "True Love": Some Concluding Reflections

Can one say what "true love" is? The philosopher Douglas Morgan in *Love: Plato, the Bible and Freud* (Englewood Cliffs, N.J.: Prentice-Hall, 1964) rejects any possibility of defining the essential nature of love. He writes:

> It is finally in order here to disavow any intention of expounding the "real meaning" or the "essence" of love. There is no such thing. Love is, as the currently fashionable phrase has it, an "open" concept. If we are to be satisfied only with a unique, universally applicable all-time definition of "love," we may as well not even enter upon our venture. Interesting words (like "love") don't usually work in ways that permit such precision (p. 3).

For anyone who has studied the history of theories of what "true" love is supposed to be, one encounters a bewildering and conflicting variety of definitions. One type of love that has fascinated man down through the ages is one that is also the most commonly scorned by moralists and by the man in the street. This is romantic love or, as Alan Lee calls it, "manic love." The phrase "manic" suggests that such love is a kind of madness, as when one speaks of falling "madly" in love. In countless plays and novels such love is pictured as a dark, violent passion over which one has no control. Such lovers seem driven to completely sacrifice their own identity in trying to form a quasi-mystical union with each other. They are, furthermore, typically insanely jealous and possessive of each other, and feel absolutely lost when they are apart. A psychiatrist would, of course, say that they are self-hating masochists who surrender themselves completely to their beloved and seek love as a means of overcoming their self-contempt. But, as I noted in the preceding section, how could one prove that this analysis applies to every romantic, including Tristan and Iseult, Lancelot and Guinevere, Antony and Cleopatra, Romeo and Juliet, or even the boy in the film *Summer of '42*?

Although the man in the street who wants to be practical and rational would typically scorn the romantic, why is it that such figures as those mentioned above have fascinated endless readers of the plays and novels in which they have been portrayed? Since such tales have typically ended in the lovers' deaths or in some other tragic way, Denis de Rougemont has argued that there is a link between the romantics' quest for the ultimate passionate experience and a secret yearning for death: He writes:

> Both passion and the longing for death which passion disguises are connected with, and fostered by, a particular notion of how we are to reach

understanding which in itself is typical of the Western psyche. Why does Western man wish to suffer this passion which lacerates him and which all his common sense rejects? Why does he yearn after this particular kind of love notwithstanding that its effulgence must coincide with this self-destruction? The answer is that he reaches self-awareness and tests himself only by risking his life—in suffering and on the verge of death. The third act of Wagner's drama represents far more than a romantic disaster; it represents the essential disaster of our sadistic genius—the repressed longing for death, for self-experience to the utmost, for the revealing shock, a longing which beyond question manifests the most tenacious root of the war instinct we nourish. . . . Why is it that we delight most of all in some tale of impossible love? Because we long for the *branding*; because we long to grow *aware* of what is on fire inside us. Suffering and understanding are deeply connected; death and self-awareness are in league; and European romanticism may be compared to a man for whom sufferings, and especially the sufferings of love, are a privileged mode of understanding.[23]

De Rougemont goes on to argue that one of the key elements in romantic tragedy is some obstruction to the happy fulfillment of love. If no obstacle occurs by chance, the romantics will invent obstacles to, say, reaching their beloved so as to heighten their passion by keeping themselves eternally frustrated. The ultimate obstacle to the consummation of their love would, of course, be their own death; this would be a further explanation for the secret death wish that de Rougemont claims to be characteristic of romantic lovers.

De Rougemont's thesis is, however, based on an examination of various romantic tales and plays, and it might be argued that seeking obstacles to the consummation of a happy love and the tragic endings of such tales are simply devices for enhancing their dramatic power. It need not follow that real-life romantics are secretly yearning to die. Indeed, a romantic would protest that de Rougemont wants to besmirch romantic love because he is interested in defending married love, something for which he thinks romantic passion does not provide a sound basis for an enduring commitment. Thus the romantics would argue that their own concept of love as a dark, violent passion is, for them, what true love is. To be sure, the romantic is perhaps often really only in love with his own exquisite passions or in love with love, but the romantic would ask why true love must necessarily be love of persons. Indeed, if (as de Rougemont admits) romantic love is "self-experience to the utmost," and is, through suffering, a privileged route to self-awareness, then it can hardly be all bad. The sociologist Alan Lee, for example, writes:

In romantic fiction the manic lover is capable of deeds of high nobility and self-sacrifice, but he is usually blind to the fate which has taken

---

23. *Love in the Western World* (New York: Harper and Row, 1974), pp. 51–52.

command of his emotions. . . . Most of my manic respondents, even those not yet fully recovered from a traumatic break-up, believed the experience had been of some benefit to them. Only a very few, if given the chance over again, knowing what they know now, would rather have not fallen in love manically. The extremes of manic love had ennabled most respondents to realize for the first time how much they could care for another person. . . . The transcendental power of manic love can lift you out of yourself. New talents may be discovered, new perspectives may be opened. You may even conclude that you could not have become a mature person without a manic experience. Instead of discarding your manic experience as a juvenile stage or a neurotic illness, it is possible to recognize this experience as a major contribution to your growth in the capacity to love. In this sense, manic love is akin to a religious conversion.[24]

I have focused on romantic or manic love as a way of illustrating how dangerous it is to say that a form of love that does not happen to suit one's own temperament is necessarily sick or unhealthy or could not be true love from the point of view of a particularly passionate sort of person. To be sure, romantic love may sometimes end tragically, but the romantic would prefer his hour of glory to the life-long tepid pleasures of the safe and sane love advocated by Erich Fromm. Fromm's ideal love is, of course, the one that is advocated by most of today's moralists who want a calm, rational love based on commitment to a life-long marriage. This may be a valid life-style for the majority of persons, but it is hardly fair to label other forms of love as sick or unhealthy because they do not sustain the life-style preferred by the masses.

Indeed, Fromm's ideal lover would to many seem utterly cloying in his obsession with being so good, trustworthy, benevolent, and the like. Fromm's safe and sane lover is so noble in his benevolence that he seems almost unreal in being devoid of those foibles that make one human and lovable. Furthermore, the sanity and goodness of Fromm's type of love could be positively unhealthy in that it seems not to recognize the darker forces of human nature. Attempting to hide or repress these forces under a facade of absolute benevolence could very well turn Fromm's so-called healthy love into a neurotic one.

What, then, is true love? I would argue that there is no one true love that is valid for everyone. The concept of "true love" is, I think, a kind of blank canvas on which we paint a picture that reveals only our own ideals and aspirations.

---

24. *The Colors of Love*, p. 106. Lee's comments would indicate that the only so-called death the romantic is seeking is the death of his old self. The romantic seeks a kind of rebirth in taking on a new identity to please his or her beloved or by absorbing the identity of his beloved.

Three

Four Philosophers of Love: Singer, Schopenhauer, Freud, and Sartre

1
Irving Singer: Love as Bestowal of Value

I wish to examine a contemporary theory of love found in the opening chapter of Irving Singer's history of love.[1] The key to Singer's highly interesting theory is his distinction between *bestowal* and *appraisal*. This distinction will be explained in detail as we proceed; roughly it means that love is not primarily a matter of appraising a person for their prospective usefulness but is rather a "bestowing" of value on the beloved for his or her own sake or person alone. Thus far there would seem to be nothing particularly novel or controversial about such a view; but when it is developed in detail, certain critical difficulties arise that one would not have expected in such a traditional, idealistic theory. (I do not mean that Singer has not been highly inventive and original in the way he develops the theory; it remains to be seen whether the difficulties the theory presents arise from the traditional distinction itself or from the particular way in which Singer develops it.)

The term *bestowal* is interesting in that one often finds it used in religious theories, for example, God's apapic bestowal of love on mankind. Let us look at a passage that nicely summarizes the concept of religious bestowal (found in Anders Nygren's classic work *Agape and Eros*) and then see how it could relate to Singer's use of the term applied to a mortal pair of lovers:

1. *The Nature of Love: Plato to Luther* (New York: Random House, 1966), pp. 3–23.

192

Christ . . . declares that God's love has no limits and is independent entirely of the merits of its recipient. "Your heavenly Father maketh his sun to shine on the evil and the good." God is free and God is sovereign. His love does not need to find desert; it is not called into being by anything which man can afford or boast. The degrees of human worth are as nothing in their finiteness to God; they do not count at all. God has the initiative and in man's relation with God it is God who gives all. Nygren sums up the meaning of Agape in the Gospel under four heads. It is spontaneous and uncaused . . . we can offer no explanation of it on natural grounds. It is indifferent to human merit. Human values have no place when God loves. God does not love the good on account of their goodness; the sinner equally with the righteous can be struck with the dart of God's love. Thirdly, it is creative in that what was without value, a minus number relative to God's positive reality, acquires value by the fact that it becomes the object of Agape. "The idea of the infinite value of the human soul is not a Christian idea at all"; such a view rather belongs to the philosophy of Eros. When, for example, God says to the sinner, "Thy sins are forgiven thee," this forgiveness creates the goodness and does not presuppose it in any way. Lastly, Agape opens the way to fellowship with God. Man of himself . . . has no way of attaining to this fellowship. It is a pure gift to man.[2]

D'Arcy also describes Nygren's contrast by adding: "Eros is motivated by beauty and value in the object. Agape *bestows* itself on what is quite unworthy, creates the value and is sovereign" (p. 74; italics mine).

This is not the place to examine certain highly controversial aspects of Nygren's presentation, such as his notion of man's utter dependence on God. I wish here only to note several interesting parallels between Nygren's presentation and Singer's description of the lover's bestowal of value upon the beloved. If there are important similarities, would Singer want to say that the beloved's value somehow derives from the bestowal the lover chooses to give? This would contradict his claim that the lover cares for the beloved for his or her sake alone, and would thus make the beloved utterly dependent on the lover for his or her value insofar as the value transcends his or her instrumental virtues. And if the beloved has such value only in relation to the lover's bestowal, is the lover as unegoistic as Singer insists he or she is? Is he in love with his beloved, or is he in love with his own power and imaginative ability to bestow value on the beloved?

Before proceeding to compare Nygren's concept of bestowal with Singer's, let us see how Singer attempts to distinguish the purely instrumental appraisals from the bestowals he links with true love. Singer distinguishes two forms of appraisal: objective and individual. An objective appraisal would be that of a used-car salesman, who bases the value of a car on how useful the public

2. M. C. D'Arcy, *The Mind and Heart of Love* (Cleveland: Meridian, 1956), p. 64.

thinks the car is. An individual appraisal, on the other hand, occurs when a certain person decides the instrumental value of a car in relation to his own needs. People themselves are also subject to appraisals, but Singer adds:

> We also bestow value in the manner of love. We then respond to another as something that cannot be reduced to *any* system of appraisal. The lover takes an interest in the beloved as a *person,* and not merely as a commodity (which she also may be). He bestows importance upon *her* needs and *her* desires, even when they do not further the satisfaction of his own. *Whatever her personality, he gives it a value it would not have apart from his loving attitude.* In relation to him, this woman has become valuable for her own sake. . . . *Only in relation to our bestowal does another person enjoy the kind of value that love creates* (p. 6; italics mine).[3]

The italicized words show a similarity to Nygren's claim that only in relation to God's bestowal does a human being acquire value as a person. But if we rely upon the kind of value that love creates—that I become valuable for my own sake—then by Singer's analysis I am utterly dependent on another's bestowal of value to have any value of my own that transcends my usefulness to others. Then Singer is open to the criticism that might be directed at Nygren, namely that the individual human soul has infinite worth, regardless of what anyone, including God, thinks of it.

A further problem that faces all theorists of erotic love who speak of loving a person for his or her own sake alone is the fact that one does not love some abstraction called a "person." This is a problem commonly faced by those who wish to describe two lovers in agapic language (agape having to do primarily with loving all mankind simply because it is composed of human beings, regardless of individuals' personal qualities). But when Joe loves Mary, how can he avoid noting her specific qualities and making appraisals of them? For presumably he selected her out of a large assortment of women; surely he did not choose at random or choose Mary out of pure charity. Singer is aware of this problem when he writes:

> For the effort (of love) to succeed it must be accompanied by justifiable appraisals, objective as well as individual. The objective beauty and goodness of his beloved will delight the lover, just as her deficiencies will distress him. . . . Individual value is rarely stable. It changes in accordance with our success or failure in getting what we want. And as this happens, our perception of the beloved also changes (pp. 9–10).

Does this mean that Singer now finds himself driven to a possible situation in which appraisal will have to triumph over bestowal, in the sense that the

---

3. Note also Singer's claim that "upon the sheer personality of the beloved, he bestows a framework of value, *emanating from himself,* but focused on her" (p. 8; italics mine).

lovers' incompatibility (in terms of meeting their mutual needs) will eventually reveal itself and they will have to part? (Agapic love of persons for their own sake does not, of course, permit this.) Singer tries to rescue himself from this problem by saving:

> Where this conjunction (of appraisal and bestowal) exists, *every* appraisal may lead on to a further bestowal. By disclosing an excellence in the beloved, appraisal . . . makes it easier for us to appreciate her. By revealing her faults and imperfections, it increases the importance of acting on her behalf. . . . Once bestowal has occurred, a man may no longer care that his beloved is not the choicest of sexual objects. Given the opportunity, he may prefer her to women who are sexually more attractive. *His love is a way of compensating for and even overcoming negative appraisals. . . . Love confers importance no matter what the object is worth.*[4]

A number of questions immediately arise about this handling of possible conflicts between appraisals and bestowals. Can all negative appraisals be overcome by "acting on her behalf"? The beloved may have qualities that do not permit such a resolution. Singer does want to say that true love will continue to confer importance no matter what the object is worth. But has love now assumed a blind quality that may be forced into self-sacrifice? (Recall, however, that earlier he said that for love to succeed it must be accompanied by justifiable individual and objective appraisals.) Purely agapic religious love, is, of course, utterly unconcerned with the relative merits of persons and everyone loves self-sacrificially. But Singer is speaking of setting up a *love relationship* between two individuals, and the requirements are much more severe than his agapic-sounding theory can meet.

Finally, we must return once again to the question of whether the lover really is attending to the person as he or she is. Or is his bestowal a product of his own imaginative projection of the value he would like to see in the beloved, regardless of what she is actually like? Recall that Singer says that "love is a way of compensating for and even overcoming negative appraisals." At another point he writes:

> In saying that to him she is perfect he merely reiterates the fact that he loves this woman. Her perfection is an honorific title which he, and only he, bestows. The lover is like a child who makes a scribble and then announces, "This is a tree." The child could just as easily have said, "This is a barn." Until he tells us, the scribble represents nothing. Once he tells us, it represents whatever he says . . . (p. 13).

4. Ibid., p. 10; italics mine. His claim that love confers importance no matter what the object is worth seems to be contradicted when he writes: "Unless the beloved satisfied in some respect, no man might be able to love her. For *she* must find a place in *his* experience; she must come alive for him, stimulate new and expansive interests . . . (p. 13).

But this is not at all like a respect for persons; using the analogy of the scribble, a man could as easily announce, "This woman is a tramp," or "This woman is perfect." Just how much is the person herself being attended to? (At one point Singer writes: "Though beauty and goodness are not in the eye of the beholder, love is" [p. 14; italics mine].)[5]

This role of the imagination is further emphasized when Singer compares a lover to an "awakened genius who chooses its materials in accordance *with its own* creative requirements (p. 16). He adds, in comparing the lover with El Greco: "What matters *is his way of seeing* as a function of his imagination, not the disposition in space of stones and mortar" (p. 17; italics mine). Thus:

> The creativity of love is primarily a *self-creation.* Lovers create within themselves a remarkable capacity for affective response, an ability to use their emotions, their words, their deeds for bestowing as well as appraising value. Each enhances the other's importance through an imaginative play within valuation itself. Indeed, love may be best approached as a subspecies of the imagination (p. 16; italics mine).

As Singer's essay proceeds to its conclusion, we see a self-interest emerging, a delight in the exercise of powers of the imagination and in the power to bestow value one wishes to see in the beloved. The beloved thus is not a person respected for herself but is rather an excuse for a one-sided or mutual indulgence in exercising one's imagination on one's "raw materials"—another human being.[6] Of course, such imaginative powers protect one from disappointments in changes for the worse in the beloved, but this is still imagination as a tool of self-interest. That is, if his beloved turns out to be much less than he had expected, he could always compensate for her lack of value in an appraisal sense by imaginatively bestowing value on her which she objectively lacks.

Finally, Singer strongly insists that his aesthetic, imaginative approach to love is to be distinguished from *knowledge,* where we always stand the chance of being duped or "blind." For the imaginative person is operating only "as if" what he creates is real. In doing so, Singer compares a lover to persons witnessing a play; they know the characters are not real, but they imagine that they are real so that they can become emotionally involved with the play. Singer feels that his imaginative portrayal of the beloved as more charming and beautiful than she really is, is a beautiful bestowal of his gift of love to her. "By his affirmative response alone, the lover places an ordinary stone within the costliest of settings. The amorous imagination bestows value upon a person as the dramatic imagination bestows theatrical import upon an actor"

---

5. Elsewhere Singer writes: "[The lover's] superlatives are expressive and metaphoric. Far from being terms of literal praise, they betoken the magnitude of his affection and *say little about the lady's beauty or goodness*" (p. 12; italics mine).

6. Singer would do well to recall Nietzsche's remark that the artist exercises his will to power, in however a subtle way, in his mastery over his materials.

(p. 20). Once again he seems to be not in love with the person for her own sake, but only with an aesthetic object of his own creation.

Indeed, could not Singer have become so emotionally involved with his creation that he begins to confuse imagination with reality? But then could not his imaginative projection of unmerited value in time wear off, and what is he then going to think of his beloved? (Imaginative people are notoriously prone to boredom, and are always seeking new outlets for their imaginative powers.) Will he abandon his beloved? If so, the tragedy would be great for the erstwhile beloved if she accepted Singer's view that only by being loved does one acquire value that transcends one's mere usefulness to others. She should realize that, Singer's view notwithstanding, one has this unique worth whether one is loved or not.

In summary, Singer's theory fails to prove that love is a benevolent regard for other persons for their own sakes. For the one who bestows value seems to primarily be in love with his own imaginative powers. ("For his love is a creative means of *making* her more worthy—in the sense that he invests her with greater value, not in making her a better human being. That may also happen. But more significantly, the lover changes *himself*. By subordinating his purposive attitudes, he transforms himself into a being who enjoys the act of bestowing," p. 16). And those who seek this gratuitous and unmerited bestowal of value are doubtlessly self-interested in seeking to be viewed in this idealized way. But they should realize they are not really being accepted as they are, and that the only true value they have is to be found in themselves alone.

2
Schopenhauer and Freud: Love as Derived from Sex

Schopenhauer is often cited as a precursor to Freud. Let us first examine Freud's theory and then determine if this is valid.

In this century Freud argued that love cannot be divorced from its sexual origins; indeed, he thought that all forms of human association have a libidinal (sexual) basis. Civilization, of course, tries to prevent direct sexual expression except with one's wife or lover; but to Freud the way friends and relatives desire to be physically close to one another is a giveaway of the libidinal basis of their relationship, however much the relationship may have been sublimated into a non-genital form.

For Freud, love was defined as "aim-inhibited" sexuality; when our sexual desires are not given full gratification, there is a surplus of libidinal energy that is sublimated into love. Were we completely gratified in all our sexual desires, as in some state of nature, presumably love would cease to exist. But civilization inhibits sexuality from its true aim—genital release of tension—and love develops as a substitute sexual form in which we can at least kiss or be close to our beloved and thus partake of some of the components of the full sexual act we really want.[7]

We noted in an earlier chapter all the differences between love and sex that Theodore Reik sets forth: that love is selective and sex is not; that love is a continuing thing, whereas sex wants the partner only when he feels the urge, and so forth. It is not clear how Freud would answer Reik's attack on his views: Perhaps he would argue that our sexual urges have become so sublimated that crude non-selective sex no longer really exists, or he might argue that we get our partner to love us so that we will be sure of having a means of release in the future; that is, we do not cease to be interested in the partner after orgasm because we know the need for gratification will arise again and again in the future.

However, the chief difficulty with Freud's theory that love is the product of unsatisfied sexual urges is that those who are sexually frustrated do not necessarily fall in love. (Freud would perhaps answer that their unsublimated sexual energy would cause them to become neurotics or else they would sublimate their unreleased urges in some other way, such as becoming artists.) In addition, those who are lovers and who are sexually fulfilled do not necessarily cease to love each other. Yet they should cease to do so if love is derived from sexual frustration. But perhaps Freud would give the same answer suggested in the preceding paragraph: They love in order to be sure of maintaining a source of release of their sexual urges. (Freud could argue that this refers to an unconscious motive for loving; the fact that lovers deny loving each other for the reason Freud gives would prove nothing if they are unaware of their true motives.)

Now let us examine the ways in which Schopenhauer might be said to be a precursor of Freud. To begin with, their theories about the nature of reality differ significantly in many important ways.

Schopenhauer, reared in the tradition of German metaphysics, argues that there is an underlying "true" reality that cannot be discerned by the senses or intellect, but only by our inner intuitive sense of being identical with this reality. This ultimate reality is called the will to live. It is an irrational force that drives us to sexual activity, but it differs from Freud's libido or underlying sexual impulse in being the one true reality, with individual creatures merely being the way it appears to our minds. Freud's libido is found in each individual, but Freud does not assume it to be some underlying metaphysical reality that is the very core of the universe. For Schopenhauer, the will to live is omnipotent and is the only "real" reality. The will to live is *one,* blind, irrational, and is the ultimate source of all that we call love between the sexes. For Freud, on the other hand, the libido or sexual impulse would be all-powerful were it not for the constraining forces of civilization. Like the Freudian libido, Schopenhauer's will to live is constantly restless in its desires, and has no concern for morality or restraint.

7. See Sigmund Freud, *Civilization and Its Discontents,* tr. James Strachey (New York: W. W. Norton, 1962).

The significant difference, however, is that Freud does not claim that individuals are basically a function of how our intellects perceive this ultimate single reality, or that individuality is ultimately an illusion or the way the will manifests itself to our minds. For Freud was a simple materialist, and he would disdain the view that individuality is ultimately illusory.

Although Schopenhauer's view of individuals was that they were ultimately illusory—like the veil of Maya that disguises the reality that underlies it—he also seems to think that individuals have a reality that requires them to preserve the species and thus satisfy the cravings of the will to live. Perhaps what he actually means is that individuals are not the *basic* reality, that they exist only to preserve the species and ultimately the will to live itself.

Schopenhauer's attitude toward reality was utterly pessimistic. Happiness for him was never positive; it could only be the absence of pain in a world governed by the will to live. The will to live drives us endlessly to fulfill our painful wants and afterwards we are left only with satiated boredom; life is an endless cycle to preserve ourselves for which the ultimate reward is death. Sexual desire torments us until it is fulfilled, and then after the climax when our tensions are released we are so let down, so bored, so satiated that we wonder why we ever went to so much trouble to seek sex in the first place. But soon sexual desire sets in again and we are forced to repeat the cycle over and over. (Freud himself often spoke of sex this way, although not quite with the cynicism and disdain of Schopenhauer. For him, too, the sexual act was a release from painfully unfulfilled sexual tensions.)

Finally, lurking behind it all is the mysterious will to live, a kind of diabolical reality that has no consciousness of its own, is not a "person," but is also not some materialistic mechanism. None of us as individuals have any free will, and our consciousness merely points the way to the gratification of this blind will. Our intellect or consciousness, he says, is like a dwarf sitting on the shoulders of a blind giant; the giant tells the dwarf where he wants to go, and the dwarf merely points the way.

We are now in a position to outline what Schopenhauer thinks love between the sexes amounts to in such a world.[8]

1. The ultimate purpose of love is not to experience the ecstasy of holding the beloved and entering into some blissful, romantic state. The lovers on the conscious level may think that they are unselfishly devoting themselves to each other, but what is really directing them to each other's arms is the will to live, which is intent upon preserving the species through procreation. (This distinction between conscious and unconscious levels and the claim that the latter determines the former is, of course, found in Freud as well.) The will to live does not care for the lovers as individuals at all, and views them only as a means to the preservation of the species. When we are no longer able to reproduce, we sink gradually into old age and death; the will to live has no more use for us, no matter how much we may want to go on living.

8. Arthur Schopenhauer, "The Metaphysics of Sexual Love," *The World as Will and Representation*, Vol. II (New York: Dover, 1958), pp. 531–567.

2. Why, then, does the will to live allow us to *think* we love each other, and to think erroneously that sex is just one expression of this love? Schopenhauer argues that self-interest, the dominant motive on the conscious level, makes us think that in loving another we are serving our own best interests through all the delights that love and sex supposedly bring. If we were aware that we are merely serving the purposes of the species rather than ourselves, we would be revolted and less likely to procreate. But love has a kind of blinding effect that leads us to marriages that often end in utter discord and unhappiness. The reason that such marriages are so often unhappy, although conceived in a rapturous overflow of powerful erotic emotions, is that nature wants to procreate not just any individual but one that is superior in combining the best features of each parent. Thus it would want, for example, to combine the intelligence of the female with the brute strength and courage of a male. (Schopenhauer was struck by the fact that he so often saw women of great sophistication mysteriously attracted to rugged but unintellectual males.) Each person seeks what he himself lacks. But such marriages usually end in discord because they are conceived in a moment of passion (as determined by the will to live) that unites two beings who are so different that harmony becomes impossible. If our conscious intellects were in control, then planned marriages based on compatibility would be the rule; but reason does not rule our lives—only irrational forces over which we have no control. Indeed, the public is bored by rational marriages and applauds two lovers eloping romantically, governed totally by feeling rather than reason. But it is only the will to live that causes us to admire such romantic passion and the procreative result.

3. The role of the will to live is further demonstrated by the sort of characteristics that cause people to fall in love with each other. Health, strength, beauty, and consequently youth are what cause romantic passion; the ugly, the deformed, the aged, the stupid are ignored or only chosen out of sheer desperation. (Even a full bosom is admired, according to Schopenhauer, because it promises the newborn child abundant nourishment.) The reason for this, according to Schopenhauer, is that the will to live wants to create individuals who will best ensure the continuance of the species and in turn ensure the continuance of the will to live itself. For the only goal of the will to live is its own continued existence. Being devoid of intellect, it does not conceive of goals; its only goal is self-preservation for sheer preservation's sake.

4. Does anyone ever escape the will to live? Schopenhauer thought there were in history a few saints and ascetics who had, through no power of their own, been able in some mystical way to pierce the veil of illusion of a world of self-seeking individuals to get a glimpse of the underlying reality itself—the will to live—and he admired them greatly. They were then able to see that, since this will is one and not many things, all of mankind was in essence basically one. They are the few who are then capable of pure compassion because they are free of the shackles of illusory individuality and egoism in seeing that we are all basically one thing. This awareness of our oneness leads to a basic sense of identification with all humanity and its sorrows. Presumably

horrified by what they see behind the veil of illusion, they turn against the will to live and cease to procreate. They are then free of the unending cycle to which our appetites drive us; frustration followed by boredom and satiety, followed by frustration, and so forth.

Schopenhauer notes that after a man has spent time and money, perhaps even his reputation, good name, and health, in order to seduce some beautiful woman, he finds that upon orgasm he is just as let down as if he had had intercourse with a common hag. We feel as if we had been duped, that all our efforts were pointless. For nature was concerned only with the birth of a beautiful, healthy child that such a sex act could produce. But as soon as we have fulfilled her purposes, we feel duped; for the exquisite joy that we sought from having sex with a beautiful, healthy creature leaves us bored and soon frustrated once again.[9] But saints, in renouncing sex, are free of feeling duped since they have conquered the will to live that drove the man virtually to destroy himself in blindly seeking sex with a beautiful woman.

The chief difficulty Schopenhauer's theory faces is why so many lovers (as well as non-lovers) seek sex but try to prevent procreation by abortions and birth-control devices. And then there are those, such as homosexuals, the very old, and the sterile, who seek sex without any possibility of procreation. If the will to live and to reproduce is all-powerful, none of these things should happen. The only sex would be procreative sex, if Schopenhauer's theory were correct.

Schopenhauer's answer to this is an exceedingly dubious one. His central argument is that nature does not permit certain persons to reproduce because the progeny would be weak or deformed or retarded in some way. He argued that the elderly and the very young would be particularly prone to produce such children; and he claimed that (from his observations) homosexuality took place primarily between elderly males and youths, neither of whom qualify to produce strong progeny with women. So nature lets them gratify their desires in non-procreative ways. And those who practice abortion, birth control, or are sterile are simply carrying out nature's wishes that they not produce defective children.

But these answers are clearly unsatisfactory in terms of Schopenhauer's own assumptions. How could a blind, unconscious, irrational will have any precognition as to who is going to produce what kind of child? And since many defective children are born, how did his omnipotent natural force fail to foresee and prevent it? Furthermore, those who have had healthy children sometimes turn to abortion or birth control, so there is no reason to think the aborted child would have been deformed. Nor does homosexuality take place primarily between older men and youths, unless Schopenhauer was speaking

---

9. Schopenhauer's idea that sex is preceded by frustration and followed by boredom and satiety is actually typical of only certain types of sexual partners, especially those who are disgusted by sex or who are disappointed because it did not provide them with some kind of salvation they were seeking. But those who enjoy sex for sex's sake, in the way one savors fine wine, approach sex with a sense of eager anticipation and are left feeling fulfilled and refreshed. Schopenhauer's lovers are more like those who use sex as a means to an end, in the way one gulps down food in order to relieve a prolonged and painful hunger, and then finds oneself suffering from indigestion.

of ancient Greece or the homosexual prostitution he may have witnessed in Germany. Some homosexuals later marry and have healthy children, just as do bisexuals. Thus, while there may be some kind of orgasmic energy that drives us to seek sexual intercourse, we seem to be able to use sex for whatever purpose we wish. How can there be an all-powerful, procreative instinct that governs the universe?

Finally, how would Schopenhauer handle the sharp distinctions between love and sex that we have already noted. Reik argued, for example, that sex (or at least crude sex) is utterly selfish, whereas love is selfish only in the innocent sense of being happy in the happiness of the other person.[10] But for Schopenhauer we are all basically egoistic since we are all manifestations or incarnations of the will to live, which cares only for its own self-preservation. Thus Schopenhauer would probably argue that both love and sex are selfish and that one cannot try to stop the reduction of love to sex in this way.

Reik also says that crude sex is undiscriminating—it will take anybody—whereas love is selective. But Schopenhauer would argue that sex is selective also, because the will to live engages in a kind of natural selection in allowing only the strongest and wisest to be born. Only those who are utterly desperate would be undiscriminating, and he might add that even the desperate have a kind of ideal fantasy before their eyes if they engage in sex with someone who has no sex appeal.

Reik also maintained that when a purely sexual act is finished the partner ceases to be interesting and is abandoned, whereas lovers stay together. Schopenhauer argued, however, that the nature of the male is to produce as many children as possible, and no sooner is he charmed by one woman, then another fascinates him. For the male can spawn as many children in a year as he wishes, whereas the female can produce only one. Since she must raise the child, the woman is inclined to constancy in love; but Schopenhauer felt that men—if they could only arrange it—would not be faithful at all. This would also be his response to Reik's claim that it sounds ridiculous to speak of swearing eternal sexual desire, whereas it does make sense to speak of swearing eternal love. But if Schopenhauer is right—at least about male love—this is not a clear distinction. And for the liberated woman, it may come to seem ridiculous to her also to swear eternal love.

Another distinction for Reik arises from his claim that "[S]ex is a passionate interest in another *body*; love is a passionate interest in another *personality*, or in his *life*. Sex does not feel pain if its object is injured, nor joy when it is happy. It is possible to possess another person in sex, but not in love. In love you cannot possess another person, you can only belong to another person. You can force another person to sexual activity, but not to love."[11]

10. Theodore Reik, *The Psychology of Sexual Relations*, pp. 17-18, and *A Psychologist Looks at Love*, pp. 31-36.

11. *The Psychology of Love*, p. 33.

Schopenhauer would argue, however, that the will to live merely makes us think we are interested in another person for his or her own sake. While it is a feeling we may have when we are in love, love is simply a way of getting a pair of bodies to procreate. Thus we only think we love the other person for his or her own sake, when actually we are only using each other in the name of the will to procreate. (Indeed, one should say that we are both being used by the will to procreate.) Furthermore, Schopenhauer would argue that mere mutual affection for each other as persons can bring no real satisfaction if sex is absent. On the other hand if the lovers constantly squabble and fight over this and that but have a satisfying physical relationship, they will be relatively content.

· The distinction Reik makes about possession in sex and freedom in love would also be challenged by Schopenhauer on the grounds that those who are seduced and are overcome by passionate love can be possessed. And while it may be true that I cannot by myself force someone to love me, the will to reproduce that is our inner essence will eventually force two persons to be duped into loving each other in order to ensure the propagation of the species.

Therefore, if one accepts Schopenhauer's particular set of philosophical assumptions about the nature of man and the universe, it seems that he can handle Reik's attempt to put love and sex into distinct categories reasonably well.[12] Where Schopenhauer does seem to flounder, however, is his unsatisfactory answer to why nature allows abortions and birth control, as well as allowing homosexuals, the aged, and the sterile to have sex when there are no prospects for propagation of the species.

Ultimately Schopenhauer is another of these philosophers who think that sex must have some ulterior purpose. Love, for Schopenhauer, is a way of getting us to have sex, and sex is a means to procreation. That sex might be relished for its own sake escapes him.

3
Sartre: Love as a Contradictory Ideal[13]

When I was a boy growing up in a small community, it was considered to be "one big happy family," especially at festivals and in response to common crises. The concept of staring at someone else had its usual connotations in such a society; you responded depending on your self-concept or your degree of self-consciousness, and you respond depending on who it was who was staring at

12. Nietzsche would argue that the will to live is not at all our primary motive; for heroic individuals, at least, risk and sometimes sacrifice their lives in order to satisfy their basic drive for power and glory. Indeed, there has been so much disagreement over precisely what our basic unconscious motives are (if there are any such things at all) that one despairs of being able to pin them down to some one basic drive. One might just as well say that many or all of our activities are governed by a "will to sleep." One could then "explain" our desire to read, eat, go for a walk, have sex, and so forth on the grounds that such things are conducive to good sleep and thus are somehow unconsciously motivated by a "sleep drive"!

13. Sartre's philosophy of love is discussed on pages 364–379 of *Being and Nothingness.*

you. If you were secure in your own being or were someone who "counted" in terms of brains or beauty or power, you were flattered at the attention; for you knew that the judgment behind the stare was a favorable one. If you were insecure or unattractive, you were embarrassed and felt like a "thing" or a curiosity of some sort. There was no need to wonder what judgment lay behind the stare, for in a small community everyone knew what everyone thought of everyone else.

Underlying the surface harmony of such a community there was doubtlessly considerable competition, backbiting, and status seeking, but the goal of the competition was such that there need be nothing feared and everything to gain in increased self-esteem from the "stare," that is, the judgment behind the stare. Of course, if you suddenly discovered another boy kissing your girlfriend in your accustomed meeting spot and if they stared back at you in disdain, you felt as if your world were slipping away from you, that you had become a mere protuberance into their world, that you had become a mere thing in their eyes to which the message was "Go away!" Or you might not know what they were thinking—perhaps they were afraid of what your response would be—but you did know your presence was being assessed, and perhaps in ways you could never fully ascertain. In Sartre's terms they were *subjects* and I was the *object* of their baleful stare; they were free to judge me as they wished and I was their victim.

There was, of course, one way I could fight back: simply stare at them in turn (with the focus on my unfaithful girlfriend) and turn them into objects who felt shame at being discovered in a compromising position. My girlfriend's identity of being a cheat would be revealed to her in its full vividness, even if she had been so engrossed in the act she had not viewed herself as such. I had, then, become in Sartrean terms a *subject* free to contemplate and judge them as I wished, and they would feel transfixed into objects "caught in the act." They would find their cozy world slipping away from them and would become mere objects lying under a tree who would feel more like clinical specimens in a Masters-Johnson study.

Suppose, however, that I were to move to some cosmopolitan center like New York City or to Paris, Sartre's home, where I was surrounded by strangers. Then the whole system of what the stares meant in my hometown would be gone; I would not know what a particular person's stare signified. Was I being admired? Scorned? Sized up for a possible mugging? I would begin to feel like the object I had made of the couple I caught kissing; the strangers in the big city were judging me in ways I could never penetrate, particularly since persons who live in large cities so often wear the kind of poker faces one finds in a card game or on a doctoral-exam committee.

Thus far I have spoken of Sartre's concept of the "stare" in strictly sociological terms; but for Sartre the stare has a kind of metaphysical reality that afflicts all human relationships. We are either stared at and become objects or we regain our freedom *only at the expense of the other's freedom* by staring back at him, that is, judging him in turn. Human relationships then become marked by conflict instead of by the community I knew in my small town, with each person now oscillating between being a subject and an object, between staring and being stared at in turn, in a contest of wills to see who will be master of the other. Even if I did succeed in finding in New York a small community of two or more persons who did not have such conflicts, there are still more strangers out there who can stare at us, and we return to conflict again. Only the numbers involved have changed.

In my hometown, however, if the boy next door gave a girl a loving stare, she would not necessarily interpret it as an attempt to possess her freedom. Perhaps she already knew that he was a good Boy Scout or that he had read Fromm's *Art of Loving,* which suggests that the primary aim of love is to give and not to receive love. If the boy did not receive a loving stare in return, he would not necessarily judge himself as some kind of superfluous protuberance in the world or as someone who had lost his sense of identity and worth.

He might, of course, be shaken if the girl was of special importance to him because of her extraordinary charm or beauty or brains; but if he were secure in himself and did not allow his sense of worth to be determined primarily by how others viewed him, he would probably say that even if no one loved him, he could face the world alone on its own terms and find significance for himself in ways other than the approval of other people. (Indeed, in an earlier section of *Being and Nothingness,* Sartre labels those who are incapable of authentically deciding for themselves the life-style they want as being guilty of "bad faith"; his classic example was of the girl who knows she is being seduced and refuses to face the fact. When her lover takes her hand, she lets it lie there as an inert object to avoid the agonizing responsibility of deciding to go ahead with the affair and please her lover or withdraw it and risk offending him.)

When we turn to Sartre's own theory of love, however, we find a curious obsession with how others view oneself, as if it were they who were the source of my identity. Even if I did "stare down" the other and reclaim this identity for myself and assume responsibility for it, it would still be an identity fashioned through someone else's eyes and not my own.

Let us now see how Sartre's philosophy of love fits in with what we have already said about the stare and how he might react to our small-town love relationships. For Sartre, the ideal love relationship would be one that is surprisingly like Fromm's: two free subjects who identify with each other without mutually attempting to possess each other as objects. But Sartre thinks this is an impossible ideal.

1. In his view, unless I am loved, I will feel like a superfluous being who is merely viewed instrumentally by others. We are all born or "thrown into the world" with no necessary reason why we should be here and with no inner essence or external scale of absolute values in terms of which we may model ourselves or ground our being. Perhaps the hometown boy who thinks he is secure within himself has merely turned himself into a kind of human rock to avoid the emptiness and estrangement he may feel at any moment should his freedom assert itself and negate the seemingly secure identity he thought he

had established for himself. As long as consciousness is free, there is the possibility that he could see that this secure self could be otherwise than it is; for human beings are not rocks, with no self-awareness of alternative possibilities. We are beings who need not be what we are, and we can all awaken some morning and find that our previous identity has lost its meaning. We are then faced with the agonizing necessity to choose ourselves anew. In his section on love, Sartre seems to posit that being loved rescues me from this forlorn sense of being cast adrift in a world where I feel no reason for my existence, where my identity can be shattered at any time by my own free choice or by another's stare. We are beset by insecurities from both within and without. We do not, of course, want to surrender our freedom, but we also want to have some firm sense of meaning or identity within ourselves and with the world. In Sartre's terms, we want to "ground our existence" in a solid way, and yet we also want to be free. But for Sartre, the fluidity of freedom and the solidity of a personal, secure identity are ultimately contradictory ideals.

2. It is by now apparent that for Sartre love is the *desire to be loved.* But since the ideal love is between two free subjects, he does not want to destroy the other person's freedom and he wants to preserve his own. Furthermore, he wants the choice of the partner to be an absolute one, as if they could say that they were created for each other alone. He does not merely want to be chosen from among others. (He could have added that if one is "chosen from among others," another more favorable choice could always come along that could leave him abandoned.) And a choice it must be; to be driven into one another's arms by a love potion would be degrading to both. Only in such ways as these is my existence, according to Sartre, given some kind of justification and protection from devaluation by the indifference or stares of others who do not love me.

However, we must recall that, for Sartre, preserving one's freedom and sense of worth means rescuing one's freedom and identity from the stares of others. And it seems I must do this even to my beloved, a free, independent being who is judging me in ways I know not. But how can I reclaim my freedom and identity as molded by my beloved without destroying her freedom in the very process and thus reducing her to an object? To do this would be to violate the ideal of love as an intimate relation between two free subjects. Thus, if I wish to capture the freedom of the beloved, I must somehow be able to do this without destroying it in the very process of capturing it and thus reducing her to an object. For who wants to be loved by a slave?

Perhaps one approach would be to pretend to present myself as a nonthreatening object: "I want to do anything for you that you desire." For if I were to approach her as a free subject, then my "stare" would on Sartrean grounds turn her into an object whose freedom I had absorbed. And this she would never consent to; my stare would be a signal for her to leave at once, for she would sense that I was trying to possess her. Thus what I would do is simply throw myself at her feet, as it were, and seem to present myself as an object who is no threat to her freedom. I would set myself up as the very meaning of her existence, with all sorts of flattery and seduction. I would try to make her see that the very meaning of her existence, her reason for living, depends on me. But now it seems clear that I have turned myself into an object by trying to be her "sweet little thing." I may, in seduction, think that I am only pretending to be an object and that I am still secretly preserving my freedom and subjectivity. But will the effort at seduction work as a ruse in presenting myself as an object while still trying to preserve my subjectivity?

Sartre thinks that language is to seduction what the caress is to sex. But we cannot really capture the other's freedom this way since we can never know how the other person is interpreting our words. The other sits in lofty silence while listening to my entreaties and is free to interpret them however he or she wishes. Someone may seem to be willing to surrender to my wishes and then at the crucial moment refrain from giving me a clear answer. The response to my words is analogous to the stare or judgment of others whose meaning I can never be sure I have penetrated and reclaimed as my own freedom and identity. Thus I am still a mere object held captive by my partner's freedom to interpret my entreaties as she wishes, however much I may think I am only pretending to be an object or her slave in order to entice her to surrender her freedom to me. But as long as I am still only an object, the ideal of love as a relation between two free beings is violated. For I am her slave, and her freedom has eluded me.

3. But what if I do succeed in getting the other person to love me? We have already noted that, for Sartre, love is the desire to be loved. The one I have successfully seduced, of course, also knows that I love her. But since love is not just the desire to possess me temporarily, but to capture my freedom permanently, she will try to do me what I tried to do her: to chain my will to hers permanently. Since I was the aggressor and seducer, she knows that such persons demand that she accept them as her supreme value, as the absolute limit to her freedom, as her reason for living. She will thus allow herself to surrender to me as a roundabout way of possessing me. But in surrendering to me she has, in effect, self-destructed her freedom and has now become my slave. But this is something which I surely do not want since I want to be loved by a free being, that is, by someone who gives her love to me freely.

On the other hand I also want to possess her freedom and identity, and chain her will to mine permanently. But a freedom which is possessed is no longer free, and this contradicts my other demand that I be loved freely and not by an automaton. Thus love, for Sartre, involves contradictory goals. He writes:

> The man who wants to be loved does not really desire the enslavement of the beloved. He is not bent on becoming the object of a devotion which flows forth automatically. . . . The total enslavement of the beloved kills the love of the lover. If the beloved is transformed into an automaton the lover finds himself alone. Thus the lover does not desire to possess the beloved as one possesses a thing; he demands a special type of appropriation.

He wants to possess a freedom as *freedom*. . . . He wants to be loved by a freedom but demands that this freedom should no longer be free (p. 367).

Elsewhere, he writes:

I demand that the other love me and I do everything possible to realize my project; but if the other loves me, he radically deceives me by his love. I demanded of him that he should establish my own being as privileged object by maintaining himself as pure subjectivity confronting me; and as soon as he loves me he experiences me as a subject and is swallowed up in his objectivity confronting my subjectivity (p. 376).

Thus in getting others to love us so that we may possess their freedom and identity as our own inevitably results in our having to reduce ourselves to mere objects or slaves in order to win the beloved. And as soon as my beloved senses that she has, in effect, become my slave, she will doubtlessly struggle to preserve her freedom, identity, and subjectivity. The lovers then engage in endless conflict, with each one engaged in a futile battle to capture the freedom of the other while still wanting to be loved by someone who is free. If I do capture the freedom of my beloved, she can at any moment regain her freedom by becoming aloof, silent, and staring at me with that Medusa-like gaze that freezes me into an object. Hence arises the perpetual insecurity of possessive lovers. As the conflict rages on, each partner alternates between being subject and object, master and slave, as it were. The ideal of two subjects loving each other, that is, two persons who mutually respect each other's freedom and subjectivity, is thus impossible, according to Sartre. For in a conflict such as this, I can, for Sartre, only become free at the expense of the other's freedom.

4. There is, finally (according to Sartre), a kind of logical incoherence in defining love. For if (a) "I love you" means "I want you to love me," then (b) "I want you to love me" entails "I want you to want me to love you." But this would mean that (c) "I want you to want me to love you" would entail "I want you to want me to want you to love me," ad infinitum.[14]

How does one go about evaluating such an intricate and pessimistic theory such as Sartre's? It seems to be a theory to which one would react in a total take-it-or-leave-it fashion, which is to say one's reaction would be based more on emotion than reason. (The same could be said for Fromm's *The Art of Loving*.) The responses would clearly depend on what one's experiences with lovers had been and how one had reacted to them. If one has suffered at the hands of a possessive, selfish lover, but still believes in love itself, then Fromm's book might be reassuring to one who wants to believe that benevolence and love are not incompatible. Another person who has suffered

---

14. Thus, in Alfred Stern's words, "Sartre concludes that the amorous relation is a system of infinite reflections, a deceiving mirror game which carries within itself its own frustration. Love is a kind of dupery." Stern, *Sartre* (New York: Dell Publishing Co., 1967), p. 155.

similar disillusionment might find Sartre's theories comforting in reassuring him that this is simply the way love is and that it is best never to love again.

Let us now attempt some evaluation of Sartre's theory that goes beyond sociological generalizations about what love is like in large urban centers whose residents live in an atomistic, noncommunal, self-centered way, who are constantly competing with each other for money or love or power, and whose motto is "Get them before they get you." Sartre is a cosmopolitan Parisian to the core, but he could note that the seeming harmony of small towns really disguises a Peyton Place atmosphere, where the grim attempt to conquer everyone else lurks behind a facade of hometown amiability.

One difficulty is that "I love you" does not necessarily mean "I want you to love me." There may be lovers who are aroused only by aloof, independent types whom they know will refuse to return love. Their refusal to become enslaved by love may make them, in the eyes of some, much more lovable than those who are all too eager to surrender or who at least take one's entreaties to be loved seriously. Furthermore, there are those who love, but who do not wish to set up a love relationship with the other because they believe that such a relation may end in a set of Sartrean contradictions. They may see each other from time to time and relish each other's presence; but they will keep their distance because they feel that too close a union would lead to mutual enslavement.

In the earlier sections of *Being and Nothingness,* Sartre speaks highly of those who authentically choose for themselves their own identity, and who do not allow themselves to escape their freedom by adopting roles in which they become frozen as things. Of course, when we become free beings we are always faced with the possibility that our old choices will pall and that our restless freedom will demand fresh choices. Does this necessarily mean that we will seek some ultimate grounding for our existence to avoid the agony of constantly being forced to break away from our old self and choose anew?

There is, for example, a kind of lover who does not seek to ground his being by leaning on his "one and only." He may feel secure enough in his being that he is not afraid, for example, to make repeated choices of lovers. Sartre might, of course, point out that there is a quest for a kind of identity here: to be a "lover" whose identity is based on a continuity of choices. Process itself would become a kind of identity. But if love holds no vital importance for him, it would be difficult to see how he is trying to use love to lend solidity to his existence. And if he does choose to become a "rolling stone," the type of lover who commits himself to no one for long, he could still be more than just a lover, unlike the waiter in a restaurant who tries to escape the agony of making choices by defining himself exclusively in terms of his social role. (Sartre's term for this latter phenomenon is *bad faith.* But such a lover need not define his whole life in terms of what he does in the evening or constantly play the role of "lover boy.")

A further difficulty arises in Sartre's claim in the section "Being-for-Others" that we see ourselves as others see us. We then attempt to regain this identity by seizing it from the other person and claiming it as our own in order to "ground one's being." But it could hardly be my own identity unless I had first fashioned it for myself. Of course, if my own self-created identity had somehow been stolen from me by another, then it would make good sense to try to regain it. (This would be true if I had been hypnotized or brainwashed.) At some points in Sartre's exposition he does seem to suggest that it is my own self-shaped identity that has been externalized (and revealed to me clearly for the first time) by the other person's stare and which I wish to recapture. But it is not clear (to me) how much he intends my own identity to be revealed and how much the other person actually gives me or shapes my identity.

If he does mean that my identity is shaped by others, I would surely not want to recapture it if it were, say, an unfavorable one. Sartre's classic example is of being caught peaking through someone's keyhole; here he seems to think the other person has revealed to me what I really am—a shameful person. But surely his stare has molded me only in the light of his own judgments about my act. And if I am the free being Sartre claims we all are, I need not feel shameful; for could I not choose to see myself in the light of my own judgments about myself and my act, and simply refuse to feel shame if I have some very good reason for peeking through the keyhole?

But there is an even deeper difficulty: What if the person who is judging me is himself someone whose identity has been shaped by others, and so on? We all thus seem to be mirror images of each other. Where is the person whose judgments are his own and who is the solid source of all our judgments of each other? But if there is no one who is really possessed of an identity of his own making, then I am not recovering any other identity as my own that was shaped by another's stare. For it is only a phantom individual shaped by others who is staring at me and whose judgments are not really his own. Why, then, should I be concerned about another's "judgment" of me? Indeed, it is as if no one had a real identity or center that I could absorb at all.

If this interpretation of Sartre is correct, then "being loved" is no way to gain any sense of solidity or identity or sense of self-worth. In trying to absorb another's identity or freedom as mine when that person has been so socialized (and by a society I may despise), I could hardly achieve my goal of regaining *myself* or any *freedom* at all.

Finally, a critic might argue that the chief difficulty with Sartre's theory of love is that love is being used as a means to an end instead of simply allowing the lovers to relish each other's presence for its own sake. We have already noted that a common failing among many philosophers of sex was that they wanted to convert it into some form of communication or way of relating to others instead of simply allowing two people to relax in each other's arms and gradually build up to a climax of lustful pleasure enjoyed for its own sake.

In our philosophical theories of love we note the same tendency: Sartre wants to *use* love to sanctify his own existence in the eyes of the beloved; the contradictions he attributes to love itself may simply be due to the way he thinks all persons treat love. If I want my lover to be a free agent who chooses to love me and if I also want to possess her freedom and identity, this does not by itself prove that love is necessarily a self-contradictory ideal. It only proves that there are some people who treat love possessively because they are frightened of being cast adrift in a world where they must choose (and perhaps constantly rechoose) their own being. But persons who are capable of self-choice would not feel like protuberances in an indifferent world whose existence can only be redeemed by being loved.

Four

Erotic Love: A Final Appraisal

Is erotic love itself "beautiful" and "good"? As we have already noted, Plato argued that it was not since love seeks out beauty and goodness; if it already had beauty and goodness, it would not be necessary to search for what it already possesses. Yet most people would probably hold that a life devoid of love was either worthless or at least sorely missing something that would make it complete.

I have, however, argued in preceding chapters of this book that erotic love is not a viable concept, that it is riddled with contradictions that set up conflicting desires within the lover and cause endless mental torture. This would then refute the claim that love or sex with love results in increased contentment and peace of mind.

Some of these conflicts, of course, can doubtlessly be resolved by a gradual change in what partners demand of a love relationship. For example, the most familiar conflict is, on the one hand, the desire for a sense of oneness with one's partner, involving a unity of heart, mind, body, and soul. On the other hand, there is the desire for freedom and independence; one doesn't want to feel possessed or smothered by one's lover. The sense of oneness with another fulfills an important psychological need that many feel, that of wanting to be lifted out of one's isolation and thus enjoying the feeling of security that one will not have to face the world utterly alone. But to have security and nothing else is deadening to the spirit; one also seeks adventure and variety, and this involves an assertion of one's independence.

Many lovers feel they have worked out a relationship wherein both these demands for security and adventure can be fulfilled. But when the supposed reconciliation of these conflicting demands is put to the supreme test, such as one lover's desire to commit adultery and thus add a little adventure and variety to his sex life, the partner will commonly protest that the sense of total oneness between them is being torn asunder by his giving his body to another. She may very well then threaten to sue for divorce on the grounds of marital infidelity. But then her mate's conflicting desires cannot be fulfilled: on the one hand, he wants the security of a loving wife; on the other hand, he wants the ultimate sexual adventure, which for him is to have an affair.

But perhaps erotic love can overcome the problems posed by this sort of example. The couple will simply reconcile their needs for both freedom and independence by holding that each can exercise his or her independence so long as it does not cause distress to the other or threaten to destroy the marriage. And perhaps even the distress caused by adultery can be overcome by convincing the mate that because two people are in love, it does not follow that they own each other's bodies; their only claim need be to each other's hearts—if even that is necessary. For one's body belongs to oneself alone, and no one has a right to possess it, be he rapist or lover.

Indeed, if love is as truly generous and as concerned for the beloved's happiness as is claimed, then the wife should allow her husband the freedom to engage in a sexual adventure now and then if he feels such a thing is essential to his happiness—and vice versa. Thus the wife should say: "You can give your body to whomever you wish, so long as you do not do so at those times when you know I want sexual satisfaction myself. After all an affair with another woman is only physical fun that is as innocent as any other sport. And by allowing you a little sexual freedom, you will probably love me even more by my granting you this independence. And if you do happen to give your heart as well as your body to another, this only proves that we did not really have a solid love relationship in the first place, so nothing has been lost."

This brief excursion into the problem of adultery shows that, with a more liberal conception of what love implies, one might be able in many cases to overcome the traditional conflict faced by lovers: the desire for oneness with one's beloved and also independence, that is, the desire for both security and adventure. But there are other inherent contradictions in erotic love that cannot be overcome. I will focus on one example I previously analyzed: Love for another claims to be predominantly altruistic, with self-interest either totally absent or, at most, a secondary consideration. And indeed it must presuppose this if it is to justify its claim to be a noble and beautiful thing. Yet I also argued that love is essentially self-interested and indeed presupposes just such essential self-interest. So we have a glaring contradiction.

By one concept of altruism, a lover should be totally free of self-interest and should give his love to whoever needs it most badly, even if that person has no particularly attractive qualities or is even positively disgusting. And he should continue to give his love to such a person even if this person responds by treating him like an animal. Thus he should have no concern for any rewards for himself at all.

But clearly, with perhaps a few rare exceptions, erotic lovers are not like this at all. They will give their love to someone who needs it only if that person also has attractive qualities which stir their emotions and gratify their own self-interest, such as the desire to witness beauty. Or they will completely ignore those who need love badly and give it to someone who doesn't need it at all, such as someone who is already loved by many others; and they will try to seduce such a person into loving them because she has the qualities they want. Furthermore, even if someone has highly attractive qualities, this is no guarantee they will be loved. Those who are extremely intelligent or extremely beautiful are often unable to attract a lover because others feel that their ego is threatened by being in the presence of someone to whom they feel inferior. Thus one's own self-interest is the determining factor in choosing a lover.

In another version of altruism, it is all right to have some self-interest, as long as giving to another is the primary motive. One must have some concern for his own self-interest; otherwise one would become a mere self-sacrificing slave willing to be exploited by others. A truly generous person must have some love for himself and thus some concern for his own interests; otherwise he would only project his own self-hate onto others and could not love them at all. Furthermore, lovers do not want to be loved out of sheer charity anyway; their pride demands that they be chosen because they have certain attractive qualities that appeal to others. They want to "win" the heart of their lover and not merely have love handed to them because they need it. Thus their being loved must be an achievement of which they can be proud.

Can we then reconcile altruism and self-interest by adopting the theory that love is primarily altruistic, with self-interest present but only as a secondary consideration? Clearly the lover does not want a selfish beloved; and on the other hand, she does not want charity. But if she does not want a purely charitable lover, she is going to have to admit that he must have some self-interest. This she would grant, but only as long as the lover is not governed primarily by self-interest; otherwise she is going to be exploited and not truly loved.

Will she be able to find the kind of lover she seeks, one who is primarily generous and only secondarily self-interested? The difficulty is that she does not want to be loved out of sheer charity but wants to merit love by having been selected for the attractive qualities she possesses. But we have already noted that lovers choose only those partners with certain attractive qualities that appeal primarily to their own needs and self-interest. But this means that the one who seeks to be loved will be selected primarily from selfish considerations. Thus the woman's desire to be not an object of charity but an object worthy of love has driven her to require that she be selected primarily for selfish reasons. But this violates her other claim that she wants her lover to be primarily generous.

Furthermore, her wish to be chosen on her merits violates another claim lovers frequently make: to be chosen as a total human being for one's own sake alone. But only a purely charitable lover claims to do this, and she does not want charity. Since she wants to merit love and wants her lover to be selective, she requires that she be viewed not as a mere human being (which we all are), but as someone special who has those unique qualities that appeal to those who are selective. But to be chosen "for one's own sake alone" is, once again, impossible since she wants to be selected for her charming qualities, and those who do select her for such qualities clearly don't do it for her own sake alone. Nor can she claim to be viewed as a total human being, since her desire to be selected for certain special qualities has violated this ideal also. A total human being is always something more than a particular set of attractive traits.[1]

Thus erotic love seems to be caught in a trap: On the one hand we want our lover to be primarily generous in order to avoid being exploited; on the other hand our desire to *merit* love drives us to want to be selected primarily for self-interested reasons. (I do not wish to rest my case on the one particular argument developed here; the additional arguments set forth in previous chapters are necessary to establish my thesis clearly.)

I now wish to continue my attack on the proponent of erotic love's claim to be primarily generous to and concerned for the total human being for his or her own sake alone by philosophically examining some factual data. To do this I will take another look at the research found in Alan Lee's *The Colors of Love*. Alan Lee is a sociologist at the University of Toronto who sent questionnaires to thousands of Canadians asking them to give their own conception of love and to analyze their own personal traits. Lee did not try to impose on his respondents any notion that there is some one thing called "true love." If his respondents claimed that this is what erotic love meant to them, he accepted it at face value and developed his types of love from their reports. Lee is, therefore, a pluralist, who believes there are many different kinds of erotic love. Other than this, however, he did not probe deeply into the philosophical implications of his findings, something which I shall try to do.

He labels the first type the *eros* lover. For this lover, physical beauty is the primary consideration in his choice of a mate. He may enjoy other qualities as well, but unless such persons are physically beautiful he will ignore them, no matter how attractive they may be in other ways. And if the beloved loses his or her physical beauty, it is likely he or she will be dropped cold. Clearly such a lover is motivated primarily by self-interest in his desire to enjoy beholding the beauty of his beloved. And to concentrate primarily on physical beauty is hardly to love the entire person for his own sake. Even if such a lover sublimated his love for physical beauty into love for spiritual beauty, the same criticisms would apply.

Alan Lee labels his second type of lover *ludus* (from the Greek word for game). For the ludus lover, love is a game of seduction to see who can win whom for a temporary intimate liaison. When the game is over he quickly tires of his lover and moves on to another. Ludus is clearly self-interested in that he is interested only in the ego-fulfillment of being a successful seducer. And

---

1. If a lover does insist that he loves the "total human person," all that this means is that he finds all her qualities attractive. And if these attractive qualities were to disappear, the lover of those qualities would disappear.

rather than being a loving human being, he seems only to love the game of love. He is, in our jargon, the typical "lover boy."

Lee's third type of lover is the *manic*. The manic is, Lee claims, filled with self-hate and insecurity that he tries to overcome by demanding absolute possession of his lover. Furthermore, he commonly despises his lover as well, perhaps because he secretly resents being so dependent on his lover to give his empty life some meaning. It is clear that he does not love his lover for her own sake, but is merely using her to gratify his desperate desire to be loved so that he can feel that he is of some worth. He is not really in love with a human being at all: he is in love with being loved.

Lee labels the fourth type of lover *storge*. Storge cares nothing for ecstatic emotions, and his love seems to be more like a deep friendship. Storge's main goal is to be a family man, and he chooses his lover on the basis of whether she will be a good companion, wife, housekeeper, sexual partner and mother. One wonders if he really loves his mate as a human being for her own sake or whether he is simply seeing her in terms of the roles he wants her to play to satisfy his desire to raise a family. He seems to be not so much in love with her as he is in love with family life. And if it becomes apparent she cannot play the roles assigned her, he drops her.

Although Lee mentions other types of lovers (none of which avoid the criticisms I have made of the others), he concludes with one type (which he labels *storgic eros*) who seems to be idealistic and unselfish. The storgic-eros lover's main criterion for choosing a mate is that she is someone who needs love. He is utterly lacking in possessiveness or jealousy, is warm and affectionate and does not demand that his love be reciprocated. Nor does he require marriage or their being constantly together; he sees her only when she feels she needs loving. And if someone else would serve as a better partner for her, he would graciously step aside without complaint.

However, someone who is loved by this type of person would clearly be dubious of a love that is based on the duty to help those in need of love. Does one really want to be loved out of someone's feeling that they are obligated to help those in need? Surely they want to merit love and not be patronized by being an object of charity. Furthermore if the storgic-eros lover so readily gives up his beloved if another partner would serve her better and if he does not feel any need for the love to be reciprocated, could he really be said to have any close attachment to her or be deeply involved with her in a erotic way at all? But these are surely things that the one who needs love wants. Thus if one thinks the storgic-eros lover is truly noble (as Lee does), he seems to be giving more of a priestlike love than an erotic love. (Lee notes that this very idealistic type of lover cares little or nothing for sex, perhaps because he feels that lustful desire is selfish). If one thinks he is not so noble, one could say that he is not really in love but is merely using his lover to satisfy his charitable drives. Rather than loving her, he seems to be more in love with the idea of giving love and the enormous ego gratification this yields to this type of person. (It should be noted that only a tiny minority of Lee's respondents claimed to have the self-giving characteristics mentioned above.)

Although Lee does not probe deeply into the philosophical implications of his work, the philosopher would note that there seems to be no one characteristic that all these love types share in common that uniquely defines love and distinguishes love from other types of human relationships. (This confirms a thesis I defended earlier in the book.) But more ominously, it becomes clear that after surveying these love types, the ideal of loving the total person for his or her own sake alone is either clearly absent or at least open to serious doubt in each case. The predominance of self-interest in each type is either obvious or could be detected by a careful analysis of motives.

Lovers, of course, often devote much time and energy to pleasing their beloved. But the owner of a new Cadillac or a fancy sports car devotes endless hours to polishing it or spends considerable money keeping it in working condition. He does these things not out of any devotion to the car but only because the thrill and ego-fulfillment of driving such a beautiful car requires that he do such things for it. And when the car begins to require sacrifices that outweigh the benefits it gives, he trades it in. He has "given" but only in order to "get."

If he continues to hold on to the decrepit car, it is perhaps only because he knows he cannot afford a better one. He might sacrifice much time and energy to "nurse" it back to health and restore it to its original qualities, but this is only so he can have the ego-fulfillment of driving a beautiful car once again. Or he may cling to it because, for some reason, it has him emotionally "hooked" even though it yields no rewards and he would really like to get rid of it. Or he may keep the car for sentimental reasons, for "old times' sake" because its presence brings back delightful memories of all the ego-gratification he once received from it; but this is still a self-interested motive, and he no longer loves the car as it is but only as a memory. Thus ego-gratification or other nonaltruistic considerations were the central motive for remaining loyal to the old car.

This example of the car applies perfectly to lovers as well: They give in order to get and if they think they aren't getting as much as or, hopefully, more than they are giving, they trade the once-beloved in on a new model, even though the rejected partner may need love badly. Or if the lover does not trade her in, it is only for the self-interested reasons analogous to those of the car owner who held on to his decrepit vehicle.

Given these considerations, why is it that most people still want to be "in love," even if they are aware of the self-interested motives for their being loved? The answers, I think, are obvious:

1. One wants to enjoy the ecstasy of the intoxicating emotions that arise from loving or being loved.

2. Either because of pride or because of social conditioning, we feel that we are worthless unless we have had our merits and attractive qualities confirmed by having been able to attract a lover.

3. In a sexist society, the male is faced with the delicious prospect of getting not just as much as he is getting but even more than he is giving. For the female has been conditioned to think that she is inferior and deserves only the minimum of gratification, and that she must honor the supposedly superior male by endless self-sacrifice. This generosity of the female does not, however, rest on any solid foundation of true altruism; it arises only from feelings of inferiority. Once sexism is eliminated, the female's self-interest will start to assert itself, and she will demand rewards commensurate with what she gives, and quite justifiably so. But this then becomes a "you scratch my back and I'll scratch yours" type of relationship, where each partner is on the alert to see that he or she is getting as much or he or she is giving. This can lead frequently to violent lovers' quarrels with one partner feeling that he or she isn't getting a fair share. This grim picture is clearly miles away from any concept of a truly altruistic relationship.

4. The final reason most persons prefer to be loved is that, even if they realize their partner is giving only in order to get, they are at least getting something, which is better than being utterly alone and getting nothing at all. They fail to realize there may be other forms of truly humanistic relationships that do not involve erotic love, which, as we have seen, seems to turn its adherents either into something vicious or at least into something far less than noble. (Despite all I have said, however, most erotic lovers will continue to insist that their love is truly altruistic; but this is only because they are blinded by the emotions of love to their lovers' true motives.)

In my concluding section on love I have chosen to focus on the egoism-altruism controversy, since it gives me an opportunity to show how the second part of my book, dealing with love, supports the central argument of the first part, dealing with sex. There I maintained that sex with a generous, considerate, and sexually adept non-lover committed to humanistic principles can provide a sexual experience that is as good as or even better than sex with a lover.

If my thesis that erotic love is essentially self-interested is correct, it is going to damage seriously the claim that sex with a lover is the supreme experience. Part of the sexual joy lovers experience derives from the feeling that the partner is truly an altruistic person who would be willing to give his all to the act even if he felt he weren't getting very much in return. But if my thesis about the motives of lovers is correct, this joy is based on an illusion.

Lovers, for example, would be on the alert to see that they are getting as much as they are giving, or hopefully, to get more than they give (as with the millions of husbands who leave their wives orgasmically and otherwise unfulfilled). Of course, the lover may do his best to thrill his beloved, but if he is essentially self-interested, this would only be in order to prove to himself that he has the virility or sexual prowess to arouse another person. Furthermore, lovers commonly consider the beloved obligated to satisfy them whenever they wish, even if the beloved isn't in the mood for sex at all.

On the other hand, a generous, considerate non-lover is capable of performing a sex act without engaging in violent quarrels if he fails to be satisfied. Nor will such a generous person so readily threaten to abandon his partner if he fails to be pleased sexually with his partner's performance. Nor will he think that it is his partner's obligation to please him whenever he wishes.

Furthermore, sex between humanistic non-lovers would not be devoid of feeling, for the partners' mutual realization that their motives are truly generous would create enormous feelings of affection for each other. And since a truly generous non-lover would stay with his partner even if he isn't receiving his so-called fair share of sexual pleasure, such a sex act would be devoid of the fears that haunt lovers if they fail to "measure up." (Such tunes as Paul Simon's "Fifty Ways to Leave Your Lover" or "Will You Still Love Me Tomorrow?" or "The Thrill Is Gone" hang over the sexual act like a black cloud.)

Why is the generous type of non-lover more likely to treat his partner better than the erotic lover? The answer, I think, is that he is free of the things I have already claimed that erotic love does to its victims, especially the violence that such a love seems to do to their altruistic nature. I conclude, therefore, that on the whole, sex with a humanistic non-lover is far preferable to sex with an erotic lover.

I now leave it to the reader to judge if I have proved the central thesis about the superiority of sex with a humanistic non-lover. And, while philosophers have traditionally avoided such topics as I have discussed here—perhaps because they could not possibly see how there could be any connection between logic on the one hand and love and lust on the other—I hope this work has also shown that philosophy can have something important to say about such things.

Suggestions for
Further Reading

Alexander, W. M. "Philosophers Have Avoided Sex." *Diogenes* 72 (1970): 56–74.

Aristotle. *Nichomachean Ethics.* Books Seven and Eight. Translated by J. A. K. Thompson. Baltimore: Penguin Books, 1962: 227–285.

Atkinson, Ronald. *Sexual Morality.* New York: Harcourt, Brace and World, 1965.

Baker, Robert. "Pricks and Chicks: A Plea for Persons." In *Philosophy and Sex,* edited by Robert Baker and Frederick Elliston. Buffalo: Prometheus Books, 1975: 45–64.

Bayles, Michael D. "Marriage, Love, and Procreation." In *Philosophy and Sex.* Op. cit.: 190–206.

Benoit, Hubert. *The Many Faces of Love.* New York: Pantheon, 1955.

Bertocci, Peter Anthony. *The Human Venture in Sex, Love and Marriage.* New York: Association Press, 1949.

———. *Sex, Love, and the Person.* New York: Sheed and Ward, 1967.

Blum, Larry, Marcia Homiak, Judy Housman, and Naomi Scheman. "Altruism and Women's Oppression." *The Philosophical Forum* 5 (1973): 222–47.

Brain, Robert. *Friends and Lovers.* New York: Simon & Schuster, 1977.

Brown, Norman O. *Love's Body.* New York: Random House, 1966.

Buckley, M. J. *Morality and the Homosexual: A Catholic Approach to a Moral Problem.* Westminster, Md.: Newman Press, 1960.

Cohen, Carl. "Sex, Birth Control and Human Life." In *Philosophy and Sex.* Op. cit.: 150–165.

Davis, Murray S. *Intimate Relations.* New York: Free Press, 1973.

de Beauvoir, Simone. "Must We Burn Sade?" In *Marquis de Sade: Selections From His Writings.* New York: Grove Press, 1953: 11–82.

———. *The Second Sex* (1949). Translated by H. M. Parshley. New York: Knopf, 1952.

de Rougemont, Denis. *Love in the Western World.* Translated by M. Belgion. New York: Pantheon, 1970.

———. *Passion and Society.* London: Faber & Faber, 1962.

de Sade, Donatein Alphonse-François. *Justine; Philosophy in the Bedroom; Eugenie de Franval and Other Writings* (1791). Translated by R. Senver and A. Wainhouse. New York: Grove Press, 1965.

Ellis, Albert. "Rationality in Sexual Morality." *Humanist* 29 (1969): 17–21.

Elliston, Frederick. "In Defense of Promiscuity." In *Philosophy and Sex.* Op. cit.: 222–243.

Feinberg, Joel, ed. *The Problem of Abortion.* Belmont, Calif.: Wadsworth, 1973.

Finnis, John M. "Natural Law and Unnatural Acts." *Heythorp Journal* 11 (1970): 365–87.

Freud, Sigmund. *Civilization and Its Discontents* (1930). New York: W. W. Norton, 1961.

———. *Three Contributions to the Theory of Sex.* New York: Dutton, 1962.

Frye, Marilyn. "Male Chauvinism: A Conceptual Analysis." In *Philosophy and Sex.* Op. cit.: 65–79.

Gendron, Bernard. "Sexual Alienation." In his *Technology and the Human Condition.* New York: St. Martin's Press, 1977: 114–133.

Goldman, Alan. "Plain Sex." *Philosophy and Public Affairs* 6 (1977): 267–287.

Gould, Carol. "The Woman Question: Philosophy of Liberation and the Liberation of Philosophy." *The Philosophical Forum* 5 (1973): 5–44.

Gould, Thomas. *Platonic Love.* New York: Free Press, 1963.

Gray, Robert. "Sex and Sexual Perversion." *The Journal of Philosophy* 75 (1978): 189–199.

Hazo, Robert. *The Idea of Love.* New York: Praeger, 1967.

Held, Virginia. "Marx, Sex, and the Transformation of Society." *Philosophical Forum* 5 (1973): 168–184.

Hunt, Morton M. *The Natural History of Love* (1959). New York: Alfred A. Knopf, 1967.

Jagger, Alison M., and Paula Rothenberg Struhl, eds. *Feminist Frameworks.* New York: McGraw-Hill, 1978.

Kierkegaard, Soren. *The Diary of a Seducer* (1843). Translated by Fick. Ithaca, N.Y.: The Dragon Press, 1932.

———. *Works of Love* (1847). Translated by David F. Swenson and Lilian Marvin Swenson. Princeton, N.J.: Princeton University Press, 1946.

———. "The Aesthetic Validity of Marriage." In *Either/or,* vol. 2. Translated by W. Lowrie. New York: Anchor, 1959.

Lewis, C. S. *The Four Loves.* New York: Harcourt, Brace Jovanovich, 1960.

Lilar, Suzanne. *Aspects of Love in Western Society.* Translated by Jonathan Griffin. New York: McGraw-Hill, 1965.

Litewka, Jack. "The Socialized Penis." *Liberation Magazine* 18 (March–April 1974).

Marcuse, Herbert. *Eros and Civilization: A Philosophical Inquiry into Freud.* Boston: Beacon Press, 1955.

Margolis, Clorinda, and Joseph Margolis. "Alternative Life-Styles and Sexual Tolerance." *The Humanist* 33 (1973): 19–20.

Margolis, Joseph. "The Question of Homosexuality." In *Philosophy and Sex.* Op. cit.: 288–302.

McMurty, John. "Monogamy: A Critique." In *Philosophy and Sex.* Op. cit.: 166–177.

McNeill, John J. *The Church and the Homosexual.* New York: Simon and Schuster, 1976.

Merleau–Ponty, Maurice. "The Body in Its Sexual Being." In *Phenomenology of Perception.* New York: Humanities Press, 1965.

Millett, Kate. *Sexual Politics.* New York: Avon, 1969.

Morgan, D. N. *Love in Plato, the Bible, and Freud.* Englewood Cliffs, N.J.: Prentice-Hall, 1964.

Moulton, Janice. "Sexual Behaviour: Another Position." *Journal of Philosophy* 73: (1976): 537–546.

Norton, David L., and Mary F. Kille, eds. *Philosophies of Love.* San Francisco: Chandler, 1971.

Ortega y Gasset, José. *On Love* (1939). Translated by Toby Talbot. New York: Meridian, 1957.

Palmer, David. "The Consolation of the Wedded." In *Philosophy and Sex.* Op. cit.: 178–189.

Pierce, Christine, and Marjory Collins. "Holes and Slime: Sexism in Sartre's Psychoanalysis." *The Philosophical Forum* 5 (1973): 112–27.

Plato. "Lysis," "Symposium," "Phaedrus." *The Dialogues of Plato,* 3rd ed. Translated by Benjamin Jowett. New York and London: Oxford University Press, 1892.

Pope Paul VI. "Humanae Vitae." In *Philosophy and Sex.* Op. cit.: 150–165.

Rapaport, Elizabeth. "On the Future of Love: Rousseau and the Radical Feminists." *The Philosophical Forum* 5 (1973): 185–205.

Reich, Wilhelm. *The Sexual Revolution: Towards a Self-Governing Character Structure.* New York: Orgone Press, 1945.

———. *The Invasion of Compulsory Sex-Morality.* New York: Farrar, Strauss, & Giroux, 1971.

Ruddick, Sara. "On Sexual Morality." In *Moral Problems,* edited by James Rachels. New York: Harper and Row, 1971: 85–105.

Russell, Bertrand. *Marriage and Morals.* New York: Liveright Publishers, 1928.

Shaffer, Jerome. "Sexual Desire." *The Journal of Philosophy* 75 (1978): 175–189.

Singer, Irving. *The Goals of Human Sexuality.* New York: Schocken, 1974.

———. *The Nature of Love: Plato to Luther.* New York: Random House, 1966.

Slote, Michael. "Inapplicable Concepts and Sexual Perversion." In *Philosophy and Sex.* Op. cit.: 261–267.

Solomon, Robert. "Sexual Paradigms." *Journal of Philosophy* 71 (1974): 336–45.

Taylor, Roger L. "Sexual Experience." *Aristotelian Society* (New Series) 68 (1967): 87–104.

Toon, Mark. *The Philosophy of Sex According to St. Thomas Aquinas.* Catholic University of America Philosophical Studies No. 156. Washington, D.C.: Catholic University of America, 1954.

Verene, D. P. "Sexual Love and Moral Experience." In *Philosophy and Sex.* Op. cit.: 105–115.

———, ed. *Sexual Love and Western Morality: A Philosophical Anthology.* New York: Harper and Row, 1972.

Vetterling–Braggin, M., F. Elliston and J. English, eds. *Feminism and Philosophy.* Littlefield, Adams and Co., 1977.

Wassertrom, Richard. "Is Adultery Immoral?" In *Philosophy and Sex.* Op. cit.: 207–221.

Wellman, Carl. "Premarital Sex." In his *Morals and Ethics.* Glenview, Ill.: Scott, Foresman: 104–132.

Wilson, John. *Logic and Sexual Morality.* Baltimore: Penguin, 1956.

Wood, Frederick C. *Sex and the New Morality.* New York: Association Press, 1968.

Index

Abortion, 2, 102, 131, 135
Adultery, 38, 46, 61, 102, 213
Agapic love, 132–33, 192–95
Alienation, 18–20, 97, 129
Allen, Clifford, 40–43
Androgyny, 89–91, 146
Aristotle, 5, 153, 159–60, 166
Atkinson, Ti-Grace, 25, 38, 115–16, 131
Authentic decisions, 4–5, 8, 13

Barrel, James, 9–10
Baumrin, Bernard, 101–07
Bisexuality, 146, 202
Bonaparte, Marie, 51
Brain, Robert, 60
Brownmiller, Susan, 56

Camus, Albert, 151
Casler, Lawrence, 25, 140
Communal sex, 54–55
Conservative sex, 118–19
Contradictions of love, 131–147, 212–19

De Beauvoir, Simone, 147
De Rougemont, Denis, 189–90

De Sade, Marquis, 40, 44–48, 51, 53–55, 125
Double-standard arguments, 4

Embodiment, 14, 61–68, 85, 102, 110–11
Existential sexuality, 4, 8, 13–14, 48–51

Feminism, 25, 28, 115–16, 131, 143
Fenichel, Otto, 162
Firestone, Shulamith, 131
Foreplay, 80–81, 83–84
Freud, Sigmund, 8, 10, 83, 133, 149, 176, 197–99
Friendship, 150, 173–81, 186–88
Fromm, Erich, 5, 137, 153, 159–66, 191, 205, 208
Frye, Marilyn, 52–53, 55

Garrison, Omar, 88–91
Gide, André, 40
Goldman, Alan, 112
Good sex, 79–117
Greenfield, Sydney, 130
Groddeck, George, 113
Group sex, 108, 110

Harmony of opposites, 33–34, 143, 145–47
Hite, Shere, 117
Homosexuality, 30, 34, 120–21, 146–47, 201–02
Human dignity, 60
Human rights, 57–60, 126
Humanism, 7–8, 15, 218–19

Incest, 102
Infatuation, 2–3, 147, 149–50, 164, 181–86
Insincerity, 76–77

Kinderlehrer, Jacqueline, 113, 116–17
Kinsey, Alfred, 41, 93, 96
Koestenbaum, Peter, 4, 8, 13–14
Kosok, Michael, 5, 17–20

Laing, R. D., 116–17
Liberal sex, 120–24
Like attracts like, 145–47, 178
Love and choice, 138–40
Love and desire, 152–53, 167
Love and emotion, 138–40, 153–55
Love and idealization, 157–59
Love and knowledge, 138–40, 156–59
Love attitude, 9–10
Love, egoism, and altruism, 132–37, 159–81, 213–19
Love, security and insecurity, 140–42, 160–61, 212–13
Lowen, Alexander, 81–83, 92
Lust, 10, 14, 16, 20, 23, 27, 49, 70–71, 74–75, 83, 106

Masters and Johnson, 93, 112, 204
Masturbation, 18, 31–33, 69–71, 74–75, 83, 106, 111–17
May, Rollo, 20–23, 162
Morgan, Douglas, 189
Moulton, Janice, 5, 93–96

Nagel, Thomas, 5, 60–69, 75, 77–78, 102
Narcissism, 68, 114–15, 178
"Natural" sex, 34–38, 43, 61, 69
Necrophilia, 30
Neo-Puritanism, 22, 78
"Neurotic" love, 152, 160–61, 189–91
Nietzsche, Friedrich, 44–45, 58, 133, 156, 163, 196, 203

Nygren, Anders, 193–94
Nymphomania, 42

Oral sex, 38, 41
Orgasm, 2–3, 22, 28, 68–70, 72, 78–89, 93–96, 114

Paradoxes of sex and love, 22–23, 131–47, 212–19
Perversion, 2, 30–78, 100, 120, 125
Pleasure and pain, 46, 51–52, 59–60
Pietropinto, Anthony, 96
Plato, 5, 153, 160, 166–72, 173–74
Private and public sex, 107–11
Procreation, 34–38, 49, 69, 77, 99–101, 170–71, 198–203
Promiscuity, 42, 102
Prostitution, 69, 71, 100, 202
Proust, Marcel, 129–30

Radical sex, 125–26
Rapaport, Elizabeth, 38, 131
Rape, 2, 18, 39, 42–60, 100, 125–26
Rational love, 138–40, 149–50, 153–54, 173
Rawson, Philip, 88–89
Reich, Wilhelm, 79–86, 92, 98, 102
Reik, Theodore, 10–11, 137, 198, 201–02
Robertiello, Robert, 95
Romantic love, 149–50, 155, 159, 184, 189–91

Sadler, William, 144
Saint Augustine, 108–09
Sartre, Jean-Paul, 5, 48–51, 69, 78, 109–10, 114, 116, 203–11
Scherfey, Mary Jane, 47, 93
Schopenhauer, Arthur, 5, 198–203
Schwarz, Oswald, 8–9
Seduction, 28, 68, 207
Sensuous eroticism, 26, 80–81, 96
Sex and communication, 15–16, 69–78, 103, 109
Sex for sex's sake, 28, 37, 59, 72, 83, 87, 92, 97–101
Sex with love, 13–23, 37, 97–98, 122–24, 212–19
Sex without love, 23–28, 123–24, 127, 218–19

Sexism, 3, 34, 38, 47, 52, 59, 115, 146, 163, 218
Sexual attitude, 9-10
Sexual appeal, 55
Sexual desire, 60-69
Sexual energy, 83-92
Sexual experimentation, 98, 121-22, 125
Sexual fantasies, 64, 76-77, 116-17
Sexual feedback, 61-63, 110-11
Sexual liberation, 4-5, 97, 120-24
Sexual morality, 39, 45-60, 101-07, 118-27
Sexual potency, 22, 96-98
Sexual surrender, 20-21, 82-84, 86, 109
Sexual technique, 12, 22, 64, 84
Simenauer, Jacqueline, 96
Singer, Irving, 5, 95, 169-70, 192-97

Singer, June, 90-91, 146
Soble, Alan, 112-13
Socrates, 40, 166-67
Solomon, Robert, 5, 16, 27, 69-79, 103, 112-13
Stendhal, 5, 157-58

Tantric sex, 86-92, 98
Transpersonal individuality, 143-45
"True" love, 3-4, 24, 148-53, 160, 181, 183-84, 191, 215
Types of love, 12, 148-53, 215-17

Vulgarity, 76-77
Whiteley, C. H. and Winifred, 8, 31
Will to live, 198-203